ROUTLEDGE LIBRARY EDITIONS: THE LABOUR MOVEMENT

Volume 10

ORGANISED LABOUR

ORGANISED LABOUR
An Introduction to Trade Unionism

G. D. H. COLE

LONDON AND NEW YORK

First published in 1924 by George Allen and Unwin Limited

This edition first published in 2019
by Routledge
2 Park Square, Milton Park, Abingdon, Oxon OX14 4RN

and by Routledge
711 Third Avenue, New York, NY 10017

Routledge is an imprint of the Taylor & Francis Group, an informa business

© 1924 G. D. H. Cole

All rights reserved. No part of this book may be reprinted or reproduced or utilised in any form or by any electronic, mechanical, or other means, now known or hereafter invented, including photocopying and recording, or in any information storage or retrieval system, without permission in writing from the publishers.

Trademark notice: Product or corporate names may be trademarks or registered trademarks, and are used only for identification and explanation without intent to infringe.

British Library Cataloguing in Publication Data
A catalogue record for this book is available from the British Library

ISBN: 978-1-138-32435-0 (Set)
ISBN: 978-0-429-43443-3 (Set) (ebk)
ISBN: 978-1-138-33626-1 (Volume 10) (hbk)
ISBN: 978-1-138-33628-5 (Volume 10) (pbk)
ISBN: 978-0-429-44311-4 (Volume 10) (ebk)

Publisher's Note
The publisher has gone to great lengths to ensure the quality of this reprint but points out that some imperfections in the original copies may be apparent.

Disclaimer
The publisher has made every effort to trace copyright holders and would welcome correspondence from those they have been unable to trace.

TYPES OF

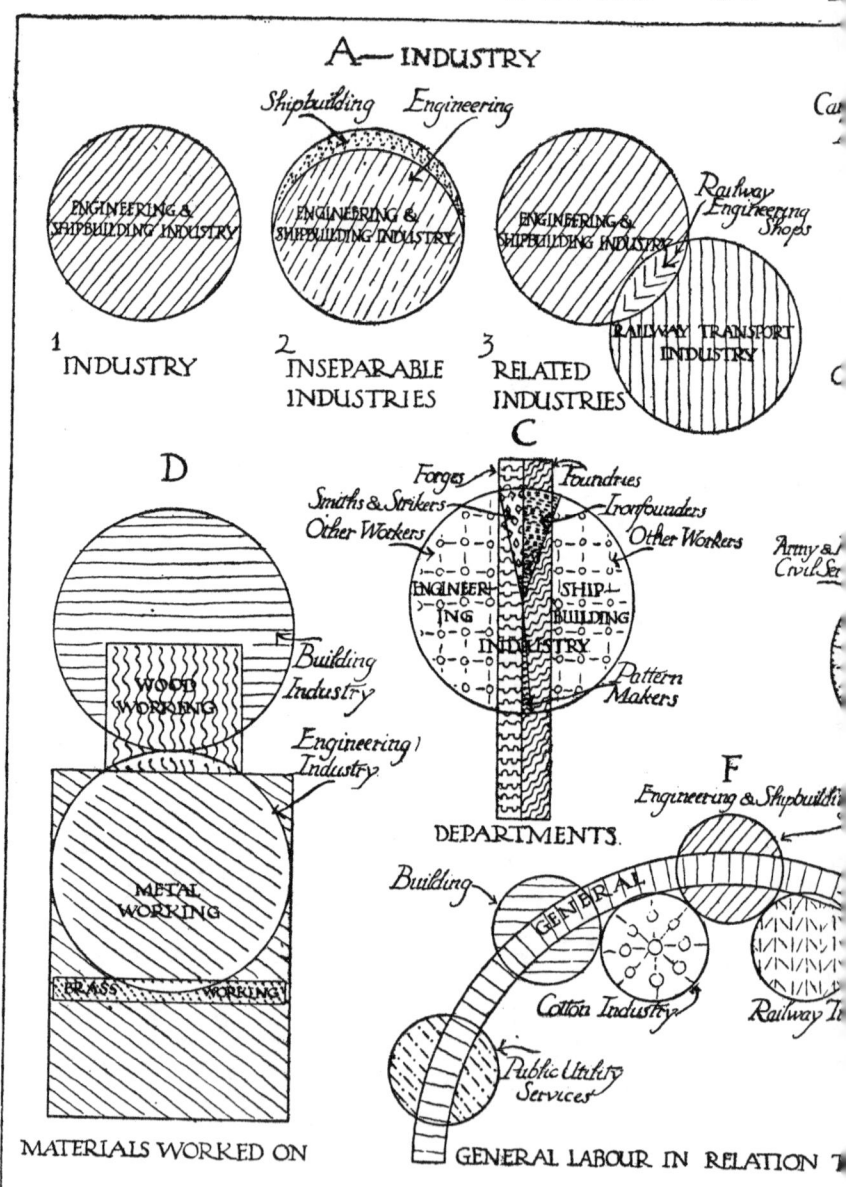

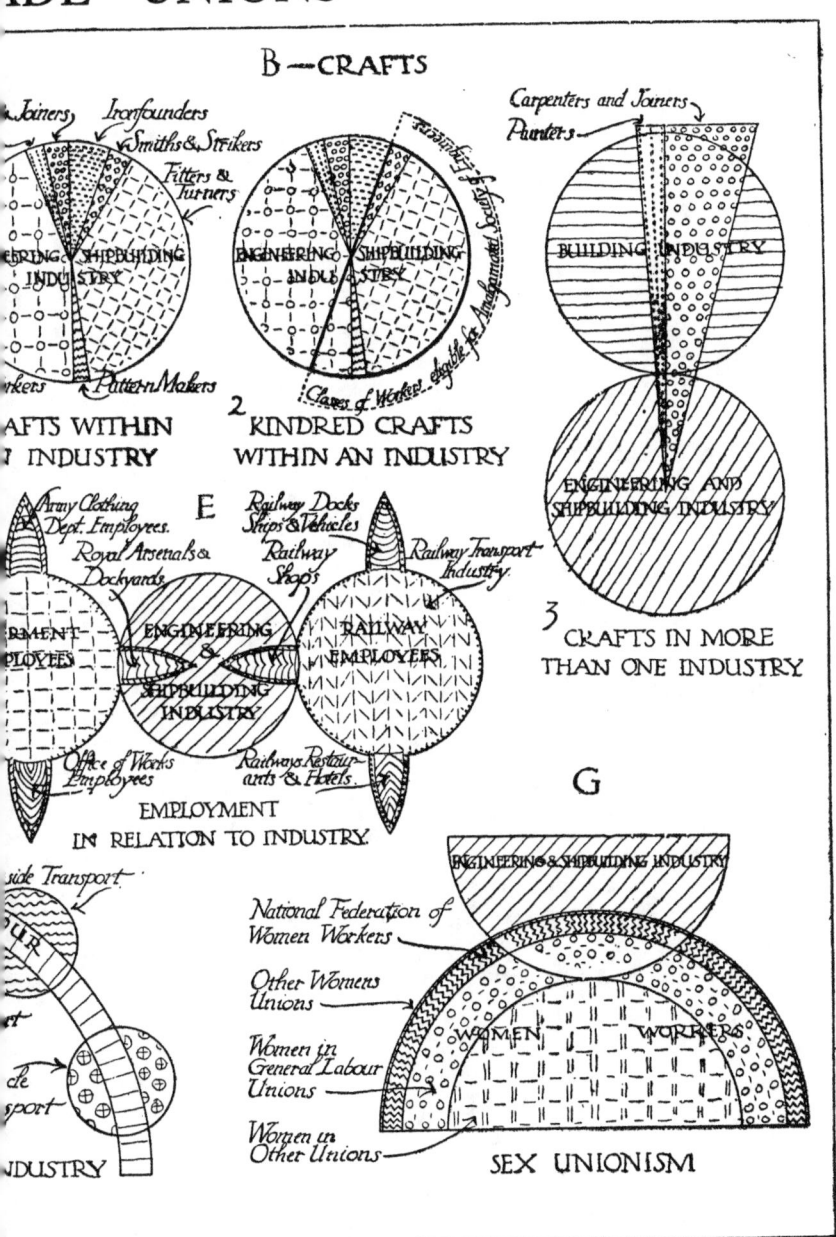

Drawn by Miss M. Pulsford from a design by G. D. H. Cole.

ORGANISED LABOUR

AN INTRODUCTION
TO TRADE UNIONISM

BY G. D. H. COLE

1924

LONDON: GEORGE ALLEN AND
UNWIN LIMITED & THE LABOUR
PUBLISHING COMPANY LIMITED

PRINTED IN GREAT BRITAIN BY THE WHITEFRIARS PRESS, LTD.,
LONDON AND TONBRIDGE.

PREFACE

EARLY in 1918 I wrote " An Introduction to Trade Unionism " in the form of a Report for the Labour Research Department. The book went on selling, though it soon became largely out of date during the period of rapid development which came after the War. Then followed the trade slump, bringing further big changes in Trade Union organisation. Now a period of greater stability seems to have been reached, and I have taken the opportunity of re-writing the whole book, and bringing it thoroughly up-to-date. Most of my figures relate to 1923, or, where this was impossible, as in the case of the official statistics, to the end of 1922. The record of facts goes up to June, 1924. What I now present to my readers is not a mere revision of my old book, but practically a new book, in which certain sections of the old are incorporated in a substantially altered form. That so drastic a re-writing should become necessary after six years is a measure of the rapidity of the changes through which British Trade Unionism has passed. I have aimed at presenting, in the Appendices, a handy statistical guide to Trade Union organisation as it is to-day.

G. D. H. COLE.

Hampstead, 1924.

CONTENTS

	PAGE
PREFACE	v
NOTE ON BOOKS	xi
PART I.—HISTORICAL INTRODUCTION	1

PART II.—THE STRUCTURE OF TRADE UNIONISM.

Section 1. The Present Strength of Trade Unionism	14
Section 2. The Unit of Organisation	21
Section 3. A Classification of Trade Unions	28
Section 4. The Area of Organisation	33
Section 5. Federations of Trade Unions	35
Section 6. Trades Councils and Local Labour Parties	38
Section 7. The Unemployed Movement	40
Section 8. The National Trade Union Movement	41
Section 9. International Trade Union Organisation	46

PART III.—THE GOVERNMENT OF TRADE UNIONISM.

Section 1. The Single-branch Union	49
Section 2. National Unions	51
Section 3. Workshop Organisation	59
Section 4. General Summary	64
Section 5. Trade Union Finance	68

CONTENTS

PART IV.—INTERNAL TRADE UNION PROBLEMS.

Section 1. Amalgamation and Federation . . . 77
Section 2. Inter-Union Relations 87
Section 3. Women in Trade Unions. . . . 93
Section 4. Supervisors and Non-manual Workers . 97
Section 5. The Problem of Democratic Control . . 103
Section 6. Political Action 106
Section 7. Trade Unionism and the Co-operative Movement 109
Section 8. Trade Unions and Education . . . 112

PART V.—TRADE UNIONS AT WORK.

Section 1. Collective Bargaining 117
Section 2. Negotiation and Arbitration . . . 120
Section 3. Strikes and Lock-outs 123
Section 4. Standard Rates and " Payment by Results " 126
Section 5. Hours of Labour 133
Section 6. The Question of Control 135

PART VI.—TRADE UNIONISM AND THE STATE.

Section 1. The Legal Position of Trade Unions . . 140
Section 2. Industrial Legislation 144
Section 3. Conclusion 147

STATISTICAL APPENDICES.

1. Total Trade Union Membership from 1892, Trades Union Congress Membership from 1866, and Trades Council Membership from 1894 . . 154
2. Membership of Trade Unions by Industries in 1892, 1900, 1910, 1913, 1918, 1920, 1921, 1922 . . 156

CONTENTS

STATISTICAL APPENDICES—*continued*.

3. Federations of Trade Unions 157
4. Women in Trade Unions at Various Dates. . . 158
5. International Trade Union Organisation . . . 158
6. International Trade Federations 160
7. National Labour Party. Membership and Electoral Record 161
8. Trade Union Income, Expenditure and Funds, 1904–1913 and 1919–1922. 162
9. Trade Union Expenditure Analysed, 1904–1913 and 1919–1922 164
10. Pre-War Expenditure of Certain Trade Unions Analysed, 1913 166
11. Strikes and Lock-outs, 1909–1923 167
12. Important Trade Union Amalgamations . . . 168
13. Summary of Trade Union Organisation arranged in Occupational Groups 170
14. Trades Union Congress General Council . . . 178

INDEX 179

NOTE ON BOOKS

THERE are full annotated bibliographies in my two narrative syllabuses published by the Labour Research Department (6d. each), dealing with " The British Labour Movement (Historical) " and " British Trade Unionism : Problems and Policy." These should be consulted by all who desire to study the subject in detail. I give here only a short list of the most useful books.

1.—HISTORY OF TRADE UNIONISM AND LABOUR.

S. and B. WEBB .	" History of Trade Unionism " (to 1920). Indispensable.
MAX BEER . .	" History of British Socialism." 2 volumes.
J. L. and B. HAMMOND.	" The Town Labourer " (for the period of the Industrial Revolution).
J. L. and B. HAMMOND.	" The Skilled Labourer " (for the period of the Industrial Revolution).
R. W. POSTGATE .	" The Builders' History " (good for 1830–1834).
W. A. ORTON. .	" Labour in Transition " (for the War period).

2.—GENERAL BOOKS ON TRADE UNIONISM.

G. D. H. COLE .	" The World of Labour."
C. M. LLOYD. .	" Trade Unionism."
S. and B. WEBB .	" Industrial Democracy."
LABOUR RESEARCH DEPARTMENT.	" The Workers' Register of Labour and Capital, 1923."

3.—LEGAL.

H. H. SLESSER .	" The Law relating to Trade Unions " (a short introduction).
H. H. SLESSER .	" Trade Unions and the Law " (a large technical work).
F. TILLYARD . .	" The Worker and the State " (for industrial legislation).

NOTE ON BOOKS

4.—Special Subjects.

G. D. H. Cole .	" Labour in the Coal-mining Industry, 1914–1921."
G. D. H. Cole .	" Workshop Organisation."
G. D. H. Cole .	" The Payment of Wages " (for " payment by results," etc.).
G. D. H. Cole and R. Page Arnot.	" Trade Unionism on the Railways " (to 1917).
Barbara Drake .	" Women in Trade Unions."
B. L. Hutchins .	" Women in Modern Industry."
Labour Research Department .	" Studies in Labour and Capital " (Railways, Engineering, Shipping, etc.).
C. L. Goodrich .	" The Frontier of Control."

5.—Theories of Trade Unionism.

G. D. H. Cole .	" Self-Government in Industry."
G. D. H. Cole .	" Labour in the Commonwealth."
G. D. H. Cole .	" Chaos and Order in Industry."
G. D. H. Cole .	" Guild Socialism Re-stated."
S. G. Hobson .	" National Guilds."
N. Bucharin and A. Preobas.	" The A.B.C. of Communism."
R. H. Tawney .	" The Acquisitive Society."

6.—Government Publications and Other Reports.

The Ministry of Labour Gazette (monthly).

Part C of the " Annual Reports " of the Chief Registrar of Friendly Societies.

" Annual Reports " of the Trades Union Congress.

Monthly Circular of the Labour Research Department.

" Year Book " and other publications of the International Federation of Trade Unions.

ORGANISED LABOUR

PART I

HISTORICAL INTRODUCTION

THIS book does not purport to be a history of Trade Unionism, or to describe the gradual emergence during the nineteenth century of an organised working-class movement for defence and aggression against the dominant capitalist system. That history has been written down elsewhere, and every one who desires to understand Trade Unionism as it is ought to study the manner and the phases of its growth. Mr. and Mrs. Webb's " History of Trade Unionism," which the authors have revised and brought up to 1921 since the previous version of this book of mine appeared, is still the indispensable basis of such a study. To it I refer the reader who realises that he cannot hope to understand the present without knowledge of the past.[1]

But, since this historical background is indispensable, I must, in this opening chapter, without attempting to write down the history of the Trade Union movement, at least indicate for reference the chief phases of its growth. This chapter is meant, not to save any one the need of studying the history for himself, but to provide certain clues to that study, and to indicate briefly the main turning-points in the career of the movement.

Trade Unions are not a recent growth. They were common in the eighteenth century, long before the period of rapid technical development which is called " the Industrial Revolution." They can be traced back beyond the eighteenth century, and analogies to them can be found, not, indeed, in the mediæval Gilds, but in many fraternities of journeymen which existed under the Gild system, and often in opposition to the Gild organisation controlled by the masters, and becoming already oligarchic and capitalistic as the Gild system decayed.

But Trade Unionism, in the sense in which we understand the term, was really born in the troublous days of the French Wars and the Industrial Revolution. The earlier journeymen's societies

[1] See also my historical narrative syllabus, " The British Labour Movement," in which are given full references for further reading.

were mostly short-lived, or were absorbed into, and subordinated to, the official Gild organisation, still supposed to rest on the solidarity of interest and outlook between master and journeyman. Even the Trade Unions of the eighteenth century were hardly Trade Unions in the modern sense, though they called strikes on occasion, and in many cases secured recognition from the masters, and negotiated price-lists and collective agreements on behalf of their members. They lacked, what is an essential element in the rise of Trade Unionism as an organised movement, a sense of class solidarity overpassing sectional boundaries, and manifesting its power in a tendency for Union, or federation, to pass beyond the limits of a single trade and to embrace many different types of workers, all animated by a common idea.

In other words, before the Industrial Revolution there were Trade Unions, but there was no Trade Union Movement, and no common impulse to create a movement. That impulse came with the miseries and disorders, the increase of class-antagonisms, the stirring of new ideas, which accompanied the revolutionary wars after 1789 and the use of steam-power and the factory system. For the first time political and industrial ideas began powerfully to interact; the struggle for parliamentary reform became inextricably interwoven with the desperate fight of miners and factory operatives against the oppression of the new industrial order. Political reformers began, as Cobbett began very definitely in 1816, to appeal to the working masses; workmen began to think politically and to apply their political thinking to their own industrial conditions. The mass of the miners and the textile operatives were, indeed, too poor and too miserable to get much chance of thinking clearly. But the men of the older crafts—tailors, shoemakers, carpenters, millwrights, and many more—were in a better position to drink in the new gospels of the time, and to react against the slavery which they saw around them. Thomas Hardy, of the London Corresponding Society, was a shoemaker; Francis Place, a tailor; Samuel Bamford, a weaver. The handloom-weavers, indeed, displaced rapidly from their old status and pride of craft by the new machines, were a typical and extreme case of men, once fairly prosperous and respected, driven into revolt by the tyranny of the new wealth-creating machine which brought to them only grinding poverty and degradation.

In this atmosphere of violent economic upheaval modern Trade Unionism was born. The old-fashioned Trade Club, half a rudimentary friendly society and half a journeymen's fraternity, began to give place to the Trade Union, formed primarily as a fighting organisation for the protection of economic interests. The French Revolution, and the Terror following it, had scared the governing classes, in Great Britain as elsewhere, into a mood of savage and irrational repressiveness. Every working-class organisation, no matter how moderate its purpose might be, was suspected of violent revolutionary designs. Police spies permeated all the factory districts, often inciting the workers to the acts of violence they were supposed to prevent. Working-class combination, tolerated hitherto and even encouraged by many of the masters as a convenient means of settling terms of employment, was now repressed with the full force of the Government. In 1799 and 1800 were passed laws making all forms of industrial combination illegal. Political societies among the workers were suppressed with still greater violence.

The Combination Acts remained in the Statute Book until 1824, by which time the renewed fears of revolution, excited by the working-class movements following the Peace of 1815, had begun to subside. During this quarter of a century, many Trade Unions continued to exist, and many more were founded, only to be broken up or speedily dissolved. The Combination Acts could not be so rigidly and universally enforced as to prevent all Trade Union activity, and the rigours of persecution were greater in the new factory and mining districts than among the craftsmen of the older towns. But any Union was liable to dissolution at any moment, and every man who was active in Trade Union organisation might at any time find himself denounced and imprisoned, or even transported. Stable organisation and open combination on any considerable scale were impossible under such conditions.

When at length, in 1824, Radical agitation, and the ingenuity of Francis Place and Joseph Hume, secured the repeal of the Combination Acts, there was an immediate outburst of Trade Unions in many trades. This led to the placing of fresh restrictions on Trade Union liberty in the following year; but there was no re-enactment of the repealed laws as a whole. Trade Unions remained lawful bodies, though the law remained swift to repress those who were too eager to use the weapon of combination. Many a Trade Union leader was still to be gaoled for conspiracy or other offences under the common law.

The period of rapid growth, which began in 1824, continued for ten years, and culminated in the great Trade Union struggles of 1834. These years were a time of intense activity among the working-class Radicals. The political reform movement was gathering force for the great contest which ended in the Reform Act of 1832. Robert Owen, already ostracised by the governing classes, to whom he had made his earlier appeals, was speaking now directly to the workers, and Owenite Societies and doctrines were rapidly permeating the younger working-class leaders.

Cobbett was at the height of his immense popularity. Hodgskin, Thompson, and other writers were developing, on a basis of inverted Ricardian economics, a theoretical basis for working-class economic claims. Co-operative Societies, intended to undertake co-operative production and lead to co-operative communities on the Owenite model, were being founded in many towns. All these, and other streams of influence, combined to create among the workers a new solidarity and a new consciousness of rights and claims. And when, in 1832, the Whigs threw over their working-class allies, and the Whig Reform Act left the workers without any share in political power, it was natural that the rejected of politics should take up their other weapon of industrial organisation, and try to strike with it a blow in support of their claims to social equality.

The sensational rise of Trade Unionism between 1832 and 1834 was the sequel to working-class disillusionment over political reform. The Potters' Union, the Builders' Union, the Spinners' Union, and many others enrolled members in thousands. And the talk, heard more than once before, but only now issuing in a popular movement, of a " General Union " to embrace all trades and link up all workers of every trade and calling in a single body, suddenly took shape in the Grand National Consolidated Trades Union, which in a few weeks enrolled, it is said, a million members. These were not, of course, all new recruits; for the " Grand National " was largely taking over existing small societies of workers in particular trades. But its growth was astounding, even when allowance is made for this.

The fall, as rapid as its growth, of the Grand National Consolidated Trades Union must be studied in the histories. Here, I can say only that behind its imposing façade was no real strength or stability. Before it had time to sort out the members it enrolled, it was engaged in half a dozen serious conflicts with bodies of employers determined to crush this new menace to capitalism before it had a chance of arraying its forces in order of battle. The Government joined in the work of destroying it, reviving in the sentence passed on the Dorchester Labourers the brutalities of pre-Reform Act times. By the end of 1834, " the Trades Union " had vanished, leaving behind it only an increased number of local Trade Clubs and a few national Trade Unions on a craft basis which held together after the general collapse. The lock-out and the " document "[1] had forced the working class to its knees.

---

[1] A form presented by the employer for signature by his workers, who are called upon to renounce membership of a Trade Union as a condition of employment.

HISTORICAL INTRODUCTION

But, while it lasted, the movement of the 'thirties was a great seeding-time of working-class aspirations, still for the most part to be harvested. The Builders' Union and the " Grand National " did not restrict their aspirations to shortening the long working day or raising the low weekly wage. Inspired by Robert Owen and his followers, they dreamed of superseding capitalism altogether, and replacing the competitive system by a system of workers' co-operation and self-employment. The Builders started a National Guild : other groups started, through their Trade Unions, producing societies, and tried to exchange their products mutually without the intervention of master or merchant. Socialism was conceived as an immediate thing, to be achieved by one great revolutionary effort. With the " Grand National " and the other great Unions perished these hopes. The producers' societies died, or languished. Trade Unionism was reduced to impotence ; and the main stream of working-class activity passed back to the political agitation which took shape in the Chartist Movement. The Owenites, however, continued their work on a less ambitious scale, and gave birth, almost against their will, to the modern consumers' Co-operative Movement. The Rochdale Pioneers, seeking to lay the foundations for an Owenite community, started their shop in 1844.

Not till the Chartist wave had begun to ebb did Trade Union organisation revive on a national scale. The surviving Trade Unions had, indeed, been slowly consolidating their position ; but the new unionism of the Victorian age really emerged with the foundation, in 1850–51, of the Amalgamated Society of Engineers, which was the model for a long series of powerful craft unions formed during the next twenty years. The new unionism of 1850 was very different from the old. All thought of revolutionary activity was put aside ; and, while the new Unions were prepared to fight hard battles on occasion in defence of the rights of combination and collective bargaining, they sought to ensure stability and strength by acting as friendly societies no less than as Trade Unions. High rates of contributions and benefits gave the members a stake in the organisation, and made for conservatism in action. The new policy also resulted in the almost complete exclusion from the Unions of those who were less skilled or paid less than a living wage ; for only the better paid workers could afford to pay the high contributions required. Trade Unionism ceased to aim at including all the workers. Its leaders openly dismissed the less skilled grades as incapable of stable organisation. The movement, save for a few exceptions, shrank up into a narrow protective organisation of a limited number of skilled crafts, making no challenge to the capitalist order of society, and seeking only, by negotiation and rare use of the strike weapon, to improve the wages and conditions of its own members.

This, indeed, was not true without reserve, or of all trades. The rise of new organisations in the 'sixties among the miners and textile operatives brought into the movement groups among which the division between skilled and unskilled was less clear and sharp than among metal workers, wood workers and workers in brick and stone. Mining and textile Trade Unionism, moreover, at least among the newly organised sections, both stood pre-eminently for political agitation, with the object of securing protective laws. Their influence modified the narrow outlook of the "Amalgamated Societies," but did not prevent it from giving to Trade Unionism its predominant character.

It was this narrow craft unionism of the Amalgamated Societies, aided by the miners and the cotton operatives, that fought, with both power and subtlety, the struggle for legal recognition in the late 'sixties and early 'seventies. An accumulation of adverse legal decisions, menacing both the right to strike and the security of Trade Union funds, forced the Trade Unions into political agitation in their own defence. Under the leadership of the "Junta," the heads of the great craft Unions, they fought this battle not, save in an isolated case or two, by putting up candidates for Parliament, but by lobbying, giving evidence before Royal Commissions, and the indirect use of political pressure. They emerged triumphant, having secured both the legal security of Trade Union funds and a much fuller recognition of the right to strike and of peaceful picketing.

This period of conflict brought into being, mainly as an instrument for use in the struggle, a central organisation for the Trade Union movement as a whole. There had long been, in some of the larger towns, local Trades Councils linking up the branches of the various Trade Unions and the purely local societies in the district. Many of these led a discontinuous existence, arising as joint "trades movements" in support of some local strike, dying out in periods of tranquillity, and arising again on a recurrence of immediate need. But by the late 'sixties a number of them had become permanent bodies, and it was to the initiative of these Trades Councils that the creation of the Trades Union Congress was mainly due. But not till, at the height of the legal struggle, the leaders of the Amalgamated Societies decided to use the Congress as an instrument of agitation did it rise to importance or attain to a really representative character.

There had been, since 1834, other attempts to unite the Trade Unions into a single body for common action on matters of

HISTORICAL INTRODUCTION

general concern. But it needed the crises of the late 'sixties to bring success. The political agitation leading to the Reform Act of 1867, which for the first time enfranchised the urban workers, and the contest of Trade Unionism with the law, changed the situation, and provided the basis for united working-class organisation. Labour representation in Parliament began with the return of two miners' leaders in 1874; but these and their successors allied themselves with the Liberals. It took another twenty-five years to bring the Labour Party into being.

Having achieved their limited purpose of securing legal recognition, the leaders of the Amalgamated Societies were quite content, and Trade Unionism fell back into the old grooves. The rise of the Socialist Movement from 1880 onwards found the Union leaders actively hostile, and made in the early years little or no impression on the established societies. But, indirectly, Socialism was destined before long to revolutionise the Trade Union movement. The Socialists, inspired by the idea of class-solidarity, could not rest content with a movement which virtually excluded from participation all the less skilled and worse paid members of the working class. Young workers, inspired by Socialist ideas, went outside the established Unions, and began to organise new Trade Unions, catering directly for the excluded sections. Unions of dockers, seamen, general railway workers, gasworkers and general labourers sprang into existence, and came forward with demands for higher wages, improved conditions, and recognition of the right to combine. The great Dock Strike of 1889 was the expression of this new movement.

Trade Union membership went up by leaps and bounds, and strike followed strike in rapid succession. There were notable victories; but the leaders of the older Unions shook their heads, and affirmed again that no stable combination was possible on the new lines. Friendly benefits and high contributions seemed to them the necessary cement of union; whereas the new Trade Unions were organised as fighting bodies, with low rates of contribution and few or no benefits save in case of strike or lockout. The wave of the "New Unionism" reached its crest in 1892.

To some extent the old leaders were right; for after 1892 began a decline. The Seamen's Union vanished altogether. The Dockers' Union sank from 23,000 to 9,000; the Gasworkers' from 36,000 to 23,000. But the "New Unionism" had come to stay, and, when the wave receded, it left a different and a far wider Trade Unionism behind. There were not many more than half-a-million Trade Unionists in 1880; there were never less than 1,400,000 after 1892. The total membership had more than doubled, and the new recruits included a large reinforcement from the less skilled and worse paid grades.

When the wave of industrial unrest subsided, the new movement took on a political shape. The period of unrest had given the Socialists a strong foothold in the Trade Union world. They now began to work energetically for the creation of a Trade Union political party. The centre of gravity shifted from the Marxian Social Democratic Federation, the pioneer body of British Socialism, to the less dogmatic Independent Labour Party, founded in 1893 mainly by the " New Unionist " leaders. And it was mainly the pressure of the I.L.P. that finally, in 1899, pushed the reluctant Trades Union Congress into the formation of a working-class political party. The Labour Representation Committee, which became the Labour Party in 1906, was formed in 1900 as the result of a Trades Union Congress decision.

The rise of the " New Unionism " did not leave the older Trade Unions unaffected. In them also the new ideas made headway, and the Trade Union movement gradually consolidated itself on a new basis. The " Old Unionism " in turn reacted on the new. The newer Unions lost much of their militancy, and, in part, assimilated themselves to the older bodies, though the necessity of keeping contributions low prevented them from developing large friendly benefits of the type paid by the " Amalgamated Societies " of skilled workers. The fusion of attitude between the two kinds of societies is not, even now, complete ; but they have long reached the stage of ready collaboration on general issues, and the rise of new societies of intermediate types has also blurred the distinction.

From the early 'nineties up to about 1910, although the industrial movement made some progress in both members and organisation, the chief developments were in the sphere of political action. About 1910, however, disappointment with the results of political action and the failure of wages to keep pace with rising prices, led to the great movement of industrial unrest and developing industrial consciousness which occupied the years immediately preceding the Great War. Again there were widespread strikes, and again the lead was taken, not by the older Craft Unions, but by Unions of the newer type. The seamen, the dockers, and the railwaymen led the way in the great strikes of 1911 ; and the miners followed their example in 1912. Again there was a rapid increase in Trade Union membership. The General Workers' Union grew in three years from 32,000 to 135,000, the Dockers from 18,000 to 48,000, the Engineers from 111,000 to 161,000. The National Union of Railwaymen, formed in 1913, by the amalgamation of three separate societies, set itself up as the "new model" of Trade Union organisation, aiming at the inclusion in one body of all the grades of workers employed in the industry. The strength of the whole Trade Union movement rose from less than two and a half millions in 1910 to nearly four and a quarter millions in the middle of 1914.

The wave of unrest was by no means spent when war was declared in August, 1914. The outbreak of war stopped the movement, and an "Industrial Truce" was proclaimed. For a time Trade Union organisation suffered a slight setback; but as the War developed rapidly into a conflict of productive capacity as well as of military operations, Trade Union activity was renewed. Industry had to be readjusted rapidly to meet war needs. Some industries were depleted; others were swollen to vast dimensions. A huge rush of men and women into the munitions trades confronted the Trade Unions with new problems of organisation. "Dilution of labour" threatened the established position of the skilled crafts. The Unions of metal-workers vastly increased their membership, and the Unions of general workers grew and grew by enrolling the less skilled grades concentrated in the munition factories. The Amalgamated Society of Engineers grew from 161,000 in 1913 to 299,000 in 1918. The general workers' Unions as a group increased their membership from 375,000 to well over a million. The total membership of all Trade Unions rose from 4,189,000 to 6,664,000 during the War.

When the War ended, and the soldiers came back to industry, there followed a period of unrest even more intense, and more definitely political, than the unrest of pre-war years. Trade Union membership grew still further, to nearly eight and a half millions in 1920. The Coal Commission and the national railway strike in 1919, the "Direct Action" movement and the miners' strike in 1920, showed the increased power and solidarity of Trade Unionism. But soon came the reaction. The artificial trade boom ended, and unemployment appeared in a form more intense than ever before. The miners suffered crushing defeat in the lock-out of 1921, and the collapse of "Black Friday," when the great Triple Alliance of miners, railwaymen, and transport workers perished, spread discouragement throughout the movement. The Amalgamated Engineering Union, into which the old A.S.E. had been absorbed in 1920, was crushed in the national lock-out of 1922. Trade Union membership fell as rapidly as it had risen. The eight and a half millions of 1920 became six and a half in 1921, five and a half in 1922, and barely five in 1923. Thereafter began a slight revival, which seems to be gathering force as I write.

Meanwhile, the strength of the political movement went on growing. The Labour Party, which entered during the War into the Coalition Governments of Mr. Asquith and Mr. Lloyd George, resumed its independence as soon as the Armistice was declared. It had already, earlier in 1918, revised its constitution so as to admit individual members as well as affiliated bodies, and proclaimed itself as the party of the "workers by hand and brain." The General Election of 1918, fought on the cries of "Hang the Kaiser" and "Make Germany Pay," brought it only a small accession of strength; but at the election of 1922 it more than doubled its numbers, and in 1923 it gained another fifty seats, and early in 1924 formed, with Liberal support in the House of Commons, the first Labour Government, though it was still only the second largest party in Parliament. The trade slump, which weakened the Trade Unions, produced an opposite effect on the political fortunes of Labour. The workers sought to achieve politically what the times made unobtainable by industrial action.

This brief review of Trade Union development shows working-class organisation growing by stages corresponding closely to the evolution of the capitalist system. In the eighteenth century, factory work is still exceptional. The typical workmen are the urban craftsman employed in a small workshop under a master directly employing only a few men, or the worker under the domestic system, carrying on his craft in his own home with his own tools and often with the aid of his family. Such conditions readily give rise to local trade clubs among the urban craftsmen, but hardly to Trade Unions extending over a wider area, or to any close union between men of different trades. There are, indeed, very rich men, and capitalism has already developed; but the great capitalist is still most often mainly a merchant, directly employing only a few workers and giving out most of his work to men who perform it in their own homes. Communication is still difficult; for the roads are very bad. The journeyman enjoys a fair amount of independence in the ordering of his work, and can often hope to become a sub-contractor or a small employer. Industrial organisation and class-antagonism have not reached the stage at which large-scale combination becomes possible.

Then come, in the textile, mining and metal-working industries, the vast changes of the Industrial Revolution. The development of power-driven machinery—first water, then steam—makes it pay better to concentrate textile production in factories rather than leave it to be carried on in the worker's home. The demand for coal and iron advances by leaps and bounds, and necessitates a further development of large-scale organisation. The making of roads and canals, and then of railways, requires a large mobile force of unskilled manual labour, largely supplied from Ireland at sweated wages. The progress of enclosures drives the peasants off the land, and crowds them and their children into the new factories. Established craftsmen, like the handloom-weavers, find themselves superseded and left to starve. War and peace add fresh factors of uncertainty. The workers, at heart either peasants unused to urban conditions or craftsmen trained in a tradition of independence, hate and resent the new factory system and the overcrowded misery of the factory towns. Independence and status are lost: wages are very low and the working day intolerably long. Naturally, the time is one of violent revolt and savage resentment, in which the more intelligent readily accept gospels hostile to the new capitalist order—from Cobbett's democratic appeals to the past of " Merrie England " to Robert Owen's preaching of Socialism and Co-operation as the principles on which a " New Moral World " must be built. They try Luddism, political Reform, Co-operation, the Grand National Trades Union, Chartism—mass violence and then political, economic, industrial and again political action in turn. They think seriously of forcible revolution. But all their efforts fail; for the working class is not yet strong enough to oppose itself to the new capitalist order, still in the heyday of youth and self-confident expansion.

In the next period, after 1848, the year of abortive revolutions in Europe, the new order has settled down and enforced its claims to service. It is rapidly increasing production and accumulating riches: it is able, out of its abundance, to provide rather better and on the whole still improving conditions for its employees. The working class, frustrated in its revolt against the system, learns the lesson of acceptance, especially as a new generation has arisen, familiar from infancy with the new conditions and knowing of the old order only as a tale that is told. The workers make the best of the new world. Co-operation changes from an attempt to create at a blow a system to supersede capitalism into a successful movement for collective trading on a non-profit basis. Trade Unionism similarly abandons its aspirations after a change of system, and seeks only to improve the lot of its members—that is, of only a portion of the working class—within the capitalist order.

But capitalism itself does not stand still. During the latter half of the nineteenth century, the industries of coal and iron gradually thrust the textile trades from their economic predominance. Their growth pushes forward the export of capital as against the export of consumers' goods. Markets are sought in the less developed lands with a view not to the exchange of products, but to the investment of surplus profits. The race for raw materials begins. Capitalism passes by stages into its phase of Economic Imperialism.

These changes administer a check to the march of Victorian progress. Economic uncertainty increases ; trade crises become more severe. Employers and workers alike become more militant again, and more class-conscious. Socialism, neglected during the preceding period, is rediscovered in its Marxian shape. The " New Unionism " arises as the industrial reflex of the new Socialist awakening. But the Unions are hard to turn into fighting organisations, or to reshape on a basis of working-class unity. Politics offers an easier chance of transcending differences of craft and skill. The more practically minded Socialists devote themselves to building up the I.L.P. and creating the Labour Party as an expression of class solidarity.

Slowly, this unity reacts upon the industrial bodies. The " new Unionism " of 1910 is essentially based on the idea of unity of all workers. The new Unions of 1889 had organised the less skilled, but organised them apart. The aim now is to bring skilled and less skilled together. But the War interrupts the new movement before it has time to gather force or become clearly articulate. It revives again after the War ; but the trade slump again diverts it into political courses, and its full effect on the form and policy of industrial organisation is delayed. Still, a great deal has been accomplished in the making of that unity in the industrial field to which all sections now at least profess their allegiance.

I wrote the little book on which this book is based in 1918, while the War was still in progress. I am struck, in re-writing it, with the extent of the changes which have come about in less than six years. Amalgamation of Trade Unions has made very big strides : at least a third of the Trade Unions mentioned in my old index have now merged themselves in new and larger organisations. The Trades Union Congress has gained greatly in power and influence, and has replaced its obsolete " Parliamentary Committee " by a General Council which is, at least, the nucleus for an effective central organisation. The Trades Councils have greatly increased in number and activity. And the slump, while it has caused a heavy loss in membership, has not counteracted this tendency towards a concentration of working-class forces. The Trade Union Movement has still a long way to go ; but it has moved rapidly in organisation during the post-war years. And I think, though the advance is less obvious, it has also moved some distance towards a broader conception of industrial policy.

In the following pages, I am studying the movement as it is. My object is rather to describe what exists than to discuss what

HISTORICAL INTRODUCTION

ought to exist. And, as this is a small book, I shall be able to do this only within rather narrow limits. I make no attempt to provide a comprehensive account even of the present structure and organisation of the Trade Union movement. I provide only a study of an introductory character, bringing out general features, and introducing descriptions of particular Societies only for the purpose of illustrating a general point here and there. But, in a special Appendix, I have aimed at giving, as shortly as it can be done, a summary of the state of organisation and a list of the main Societies with their membership. In order to guide the reader who desires to make a fuller study, I have also added a bibliography. Reference should be made throughout to the statistical appendices, in which I have given more fully information which is very briefly summarised or interpreted in the text.

PART II

THE STRUCTURE OF TRADE UNIONISM

Sect. 1. The Present Strength of Trade Unionism. Sect. 2. The Unit of Organisation. Sect. 3. A Classification of Trade Unions. Sect. 4. The Area of Organisation. Sect. 5. Federations of Trade Unions. Sect. 6. Trades Councils and Local Labour Parties. Sect. 7. The Unemployed Movement. Sect. 8. The National Trade Union Movement. Sect. 9. International Trade Union Organisation.

Section 1.—THE PRESENT STRENGTH OF TRADE UNIONISM

AT the end of 1923, the total number of workers enrolled in Trade Unions was something over five millions. At the end of 1922, the last year for which accurate figures can be given, it was over five and a half millions, and at the end of 1920 nearly eight and a half millions. The figure for 1920 represents the crest of the great wave of increase which began in 1911 and gathered force during the War and the period immediately after the War. The loss of three and a half million members since 1920 shows the full force of the trade slump which set in at the beginning of 1921. The point reached at the end of 1923 represents the low-water mark, and with 1924 Trade Union membership has again begun to increase. It is notable that even the 1923 figure shows an increase of nearly a million members over 1913, and of more than two and a half millions over 1910. Waves of organisation may recede; but each wave leaves Trade Unionism on the ebb a good distance further up the beach.

It is, unfortunately, impossible to give any accurate idea of the proportion which these five millions of organised workers bear to the whole number eligible for Trade Union membership. In 1921, when the last census was taken, the Trade Unionists were over 14 per cent. of the total population of the United Kingdom, and about 45 per cent. of the male wage and salary earners, including non-adults. Women Trade Unionists were about $4\frac{1}{4}$ per cent. of the total female population, and about 17 per cent. of the female wage and salary earners. But these figures give a very inadequate idea of the real strength of the Trade Union Movement; for young workers are largely unorganised, and the proportion of organised workers is highest in just those industries and services whose smooth running is most essential. In practically all the

THE STRUCTURE OF TRADE UNIONISM

great industries, except agriculture and distribution, a dominant proportion of the workers is organised. On the other hand, many of the smaller industries, carried on in scattered factories up and down the country, are without strong Trade Unions.

It remains true to-day, as in 1892, when the first detailed survey of Trade Unionism was made, that Trade Union membership is especially concentrated in certain districts as well as in certain industries. It is exceptionally strong in Lancashire, in the West Riding of Yorkshire, on the North-East Coast, in the industrial belt of Scotland, in South Wales, in the South-West Midlands, in London, and in certain other districts, while there are large rural areas in which the number of Trade Unionists is exceedingly small and some into which Trade Unionism hardly exists. But, although this concentration still remains, one of the most significant features in the recent growth of Trade Unionism is its penetration of the less industrial districts. During the years of boom, branches, particularly of the general and agricultural workers' Unions, and Trades Councils and local Labour Parties, sprang up even in the more remote areas, and, although many of these recruits have been lost during the period of depression, a nucleus of organisation, often centred round a local Labour Party, is now to be found in many of the most backward districts.

Trade Union organisation is concentrated not only in particular districts, but also in particular industries, notably coal-mining, the textile industries, engineering and shipbuilding, and transport. During the boom the remarkable growth of organisation on the railway service, among general labourers, shop-assistants, clerks, employees of public authorities, and women, added a considerably larger percentage to the membership of Trade Unions in these groups than in others. At the same time, organisation in coal-mining, textile, engineering, and shipbuilding industries, in which the Trade Union movement has long been most strongly established, grew so greatly that the numerical predominance of these groups was hardly shaken, and they still include not much less than one-half of the Trade Union world. The tables given in the Appendices to this volume will give in figures the fullest corroboration of this concentration of the Trade Union movement in particular industries.

Among the large industries the least strong organisation in 1924, as in 1892, is that of the agricultural labourers, who in 1923 still muster only an aggregate membership of about 45,000. No group has suffered so severely as agriculture from the recent slump. In 1910 the organised agricultural workers numbered only 4,000, and in 1913 only 22,000. By the end of the War, helped by the enactment of an agricultural minimum wage under the Corn Production Act of 1917, they had shot up to 125,000, and in 1920 they reached 211,000, not including at least 50,000 organised in the general workers' Unions. Then came the decline, accompanied by the repeal of the minimum wage. Membership fell to 149,000 in 1921, 93,000 in 1922, and about 45,000 in 1923. From the days of the Consolidated Trades Union of 1834, agricultural workers have been the hardest class to organise on any stable basis. Joseph Arch enrolled them in the period of Trade Union boom in the 'seventies. New Unions sprang up in the early 'nineties, under the same impulse as created the new Unions of general workers. But on both occasions organisation was short-lived. It remains to be seen whether the National Union of Agricultural Workers, which had sunk to 30,000 members in 1923, will be able to regain its position in the revival which is beginning as I write. That the task is not impossible is shown by the stability of the Scottish Farm Servants' Union, which has successfully held most of its members right through the slump.

Even after the decline, some Trade Union organisation survives in most of the rural districts, a clear gain and expansion of Trade Union scope.

A further significant development of Trade Unionism during recent years is its considerable extension from the manual workers to other classes of workers, such as the supervisory grades on the railways and in the Post Office, and to some extent in private industry, clerks and many groups of professional workers who are in low-paid occupations, notably teachers, nurses, and others. The teachers' associations, headed by the National Union of Teachers, are now practically Trade Unions, and the doctors have taken a leaf out of the Trade Union book, and made of the British Medical Association a powerful and aggressive combine in defence of their claims under the National Insurance Acts. These groups have, indeed, no organised connection with the Trade Union movement as a whole, and the doctors at least would strongly repudiate such a connection. But other groups of non-manual workers, such as the Association of Engineering and Shipbuilding Draughtsmen, have connected themselves with the Trades Union Congress, or, like the National Union of Journalists, with the Federation of the industry—printing—with which they are closely concerned. Organisation has also developed greatly in the Civil Service. Certainly non-manual organisations play a much larger part than at any previous time in the Trade Union world. They are more active and numerous, and the barriers between them and the manual workers are being steadily broken down. The Trades Union Congress, since 1921, includes the

THE STRUCTURE OF TRADE UNIONISM

non-manual workers in a special group, and the National Federation of Professional, Technical, Administrative and Supervisory Workers, formed in 1920, has done much to bring the scattered Societies together.

It will be well now to glance briefly at the strength and organisation of a few of the principal industries in order that we may get a better estimate of what the general figures of Trade Union membership mean in terms of concrete organisation.

The most strongly organised industry in the country is coal-mining. Here the Miners' Federation of Great Britain holds a predominant position, including at least 800,000 out of a total of 1,267,000 persons employed in coal-mines. The Miners' Federation is a national federation, consisting of a number of district organisations in England, Wales, and Scotland. It is strongest among underground workers, but also includes in most districts the bulk of the workers at the pit top. The various types of craftsmen employed in the mining industry are in most cases eligible for membership in the Miners' Association, but the majority of them still preserve their separate Craft Unions of deputies, enginemen, mechanics, and in some cases cokemen, while a small number are organised in unions of craftsmen which draw their membership not only from the mines, but also from other industries, *e.g.*, the Amalgamated Engineering Union, the National Union of Enginemen, the Electrical Trades Union, the National Union of Cokemen, and some of the Unions of colliery enginemen, are affiliated to the Miners' Federation of Great Britain. But others of the Craft Unions are outside, and the Deputies, Mechanics, and Under-Managers are linked up in separate National Federations, which aim at upholding the claims of the smaller crafts. Relations between the Miners' Associations and these Craft Unions vary widely from district to district. In some cases, as in Durham, Northumberland, and North Staffordshire, they are federated, and act jointly on the majority of questions. In other districts, where the Miners' Association has adopted an " industrial " policy and aims at including all workers employed in or about the mines, its relations with the local Craft Associations are far from cordial. The Craft Associations confined to workers employed in the mining industry have together a membership of something like 50,000, of which rather less than 20,000 are in societies affiliated to the M.F.G.B.

The railway service must now be regarded as one of the better organised industries, having reached that position shortly before the War as a result, first, of two national movements, secondly, of a strike, and thirdly, of the amalgamation of three railway unions into the National Union of Railwaymen. There are now only three Unions of any importance on the railways, apart from the railway engineering, carriage, and waggon shops : the N.U.R., which seeks to organise all workers employed on railways, the Associated Society of Locomotive Engineers and Firemen, which includes a majority of the workers in the grades of drivers, firemen, and cleaners, the remainder being in the N.U.R. ; and the Railway Clerks' Association, which now includes a considerable majority of the employees in the railway clerical departments and a goodly number of station-masters and other supervisory workers. Attempts at the amalgamation of these unions have so far failed, and the relations between the N.U.R. and the " Associated Society " are distinctly bad. The N.U.R. and the R.C.A. also at times fall out over the organisation of clerks and supervisors. The great outstanding problem on the railways is that of the railway shopmen ; for the railway engineering and other shops employ large numbers of workmen who are organised in the various Craft Unions of metal and wood workers. Repeated attempts have been made to secure an adjustment of the differences between the N.U.R. and the Craft Unions by some scheme of mutual delimitation of membership. These, however, have so far secured no result, and the present position is one of considerable strain on both sides, which the attempts of the Trades Union Congress to secure an adjustment have so far done little to relieve. The three railway Unions include about 470,000, and the Craft Unions have probably another 50,000, out of a total of 680,000 railway employees. The industry is thus well organised in a numerical sense, although inter-union difficulties rob it of some of its strength.

The engineering and shipbuilding industries are remarkable for the extraordinary number of separate unions which they contain, as well as for the complexity of their own organisation. The shipbuilding section is well organised from a numerical point of view, and the engineering section was, until the very severe slump of the past two years, also well organised ; but the advantages of a large numerical membership are largely offset, especially in the engineering industry, by inter-union difficulties. By far the largest Union is the Amalgamated Engineering Union, with 256,000 members. Next in size in the engineering group stands the National Union of Foundry Workers, with 40,000 members, followed by the Electrical Trades Union with 25,000, and so on, down to societies with only a couple of dozen members. On the shipbuilding side the chief society is the United Society of Boilermakers, with about 90,000 members, followed by the Shipwrights' Association with nearly 40,000. To this group may also be assigned the Associated Blacksmiths' Society with about 14,000.

THE STRUCTURE OF TRADE UNIONISM

The less skilled workers in the engineering industry are mainly organised in general labour Unions, which grew enormously during the War period, as a result of the peculiar conditions associated with the production of munitions of war, and have since suffered a corresponding decline. It is impossible, unfortunately, to give any figures of membership of general labour Unions in the metal-working industries; but it can hardly be less than 100,000, even after the late slump.

The position in one or two other industries can be very briefly summarised. In the building industry organisation has greatly improved. The largest Union is the Amalgamated Society of Woodworkers, with 116,000 members, many of whom are actually employed in the shipbuilding and other industries outside building. Each craft in the building industry has, as a rule, its own Union, and in some cases there are separate Unions for England and Scotland. The builders' labourers, where they are organised, are for the most part in separate Unions of their own, but a certain proportion are included in general labour Unions. The great improvement in Trade Unionism among the builders dates from the formation, in 1917, of the National Federation of Building Trades Operatives, which has become one of the few really effective Federations in the country. It includes nearly all the Unions, and acts as a single body in all negotiations and strike movements affecting the industry as a whole.

In the printing industry there exist a large number of Unions catering for distinct crafts. There is very little overlapping, since, where more than one Union exists in a craft, as in the case of the compositors, the Unions deal mainly with different localities, *e.g.*, the Typographical Association, which has its main strength in the provinces, the London Society of Compositors, the Scottish Typographical Association, and the Dublin Typographical Society. There is practically no general labour in the printing industry, but the less skilled workers are organised mainly in the National Union of Printing, Bookbinding and Paper Workers and the Operative Printers and Assistants' Society. The total proportion organised is comparatively high, and the Unions have largely maintained their position during the slump.

The iron and steel industry was largely reorganised from a Trade Union point of view in 1917, when an effective organisation speaking for the greater part of the industry was called into being. This is the Iron and Steel Trades Confederation, which we shall deal with more fully at a later stage in speaking of the government of Trade Unions. It is in form a confederation of several societies, but it acts as a single body. Outside it now remains only one society of importance, the National Union of Blastfurnacemen, which covers the blastfurnacemen in England and Wales. Scottish blastfurnacemen are in the Confederation.

General labour Unions have also a certain number of members in the industry, especially in the tinplate section, in which the Transport Union has a strongly organised membership. The mechanics are for the most part organised in the engineering Craft Unions. The improvement in numbers resulting from the confederation has been very marked, and the industry has rapidly raised itself to the level of the best-organised industries.

Other groups in which the proportion organised is high are the Post Office and Civil Service. These present very special conditions, and most of the associations exact only a low rate of contribution and do not pay benefits. The cotton group, with its close network of Craft Unions, covers practically the whole industry in Lancashire and Cheshire, but rather tends to ignore the outposts of the industry in Yorkshire and other districts. The dyeing Trade Unions are strongly organised, both in the cotton and in the woollen districts. The boot and shoe industry is strong in Leicester, Northampton, and Kettering, and one or two other towns, but weak in the outlying districts.

In the road and waterside transport group organisation has greatly improved of late years, and the Transport and General Workers' Union, formed in 1921, is now a strong and effective body speaking for the majority of both dockers and vehicle workers. The seamen, separately organised, are linked up with the land transport services in the Transport Workers' Federation, which however, has lost much of its importance since the formation of the T. and G. W. U. The rise of these sections in the Trade Union scale is among the most remarkable achievements of the past few years.

In the woollen industry there is still considerable room for advance, although here again the growth during and after the War was very marked. Still weaker numerically is Trade Union organisation in such industries as distribution, despite the growth of the Shop Assistants' Union and the National Union of Distributive and Allied Workers, and among clerks, where the National Union of Clerks and the other societies still cover only a tiny fraction of the numbers employed. In all these industries organisation is to some extent retarded by difficulties between one Union and another. Into these difficulties we will not enter here, since they will be dealt with more fully in other Sections of this book.

It is, however, necessary to mention that often the actual numbers organised in a particular industry do not furnish an accurate account of the real state of Trade Union organisation,

THE STRUCTURE OF TRADE UNIONISM

both because the Unions do not follow industrial lines, and therefore figures based on the total membership of groups of Unions may often inflate one industry and deflate another, while the proportion in different industries organised in general labour Unions is entirely variable, and, secondly, because there is always, and particularly in the weaker industries, a considerable in-and-out membership, which rushes into the Unions in times of difficulties and out of them as soon as things settle down again. This floating membership, however, can hardly be regarded as a real accession of strength in normal times.

Section 2.—THE UNIT OF ORGANISATION

How many Trade Unions are there? According to the Ministry of Labour, there were 1,190 at the end of 1922, the latest date for which figures are available. But this really tells us little; for it all depends on what is regarded as a Trade Union. The problem is not with the bogus Trade Unions or societies subsidised by employers; for in Great Britain, unlike some Continental countries, these are few and unimportant. The trouble is that it is not easy to draw the line between a Trade Union and a Federation composed of distinct autonomous Trade Unions.

The official returns are largely arbitrary in dealing with this point. For example, the organisation of the spinners and the weavers in the cotton industry is closely similar. Each group is organised in an "Amalgamated Association," made up of a number of regional and local societies. But, whereas the Spinners' Amalgamation is registered and counted as a single Trade Union, each of the local societies of weavers is counted separately. So is each section of the Cardroom Amalgamation, the third large Trade Union in the cotton industry.

In all these cases the local Associations are not mere subordinate branches, but local societies, preserving their separate existence, large local funds, and a considerable degree of autonomy. But in all industrial matters of more than local concern these societies are subject to the policies decided on by the "Amalgamations," which are in effect single Craft Unions covering the whole of their sections of the Lancashire cotton industry. As friendly societies providing sick and other benefits, the local societies are separate bodies; for Trade Union purposes they merge their identity in the "Amalgamations."

Or, again, take the case of the Miners' Federation of Great Britain. This consists of about thirty distinct societies, some of them partly federal in structure, which are counted as separate Trade Unions in the official returns. But, on all questions of a national character, the Miners' Federation acts as a national unit, though its local Associations have their own finances and an independent power of action in local concerns.

There are other instances largely similar to those of the miners and cotton operatives. The Iron and Steel Trades Confederation, for example, is practically one Union, though nominally it consists of several overlapping bodies. In other cases, Federations which were practically single Unions have recently completed the process of fusion, and become national Trade Unions in name as well as in fact. The National Union of Blastfurnacemen and the National Union of Sheet Metal Workers may be cited as examples.

In short, there is no way of determining at all precisely how many Trade Unions there are. If we are to regard the numerous local societies of cotton weavers as separate Trade Unions, there is no adequate reason why we should not so regard as well the innumerable District Committees of Trade Unions, such as the boilermakers and the engineers, which allow a good deal of local autonomy to their constituent groups. But, if that were done, the total number of Trade Unions would seem to be, not eleven hundred, but at least several thousands.

While the official figures do not really tell us how many Trade Unions there are, their variations are worthy of study for purposes of comparison. In 1892, the first year for which particulars exist, the official returns gave a total of 1,208 registered and unregistered Trade Unions. The number then rose steadily to 1,337 in 1897. Thereafter it fell, with only one slight interruption, to 1,106 in 1915. The earlier part of the fall was largely due to the collapse of mushroom Unions started in the earlier 'nineties; but the latter part was mainly the result of consolidation, the amalgamation of separate societies into larger units. The average size of a Trade Union shows a membership of 1,250 in 1892, as against 2,000 in 1910 and 3,750 in 1913. After 1915 the number of Trade Unions began again to rise, reaching 1,425 in 1920. The process of consolidation did not stop, though it was checked, during the War years; but its effect in reducing the number of separate Unions was far more than offset by the creation of new ones, especially among the non-manual workers. The non-manual groups, including workers in the distributive, commercial and public services, accounted for less than a hundred Unions in 1913. In 1921 they accounted for 374. The slump which began in that year both checked the formation of new societies and caused many of the smaller bodies to collapse or amalgamate. The total number of Unions fell again to 1,190 in 1922. And, while these totals mean little, the variation does mean something; for the figures are compiled throughout on much the same basis.

THE STRUCTURE OF TRADE UNIONISM 23

The average number of members per Union rose to 6,000 in 1920, but, owing to the rapid creation of new Societies, the rate of increase did not keep pace with the rise in total membership. After 1920 the average membership fell to 4,500 in 1920, an increase over 1892 of about 260 per cent., which is almost precisely the same as the percentage increase in total Trade Union strength. In other words, according to the official figures, the number of Unions increases at practically the same rate as the number of members. It looks from this as if there were no real progress in the consolidation of Trade Union forces.

This, however, is not the case. There is a steady movement of consolidation in the big industries, which are the real controlling factors in the Trade Union world. A very small number of Trade Unions or effective industrial combinations now include a large proportion of the total membership of all Trade Unions. Thus there are now ten bodies, each with more than 100,000 members, which between them include about half the total number of Trade Unionists in Great Britain.[1] A further fifth, or nearly a million, are in thirteen other Societies with more than 50,000 members each.[2] And four and a half millions out of about five millions of organised workers are enrolled in a total of seventy Societies. In other words, nine-tenths of the members are enrolled in less than one-sixteenth of the number of Trade Unions given in the official returns. This is partly because of the returning of local units of national bodies as separate Societies, and partly because there are many very small Societies, especially among non-manual workers. There are not, in all, more than a hundred Trade Unions, including the unified bodies which we have described, that play any effective part in the work of the movement as a whole, or add anything considerable to its bargaining strength.

Yet, though amalgamation and consolidation have made big progress, there is still no single principle clearly at work which dictates the basis on which Trade Union organisation is to proceed. The British Trade Union movement is distinguished from the

---

[1] Miner's Federation (800,000), National Union of General and Municipal Workers (500,000), National Union of Railwaymen (350,000), Transport and General Workers' Union (300,000), Amalgamated Engineering Union (256,000), Amalgamated Weavers' Association (171,000), Workers' Union (140,000), National Union of Teachers (120,000), Amalgamated Society of Woodworkers (116,000), Iron and Steel Trades Confederation (103,000).

[2] Distributive Workers (90,000), Boilermakers (90,000), Post Office Workers (80,000), Cardroom Operatives (76,000), Boot and Shoe Operatives (76,000), Printing, Bookbinding and Paper Workers (70,000), Building Trade Workers (61,000), Locomotive Engineers (60,000), Railway Clerks (60,000), Sailors and Firemen (60,000), National Union of Textile Workers (60,000), Painters and Decorators (58,000), Tailors and Garment Workers (56,000), Spinners' Amalgamation (51,000).

Trade Union movements in most Continental countries by the fact that it has not been created by some central organisation or under the inspiration of some single purpose, but has grown up almost haphazard over a long period to meet special needs and to deal with immediate difficulties. The result of this is that in the main the organisation rests upon no common principle, and disputes between Unions, not merely on points of detail, but on points affecting the vital principles of organisation, are very frequent. There are, in the main, two rival principles of organisation which are at present contending for supremacy in the Trade Union movement, Craft Unionism and Industrial Unionism. These two principles, however, seldom appear in a pure form, but are generally complicated by subordinate considerations, so that it is very difficult to get a clear view of the precise questions at issue in any actual case of inter-union dispute.

Up to 1889, as we saw, the Trade Union movement, apart from one or two industries, consisted almost entirely of skilled workers, and was dominated at the Trades Union Congresses by the organisations representing skilled workers alone. In the late 'eighties the less skilled workers for the first time began to organise on a considerable scale. Finding in the field already strongly established organisations consisting of skilled workers alone, and faced by the vested interests and prejudices of these skilled organisations, they were compelled to form separate Unions of their own, apart from those which already existed. Thus there grew up the great general workers' Unions, including not merely all grades of workers in certain industries which had not previously been organised, *e.g.*, waterside workers, but also to an increasing extent the unskilled workers in those industries in which effective Craft Unions already existed. This movement did not affect certain industries, notably mining and the textile and printing industries, in which the division between the craftsman and the unskilled worker was not clear, and in which no body of unspecialised general labourers could be said to exist. But over a large part of industry there appeared in the late 'eighties, and remains up to the present time, a wide cleavage in the methods of organisation, the skilled workers being organised in a group of Craft Unions of their own, while the unskilled are organised in a number of overlapping and rival Unions of general workers. We noted that when the movement amongst the unskilled workers first gathered force in the late 'eighties the spokesmen of the skilled Trade Union organisations were perfectly confident that it would prove to be only a passing wave of revolt, and that, once the momentary enthusiasm had passed, the general workers' Unions would collapse, because they had not, to bind them together, the

THE STRUCTURE OF TRADE UNIONISM 25

close community of craft interests, high contributions, and high benefits upon which the skilled Unions rely. We know to-day that this diagnosis of the situation was incorrect, and that after a temporary set-back the movement of organisation amongst less skilled workers has persisted until to-day, the less skilled workers now constituting an important section in the Trade Union movement.[1] It is none the less important for this reason to point out that the belief which was widely prevalent among the craftsmen in the 'eighties and 'nineties that permanent organisation amongst unskilled workers was impossible, is principally responsible for the present situation in the Trade Union movement, which sharply divides the craftsman from the unskilled worker. The essential difference between Craft Unionism and the rival forms of organisation which are now threatening its supremacy is that Craft Unionism aims at organising only the skilled workers, or at least at organising skilled and unskilled in separate Unions; whereas Industrial Unionism aims at embracing within the ranks of each Union the whole *personnel* of the industry with which it is concerned, including skilled and unskilled workers indifferently. Clearly the ease with which an industrial Union can come into being depends largely on the sharpness of the distinction between skilled and unskilled in the industry concerned. Thus in the mining and textile industries, as we have already noted, there is no very sharp distinction between the two classes of workers. In mining the boy who enters the pit has every chance of passing, before many years have gone by, into the ranks of the coal-getters, who form the skilled section of the coal-mining industry. There is no sharp division or cleavage of interests between the main sections of the mining community. Promotion runs easily from one grade to another, and therefore it is the easier to realise a form of combination in which all these various sections are grouped together in a single industrial organisation.

This does not apply with equal force to the small specialised sections of craftsmen who are employed in and about the mines, and, as we have seen, separate organisations persist among colliery enginemen, mechanics, deputies, and certain other sections of mine-workers; but these form altogether only a comparatively small section of the mining industry, and by reason of the absence, so far as the main groups of mine-workers are concerned, of any clear cleavage between skilled and unskilled, the mining community has been the first to realise something like an effective form of "industrial" organisation.

The railway service is to some extent in a similar position. If

[1] The general labour Unions include about 650,000 out of about 5,000,000 organised workers.

we leave out for the moment the special problem of the mechanics in the railway shops, there is only one section amongst the manual workers on the railways which has a very definite craftsmanship and a clear separate sectional interest. This section is, of course, the locomotive section, including drivers, firemen, and cleaners, among whom promotion proceeds from one grade to another apart from the general body of railway workers. Trade Unionism among railway employees has only become strong at a very recent date—since the all-grades movement of 1906. Since then the great mass of the grades employed in railway work have combined into an effective industrial union, but more than half the workers employed in the locomotive crafts have remained in their separate Union—the Associated Society of Locomotive Engineers and Firemen. In addition to the N.U.R. and the " Associated Society," there is, of course, a further separate organisation in the Railway Clerks' Association, now including the great bulk of the clerical staffs of the various railways, and a good proportion of the stationmasters and supervisory grades. This Association again represents a very distinct section of railway employees, and it is significant that in recent years it has shown an increasing tendency to work in co-operation with the Unions of manual workers, although the majority of its members are still apparently unwilling to go to the length of complete amalgamation.

The problem of the railway shops is a separate question of very great complexity ; for the railway shops may be said to form in some sense a link between the industry of railway transport and the industry of engineering. They employ a large number of craftsmen belonging to various metal-working and wood-working Craft Unions, and also a considerable number of less skilled and unskilled workers. So far as the metal-working trades in the railway shops are concerned, the fully skilled men belong principally to the various Craft Unions in the engineering industry. The less skilled workers, on the other hand, and also many of the wood-workers, and a growing minority even of the engineers, are already members of the N.U.R., and the principal struggle in the Trade Union movement in recent years has been concentrated round the claim of the N.U.R. to control the whole body of workers employed in the railway shops.

The mining and the railway industries are the most obvious cases in which a form of organisation following the line of industry rather than craft is clearly dictated by the conditions of employment and the absence of a clear line of separation between skilled and unskilled workers. It is therefore in these industries that the movement towards industrial organisation has found its clearest expression, and the struggle between craft and industrial organisa-

THE STRUCTURE OF TRADE UNIONISM

tion has appeared in its most acute form. In certain other industries, notably in the textile and printing industries, the struggle between the two forms of organisation either does not exist or assumes quite different forms. In these cases there is no large body of unskilled workers separate from the body of craftsmen employed in the industry, but, on the other hand, there is a sharp distinction between a number of crafts, sections, or departments, which together include the great bulk of workers in the industry. The cotton workers will serve as an example of what is meant. The spinners and piecers, the card and blowing-room operatives, and the weavers each form a separate section or department of the cotton industry. Each section is now organised in what is usually called a Craft Union, but these Craft Unions are in a very different position from the Craft Unions in such an industry as engineering, since among them they do include the great bulk of the whole *personnel* of the industry concerned.[1]

There has, therefore, been in these industries practically no opening for the entrance of the general workers' Unions, since there is no mass of unspecialised workers for these Unions to organise. This does not abolish the distinction between Craft and Industrial Unionism, or prevent the emergence of a movement making for effective combination of the whole *personnel* of the industry in a single organisation; but it does mean that these movements are very greatly simplified, and they become simply movements for the amalgamation of existing Craft Unions, not complicated by the demand that large bodies of workers at present included in general workers' Unions not confined to any particular industry should surrender their present Trade Union allegiance and throw in their lot with the industry in which they are for the moment employed.

The third group of industries is that around which conflict between Craft and Industrial Unionism is likely to concentrate in the future, even if the present conflicts in the railway and mining industries are satisfactorily settled. In these industries we find a number of Craft Unions including skilled workers only. We find also a number of general workers' Unions, or in some cases of specialised labourers' Unions confined to a particular industry, which include the great bulk of the less skilled or unskilled workers. Attempts to secure organisation on the lines of Industrial Unionism in these cases have obviously very much greater obstacles to over-

[1] There are a number of small Craft Unions in the cotton industry, but these Craft Unions follow the same principle of organisation, and if we take the seven or eight Craft Unions in the cotton industry together, almost the whole effective *personnel*, except the mechanics and enginemen, employed in the cotton industry in Lancashire and Cheshire is included in one Union or another.

come. Union by industry in these cases is not only a question of amalgamation or fusion of interests between a number of Craft Unions, but also involves the bringing into the organisation of those less skilled or unskilled workers who are at present organised in general workers' Unions not confined to the particular industry concerned. The metal and building industries are the outstanding instances of this type.

This enumeration of the particular difficulties prevailing does not suffice to present any general picture of the present conflict in the Trade Union world. It is, therefore, necessary to deal with the question rather more analytically, and to try to sum up under a number of heads the actual forms which Trade Union organisation at the present time assumes.

Section 3.—A Classification of Trade Unions [1]

(1) *The Craft Union.*—A Craft Union in its pure form consists of persons following a particular calling or occupation, possessing in common a certain skill, and aiming in common at the general enforcement for their trade of a certain set of conditions of employment. Instances of such combination are found in such Unions as the United Patternmakers' Association or the Associated Blacksmiths' Society in the engineering industry; the societies of overlookers or tape-sizers in the cotton industry; those of plumbers or plasterers in the building industry, and many others. Often, however, the Craft Union form does not appear in such purity as this, and we find associated in a single union a number of kindred grades. This is the case, for instance, with the boilermakers, who include angle-iron smiths, platers, caulkers, riveters, and various other sections. The Amalgamated Engineering Union includes fitters, turners, machinists, millwrights, smiths, electricians, planers, borers, slotters, patternmakers, and a large number of other grades; the Weavers' Amalgamation includes weavers, winders, warpers, and a number of other grades; and there are other cases of the same kind. Thus, an organisation which is based on the craft principle may have either a very narrow or a very wide basis of membership. It may be confined to a single narrow specialised occupation, or it may include a large number of kindred crafts. In this connection it is important to notice that disputes may arise not simply between "craft" and "industrial" organisations, but also between craft organisations on a wider or narrower basis. Thus the A.E.U. is at present a kindred Craft Union, though it includes a certain number of

---

[1] Throughout this Section reference should be made to the chart reproduced as a frontispiece to this book.

semi-skilled workers, but it falls frequently into dispute, not simply with those who advocate the "industrial" basis of organisation, but also with those who advocate a separate Trade Union for each distinct craft group. The A.E.U. has frequently contended for the wider basis as against the blacksmiths, pattern-makers, and other specialised Craft Unions, and it does actually cater for the crafts which these specialised Craft Unions also attempt to organise.

A further complication of "Craft" Unionism occurs where a single craft is found in a number of different industries. Thus there are mechanics or millwrights in almost every industry, and much the same can be said of enginemen. Clerks, too, occur in all industries as well as in commerce and in the public services. Carpenters and joiners are found not only in the building industry, but also in large numbers in the shipyards, and the same applies to painters, plumbers, and various other classes of workers. Thus such Craft Unions as the Amalgamated Engineering Union, the National Union of Enginemen, the National Union of Clerks, and the Amalgamated Society of Woodworkers have a membership scattered through many industries.

(2) Akin to the craft basis of organisation is a basis of organisation which it is not easy to define. I will call it for the moment Material Trade Unionism. This form of organisation follows the line not of the precise craft followed by the worker concerned, but of the material on which he or she may happen to be working. Thus, there are many who advocate that all the various sections of skilled woodworkers (carpenters, cabinet-makers, and joiners, furnishing trades, wood-cutting machinists, packing-case makers, etc.) should amalgamate into a single union, not on industrial lines, but on the lines of the material on which all these crafts in common work; and this idea seems to have been in the mind of those who adopted the name of Amalgamated Society of Woodworkers for the new body formed by the joiners and cabinet-makers after their fusion a few years ago. It is interesting to note that this is actually the form of organisation adopted by the largest Trade Union in Germany—the Union of Metal-workers. This Union, however, organises not only the skilled metal-workers, but also the labourers and less skilled grades. Again, it is worth noting that, even assuming Material Trade Unionism as a basis, the spirit of organisation may be wide or narrow. For instance, it is possible, as in Germany, to have a Metal-workers' Union including workers on all forms of metal. But it is also possible, as in this country, to have specialised Trade Unions, including only workers on some one kind of metal, *e.g.*, brass workers, copper workers, iron and steel workers, etc., and disputes may arise here, too, between the

narrower and the wider forms of organisation without any question as to the general basis on which organisation is to proceed. Material Unionism is not necessarily allied with Craft Unionism. Indeed, in Germany, the Metal-workers' Union is far more nearly akin to an Industrial than to a Craft Union. In this country, however, advocates of Material Unionism have generally stopped short at the advocacy of a union of skilled men working upon the material concerned, and they thus find themselves in alliance with Craft Unionism of the A.E.U. type. Indeed, it is often difficult to distinguish the plans for an amalgamation of skilled workers on a " material " basis from plans for a kindred craft organisation of a number of associated crafts which are employed in, say, woodworking processes.

(3) Broadly contrasted with Craft Unionism in all its various forms is Union by Industry, which again may assume a number of different forms. Advocates of Union by Industry, broadly speaking, set out to combine in a single Union all those workers who co-operate in producing a common product or type of product, or in rendering a common service, irrespective of the degree of skill which they happen to possess. Thus they aim at creating one Union for the railway industry, one Union for the mining industry, one Union for the building industry, and so on. This form of organisation, however, is difficult to distinguish clearly from a form of organisation which aims at copying exactly the present capitalist structure of industry, and at grouping in a single Union all those persons who work under a common employer or group of employers. The tendency is found to varying extents in different industries. It is especially strong in those cases in which a particular group of employers is clearly marked off from other employers either by some public or semi-public status, or by some other special consideration. Thus, when a Union sets out to combine in its membership the whole *personnel* of the railway industry, it does not limit itself to organising only the traffic grades, but seeks also to combine in membership all those persons who are employed by railway companies, whether they are engaged directly in railway transport, or are producing some product required for such transport, *e.g.*, locomotives or railway trucks, or are rendering some different kind of service, *e.g.*, serving on ships or in hotels. In this case organisation by type of service does not coincide with organisation following the lines of the employer by whom the workers are employed ; but the two forms of organisation do approximate sufficiently to enable them to be very difficult to distinguish. Thus in those particular cases where, as on the railways, a clearly marked group of employers undertakes productive work distinct from, but necessary to, the service with which it

THE STRUCTURE OF TRADE UNIONISM

is chiefly concerned, Union by Industry in the narrower sense, which groups together all the workers who co-operate in rendering a common service, easily inevitably runs into what we will call " Employment " Unionism, which aims at following the lines of the employers' organisation. In other cases, however, " Employment " Unionism diverges very widely indeed from Union by Industry. For instance, there are large numbers of tramway undertakings or electricity undertakings which are owned by municipalities, and large numbers of others which are owned by private companies. On the lines of " Employment " Unionism the employees in municipal tramways or electricity undertakings would be linked up with other municipal employees in a Union of municipal workers; whereas, on the lines of Union by Industry, the whole body of workers employed in rendering service in the running of trams or the production of electricity would be grouped in a single Union irrespective of the type of employer under whom they happened to be working. Similarly, in the Co-operative Movement, the attempt to unite in one Union all grades of Co-operative employees, productive as well as distributive, cuts right across the lines of Union by Industry; for, in the first place, it separates the distributive workers employed by Co-operative Stores and Wholesale Societies from other distributive workers employed by retail shops and warehouses privately owned, and thus divides the *personnel* of the distributive industry into two distinct sections. Moreover, the Co-operative Movement also engages largely in productive work, and therefore an inclusive Union of Co-operative employees would have to organise in its ranks large numbers of productive workers employed in the boot and shoe, clothing, food and drink, and other industries. We see thus that the principle of organisation by industry in some cases coincides or nearly coincides with organisation by employment, while, in other cases, a wide divergence appears between the two forms of combination.

There is also a further difference which must be noted. The principle of organisation by industry is applicable in practice without great difficulty over almost the whole of the industrial population. Organisation by employment, on the other hand, is only easily practicable in certain cases, in which there exists a clearly marked type of employer differentiated from the general body of outside employers; *e.g.*, the State, or the Postmaster-General; the Local Authority; the Co-operative Movement, the Railway Companies. Organisation by employment could hardly be applied to the great mass of privately owned industries, whereas union by industry is at least far more widely applicable.

The conflict between rival principles of organisation in the Trade

Union movement has been described in terms of Craft Unionism and Union by Industry, because it is round these forms of Trade Union organisation that the conflict is mostly centred. There are, however, certain other forms of Trade Union structure which demand special mention. Where, in an industry employing a considerable proportion of unskilled labour, Craft Unionism or Kindred Craft Unionism is adopted as the principle of organisation, it necessarily follows that the less skilled workers will remain unorganised, or else that they will form separate Unions of their own. In Great Britain, since the 'eighties, the latter, as we have seen, has been the case, and there have grown up powerful Unions of unskilled workers. In some cases these have been Unions of labourers attached to a particular craft or industry, *e.g.*, builders' labourers. In other cases, and this is the position in the majority of cases, the less skilled workers have grouped themselves together irrespective of craft or industry in organisations which attempt to combine all those workers for whom no specialised Craft or Industrial Union exists. Thus, the general workers' Unions in this country, which now have a membership of about 650,000, include amongst their members a number of distinct types of workers : (*a*) unskilled workers in industries in which specialised Craft Unions of skilled workers exist, *e.g.*, engineering labourers, builders' labourers, etc. ; (*b*) workers of all sorts in industries or trades for which no effective special organisations exist, *e.g.*, laundry workers, chemical workers, brewery workers, etc. ; (*c*) workers in trades or industries for which, although special organisations exist, these special organisations do not cover the whole country, or have not been able to establish their claim to organise all the workers employed in a particular trade or industry, *e.g.*, transport workers, workers in certain of the textile industries, etc. Sometimes these Unions go still further, and enrol workers who are clearly eligible for strong and recognised Craft or Industrial Unions. This tendency has become considerably more marked during recent years, particularly in the case of the Workers' Union, which, in the minds of some of its members and officials, seems to be regarded as a sort of embryonic Industrial Workers of the World, with all Labour for its province. Apart from this tendency, the general workers' Unions to-day tend to be amalgamations of all the workers in the less specialised trades and industries, together with the great mass of less skilled workers in certain highly specialised and organised industries.

A further type of Union, now nearly extinct in this country, is that which follows the line of sex. The majority of skilled Craft Unions admit only male workers, and would refuse to accept women on grounds of sex alone, even if they were otherwise

THE STRUCTURE OF TRADE UNIONISM 33

eligible for membership. This is, in effect, a sex distinction, and constitutes the Unions which do this sex unions, though they would not be generally recognised as being so. A clearer case is found in the Unions which organise only women. These may be of any type, either Craft Unions, as in the case of the Manchester Union of Women in the Bookbinding Trades; Unions on an "industrial" basis, as in the case of the Independent Women Boot and Shoe Operatives' Union; or they may be general Unions. Of late years, these separate women's societies have been rapidly disappearing. By far the largest, the National Federation of Women Workers, amalgamated shortly after the end of the War with the National Union of General Workers, forming a special Women's Section within the larger body. All save an insignificant fraction of the 800,000 women organised in Trade Unions are now enrolled in Unions which include both men and women, *e.g.*, the Weavers' Amalgamation and other textile Unions; the National Union of the Printing and Paper Workers; the National Amalgamated Union of Shop Assistants, Warehousemen and Clerks; the National Union of Distributive and Allied Workers, etc.

There is one further type of union which it is only necessary to mention in order to dismiss it with a word. This is the type which endeavours to include in a single organisation all workers irrespective of trade, craft, industry, sex, or any other consideration, on the basis merely of their own status within the capitalist system. Of this type is the organisation known as the Industrial Workers of the World. But since the two, or perhaps three, organisations in Great Britain which have passed under this name have had between them only the most insignificant membership, it is only necessary to record the type as one that is possible without laying any special stress upon it. Even in America and Australia, where the I.W.W. has been strenuous, it has, in fact, only succeeded in combining in its ranks a tiny fraction of the workers, including, in the United States, mainly immigrants from Southern and Eastern Europe.

Section 4.—THE AREA OF ORGANISATION

No survey of the character of Trade Union organisation could be complete without a glance at the geographical area covered by the typical Trade Unions of to-day. A quarter of a century ago, there were already in most cases national Unions for the principal crafts extending over the whole of England and Wales. This national form of organisation has been maintained, and in a number of cases the separate Scottish and Irish Unions which existed a quarter of a century ago have been absorbed in the English organisations. Scottish Trade Unionism still preserves, however, to some extent, its separate national organisation with national characteristics of its own. The Scottish Railway Servants' Union was absorbed by the English Society in 1892, and the Associated Carpenters and Joiners of Scotland amalgamated with the leading English Society in 1911, while the National Union of Scottish Mine-Workers forms a district of the Miners' Federation of Great Britain. On the other hand, in several of the building trades and in the textile and printing trades, and in agriculture and some of the small metal trades, separate Scottish Societies still exist, acting sometimes in entire independence of the English Societies, and sometimes in close relation to them. Most of the engineering and shipbuilding societies, however, cover Scotland as well as England and Wales, while in a few instances separate Scottish Unions compete with Unions covering the whole of Great Britain. It is noticeable that there are no special Scottish Unions of general workers. The Unions organising these grades are common to the whole of Great Britain.

It should be noted that many of the Unions covering the whole of Great Britain maintain Scottish Advisory Councils or District Councils, with varying degrees of autonomy and powers of separate action. The tendency of late years has been towards the fusion of the separate English and Scottish Societies, but at the same time towards a greater measure of autonomy for the Scottish districts of all-British Unions. In many cases, these district organisations, as well as the separate Scottish Societies, are affiliated to the Scottish Trades Union Congress, a body of growing importance and influence.

Of Trade Unionism in Ireland it is far more difficult to speak, because recent political movements and changes have produced, and are still producing, their effects on industrial organisation. In Belfast, the great majority of the organised workers belong to Societies which have their headquarters in Great Britain. The Ulster textile area is mainly organised by purely Ulster Societies, mostly weak and not very effective. In the Irish Free State, the Trade Union Movement is dominated by one big Union, the Irish Transport and General Workers' Union, with 100,000 members, including a small number in Ulster. This body, which sprang into prominence in 1912 under the leadership of Connolly and Larkin, has grown very rapidly, absorbing many of the small local Societies which used to be a feature of Irish Trade Unionism, and also gaining many members from the British Trade Unions which have Irish districts. Until the rebirth of Irish Nationalism, Irish workers were largely unorganised, the organised sections being mostly in British Unions, with a minority

THE STRUCTURE OF TRADE UNIONISM   35

in small local Societies. The British Unions, though they have lost ground relatively, still have many members in the Free State, and in most cases have been compelled to form Irish Councils with fairly wide autonomous powers. In some instances, there are rival British and Irish Unions trying to organise the same groups of workers. In others, as in the Post Office, the British Unions have agreed that their Irish District should pass over to a purely Irish Union. The Irish Trade Union Congress and Labour Party, which aims at covering Ulster as well as the Free State, but has its main strength in the latter, includes branches and districts of British Unions as well as the Irish Societies. It is, however, dominated by the Irish Transport and General Workers' Union, which accounts for a majority of the total membership of all its affiliated Trade Unions.

Wales has hardly any separate Unions, unless such bodies as the North Wales Miners' Association and the South Wales Miners' Federation, which both form part of the Miners' Federation of Great Britain, are so regarded. But, again, a number of Unions have Welsh districts, and of late years there have been several attempts to create a common federal organisation for industrial purposes over the Principality as a whole. There is a North Wales Labour Council, and occasional Conferences of Welsh Unions and Districts have been held. But, on the whole, the Trade Union Movement in Wales is not clearly marked off from the British movement.

A few of the great Craft Unions, such as the Amalgamated Engineering Union and the Amalgamated Society of Woodworkers, do not confine their organising activity to the United Kingdom, but have branches and districts overseas, in Australia, Canada and South Africa, or even outside the Empire. These are mainly the result of the emigration of skilled craftsmen, and, while the few Unions with such overseas organisation show no sign of abandoning it at present, save in the United States, there is no tendency for their example to be followed. In the main, the various countries within the Empire have their own Trade Unions, with only fraternal links with the Unions in the United Kingdom.

Section 5.—FEDERATIONS OF TRADE UNIONS

We have so far been considering the various Trade Unions chiefly as separate bodies, each with its own independent structure and form of government. But we have seen already that it is not always easy to tell the difference between a separate Trade Union and a close Federation of Trade Unions. Just as the

United States or the Commonwealth of Australia is from one point of view a single State, and from another a federation of distinct States, so there is difficulty in drawing a clear line of division in the Trade Union world. Above we have treated as being in effect single Trade Unions those federal bodies which on all industrial matters of importance follow a common policy and accept a common direction. Federations of this degree of unity are, however, comparatively rare, and belong, as we shall see, in all cases to a single type. The great majority of the Federations in the Trade Union movement are of far looser structure, and group together for a limited range of purposes separate Unions which are clearly independent bodies.

(a) The Federations, such as the Miners' Federation of Great Britain and the Weavers' "Amalgamation," which we have regarded as being in effect single Trade Unions, all consist mainly of localised societies, each covering a defined area of its own narrower than the area covered by the Federation. Thus the Miners' Federation consists mainly of the district miners' Unions in Yorkshire, Durham, Scotland, South Wales, and other coal fields; the Weavers' "Amalgamation" of local weavers' Societies in the various Lancashire towns. In these cases there is no overlapping, or practically none, between the federated Societies. The only inter-union question that arises is the degree of autonomy to be recognised within the national combination.

(b) On the other hand, such Federations as the National Printing and Kindred Trades Federation, the National Federation of Building Trades Operatives, or the Northern Counties Textile Trades Federation, consist of a number of national Unions, largely covering the same geographical area, but catering in the main for distinct sections of workers within a given industry. Thus the Printing and Kindred Trades Federation consists of Unions of compositors, bookbinders, printing-machine managers, pressmen, lithographers, etc., while the Northern Counties Textile Trades Federation consists of Unions of weavers, beamers, twisters and drawers, overlookers, etc. In such Federations as these there is, again, little or no overlapping. What the Federation itself does is to group together, on a more or less " industrial " basis, a number of distinct Craft Unions, each catering for its own section of workers within a particular industry.

(c) Sometimes hard to distinguish from this second type is a third type of Federation, consisting largely or mainly of overlapping or rival Trade Unions. Thus such bodies as the National Federation of General Workers and the Engineering and Shipbuilding Trades Federation consist of a number of Unions, many of which cater for the same class of workers and actually compete

THE STRUCTURE OF TRADE UNIONISM 37

one with another to secure members amongst these workers. In these cases overlapping between Unions exists on a large scale, and the Unions come together not because they represent distinct grades of workers who can benefit by co-operation, but because, even although they are competing one with another for members, they can increase their industrial strength in bargaining, and perhaps even settle their disputes one with another, by means of federal action. The National Transport Workers' Federation, formerly of this type, has, since the fusion of many of its affiliated bodies into the Transport and General Workers' Union, come to approximate rather to the second type of Federation.

Of course, any of these forms of federation may cover a wider or a narrower geographical area. Thus the Midland Miners' Federation, which consists of local miners' associations in North Stafford, South Stafford, Warwickshire, and four other districts, is a federation of the first type, consisting of Unions covering a smaller geographical area than the Federation which they compose. The Local Textile Trades Federation in Burnley or Blackburn is of the second type, and consists of specialised Craft Unions which do not overlap; while a local Engineering and Allied Trades Federation, consisting largely of overlapping Trade Unions, falls under the third type.

The strength of the various Federations depends largely on the particular type to which they belong. It is obvious that it will be far easier to secure effective common action where there is no overlapping between the Unions which constitute the Federation, and that where overlapping exists there will be a constant tendency for the constituent elements in the Federation to quarrel one with another concerning membership, etc., instead of presenting a united front to the employers on industrial questions. Therefore, Federations of the first two types tend to be considerably stronger and to assume larger industrial functions than Federations of the third type, which are almost necessarily weak in dealing with questions of industrial relations. Again, Federations of the first type tend to be stronger than Federations of the second type, since the Unions which compose them are homogeneous in character and consist of almost exactly the same type of members in every area. There is, therefore, comparatively little room for divergence of policy between the various local bodies composing Federations of the first type. Federations of the second type stand in an intermediate position. Any section may hold and put forward a distinct policy of its own in contravention of the policy of the other sections. But this tendency to differ is not so fatal to effective federal action as the existence of strong differences between the Unions composing a Federation of the third type, in consequence of overlapping, rivalry, and competition for members. The degree of solidarity achieved since the War by the National Federation of Building Trades Operatives, which acts as a single unit for negotiatory purposes, pools its organisers in times of dispute, and actually starts mixed branches in small centres under its own control, shows how great a step towards solidarity may be made by a body of the second type if strong personalities are at its head.

Federations of one or the other of the above types are found in the great bulk of the industries of the United Kingdom, and in greater or less degree it may be seen that these Federations serve to reduce still further than was suggested in our opening sections the number of effective Trade Union combinations from a negotiating point of view. In most industries where there is more than one Trade Union concerned, each Trade Union does not meet the employer singly. A number of Unions, through a Federation or joint association of some sort, meet the employer together and adopt a common policy. This co-operation tends to be applied to local as well as national negotiations. This is a marked feature of Trade Union action in most industries, and, unless its importance is recognised, the observer will tend to exaggerate the amount of disorganisation which at present prevails in the British Trade Union movement. The Table given in Appendix III., showing to what extent Trade Unions in certain of the big industries combine for purposes of industrial negotiation, will serve to drive home most strongly the point that there is nothing like the amount of disorganisation in the British Trade Union Movement which is often deemed to exist.

Section 6.—TRADES COUNCILS AND LOCAL LABOUR PARTIES

The vast mass of organised workers in Great Britain belong to Trade Unions which extend either over the whole country, or at least over a wide area embracing many distinct towns and villages. This involves local organisation—the division of the Union as a whole into branches, and often into districts uniting a number of branches within a manageable area. As we shall see, these branches and districts of national Trade Unions, while they are usually for strike purposes under the control of the national Unions, have certain limited powers of their own. One use which they make of this power is to form locally federal organisations not confined either to a group of crafts or to a single industry, but designed, through wider combination, to emphasise and organise the essential solidarity among all sections of the working class. This tendency finds expression on its industrial side in the local Trades Councils—federations of local Trade Union branches

THE STRUCTURE OF TRADE UNIONISM 39

and independent local Trade Unions in each particular district. The organisation of Trades Councils has proceeded apace during each period of intense industrial activity in the Trade Union movement; *i.e.*, after the Dock Strike of 1889, in the movement of 1906 and the following years, and again during recent years. It is particularly rapid at the present time, and it is now safe to say that there are not many towns or districts of any industrial importance throughout Great Britain in which Trades Councils do not exist, unless it be under special circumstances such as are mentioned below. In many cases these Trades Councils used to fulfil not only industrial, but also political functions, taking the place in the latter case of Local Labour Parties. In nearly all districts there now exists not merely a Trades Council, but also a Local Labour Party, which unites the Trade Union branches with the Socialist Societies and other similar bodies in the district for the purpose of local or national political work. Where no Trades Council exists, the Local Labour Party may also assume industrial functions. The number of Local Labour Parties has been very largely increased since the reorganisation of the Labour Party under its revised constitution of 1918, of which the outstanding feature was the admission to the Local Labour Parties of individual members as well as affiliated bodies.

It is worthy of notice that, during the last few years, there has been a considerable movement among Trades Councils, as distinct from Local Labour Parties, towards federation. Thus Federations up in Lancashire and Cheshire, Yorkshire, Kent, South Staffs, and a number of other districts, and in two cases, Lancashire and Cheshire and Yorkshire, there are two county Federations, one of Trades Councils and the other of Local Labour Parties. Moreover, a number of the leading Trades Councils have, since 1921, been linked up in a National Federation of Trades Councils, independent of the Trades Union Congress. The rise of this movement led the Congress in 1924 to give fuller recognition to the Trades Councils, and the General Council of the Congress took the initiative in establishing a Joint Advisory Committee, representing on the one side the General Council and on the other the leading local Trades Councils. The object of this step was, doubtless, both to check the rise of a separate Trades Councils movement under Communist leadership, and to equip the Congress with much needed machinery for local action in demonstrations, campaigns for securing new members, or pushing some feature of Trade Union policy, and similar work. The desire, however, of the Trades Councils to regain the strict representation at the Trades Union Congress which they lost in 1895 has not been satisfied. The national Unions take objection to this on the ground of overlapping, although Local Labour Parties, which overlap in much the same way, are directly represented at the Labour Party Conference. Councils have sprung up all over the country, with little or no central guidance, performing, in the majority of cases, very useful work in serving to emphasise what greatly needs emphasis in the Trade Union Movement—the essential community of interest among all sections of workers. They have suffered from a weakness resulting from inadequacy of funds and lack of definite functions, but against this weakness they have struggled with considerable success, and there can be no doubt that their accomplishment in the past has been on the whole a notable one, or that, given further recognition, both by the Congress and by the national Trade Unions, they are capable of still more useful service.

The functions of Trade Councils in the Trade Union Movement have never been at all accurately defined, and there seems to be very little approach to a clear idea on the subject among Trade Unionists themselves.

Section 7.—THE UNEMPLOYED MOVEMENT

At periods of acute unemployment, special organisations of unemployed workers have made their appearance more than once in the history of the working-class movement. The unprecedented unemployment of the past few years has called a proportionately active unemployed movement into being. Many of those who are out of work, especially among the returned soldiers, have no definite trade and have never been members of a Trade Union, and many more have dropped out of the Trade Unions after exhausting their claims to unemployment benefit. Moreover, though most Unions provide unemployment benefit in some form, or administer the benefits provided by the State under the Unemployment Insurance Acts, they are principally engaged in safeguarding the position of their members who are employed. Many active Trade Unionists who have fallen out of work have, therefore, felt the need to create distinct organisations chiefly for purposes of agitation and also in order to promote among the unemployed a sense of solidarity among themselves and with the working-class movement.

In town after town, therefore, there have sprung up Unemployed Workers' Committees or Movements. In 1921 a National Conference of the Unemployed was held, many of the delegates marching on foot to attend it. This Conference created a National Unemployed Workers' Committee, with which many of the local committees are connected. In a fair number of cases, provision has also been made for the local Unemployed Workers' Committee to become affiliated to the local Trades Council, while the Trades Union Congress General Council has formed a Joint Advisory Committee with the N.U.W.C.M., and this joint body has issued a national programme of demands. The Unemployed Workers' Movement is not fully representative of those who are out of work, and has come in fact, very naturally, under left wing and largely Communist leadership. It is unlikely, as a separate organisation, to outlast the depression which called it into being; for unemployed workers are naturally very short of money, and therefore find it difficult to build up stable organisations. The personnel of such a movement is, moreover, necessarily shifting; and it is liable at any time to lose its leaders as they find regular employment. The movement has largely copied the regular Trade Union structure; but, valuable as it may be for purposes of agitation, it is by its nature prevented from acquiring the stability characteristic of Trade Union organisation. There are many who regret that the Trade Union movement did not itself take up the task of organising the unemployed, instead of leaving them to form a necessarily weak and unstable organisation of their own.

Section 8.—THE NATIONAL TRADE UNION MOVEMENT

The unifying national organisation for the Trade Union movement as a whole is the Trades Union Congress. The Congress includes about four-fifths of the whole membership organised in Trade Unions. Among the manual workers, there are few Unions of importance outside it. The largest is the Amalgamation of Card and Blowing Room Operatives, which seceded recently because it refused to pay the levy imposed by Congress for the support of the *Daily Herald*. The rest of the non-affiliated bodies are either small, or are Unions of non-manual workers, such as the National Union of Teachers. A good many non-manual workers' Societies are, however, affiliated to Congress, and the tendency is for more to come in. Congress is an annual combination of delegates from affiliated Trade Unions, meeting for a week and then dispersing for the rest of the year unless it is called specially together to deal with some urgent problem. It appoints a General Council which meets at least monthly throughout the year to deal with current problems, and this General Council is the nearest approach to a central executive authority which the Trade Union Movement at present possesses. Its weakness is that it is not in a position to enforce any obligation upon the affiliated societies, and that although it has authority to speak for industrial Labour on general questions, it has not the power or the authority to deal effectively with disputes between one Union and another, or between Unions and bodies of employers.

But, while the power of Congress and its General Council is limited, and attempts to make it a real controlling authority for the whole movement are still firmly resisted by many of the great Trade Unions, its power has notably increased during the past few years. Until 1921 there was no General Council, only a much weaker " Parliamentary Committee " with very restricted functions, largely engaged in going on deputation to Ministers in support of resolutions passed at Congress, and almost wholly ineffective as a co-ordinating industrial authority. The need for closer unity was at length realised after the War, largely in connection with big disputes, such as the national railway strike of 1919, to deal with which special *ad hoc* organisations had to be called into being.

The result was a radical change in the organisation of Congress. The Parliamentary Committee, a legacy from earlier times, was replaced by the Trade Union General Council, explicitly designed to act as a co-ordinating industrial authority. Membership of this body was rearranged so as to give direct representation on it to the principal groups of Trade Unions, and two places were specially reserved for representatives of women Trade Unionists. It was, however, provided that the members, though they were to be drawn from the different occupational groups, should all be elected by the vote of the Congress delegates as a whole.[1]

The new Standing Orders of Congress, which came into force in 1921, gave the General Council greatly enlarged functions and powers, but still withheld from it any decisive control over the actions of its affiliated Trade Unions. Attempts in 1922 and 1923 to give it this additional authority broke down before the resistance of the big Unions, which jealously guard their independence and their right to conduct disputes and negotiations in their own way. It is clear that, if Congress is destined to develop into a decisively controlling agency for the whole movement, it will do this only by a gradual accretion of powers, largely by the method of trial.

The real extension which has taken place in the powers of Congress, even without definite sanction under its constitution, has been seen on several occasions since the War. Thus, in 1920, when there was danger that the Government might involve Great Britain in the Russo-Polish War, the Congress, jointly with the Labour Party, formed a Council of Action, and threatened to declare a general strike. It also on this occasion successfully

---

[1] For scheme of representation and sub-committees of the General Council, see Table in Appendix XIV., p. 178.

THE STRUCTURE OF TRADE UNIONISM 43

collected a levy from its affiliated Societies in support of the Council of Action. In the event, a strike was not required; but the incident really established the right of Congress to call one in case of need. The right to levy affiliated Societies was again successfully affirmed two years later in the levy imposed on the Unions on behalf of the *Daily Herald*, when it became the official newspaper of the Labour Party and the Trades Union Congress.

Congress has also become a much more, though not yet a fully, effective authority for dealing with disputes between rival Trade Unions. Increased prestige has brought it increased power, and there is a greater inclination to treat its decisions as authoritative.

The Trades Union Congress claims to speak for Great Britain as a whole; but there is a separate Scottish Trades Union Congress, including both purely Scottish Trade Unions and branches and districts of Unions which have their headquarters in England. The Scottish Congress represents about a quarter of a million members, of whom considerably more than half are in distinct Scottish Societies. It seeks to act as a co-ordinating authority for the movement in Scotland, and has recently (1924) put forward a very advanced programme. But the fact that many agreements and disputes extend to England and Scotland alike prevents it from acquiring a fully independent power of co-ordination.

The Irish Trades Union Congress and Labour Party, which combines industrial and political functions, represents about 200,000 workers, of whom a full half belong to one Society—the Irish Transport and General Workers' Union—another 50,000 to other purely Irish Unions, and less than 40,000 to Unions with headquarters in Great Britain. The Irish Congress is a wholly independent body, and is usually unaffected by British agreements and disputes.

Both the Scottish and Irish Congresses include Trades Councils as well as Trade Unions. The Scottish Congress has about six Trades Councils affiliated to it; the Irish thirty-five.

Second of the great co-ordinating authorities in the Trade Union Movement is the National Labour Party, with its Scottish Advisory Council. This is a Federation of Trade Unions, Socialist and other Societies, and Local Labour Parties, together with a number of Trades Councils admitted before 1918. The Trade Unions possess in this body the overwhelming preponderance of affiliated membership and voting strength.[1] We need not here enter in detail into the functions of this body, since it confines itself to political questions, and leaves purely industrial matters exclusively to the Trades Union Congress.

[1] See pp. 106 and 161.

Between these two bodies, the Trades Union Congress and the Labour Party, there exists a very close working arrangement, concluded shortly after the reorganisation of Congress which we have noticed above. Each body maintains its own separate annual meeting—the Trades Union Congress and the Labour Party Conference are the two great Labour gatherings of the year. Each also has its own executive authority—the General Council of Congress and the Executive Committee of the Labour Party. But between these two bodies and the Labour Members of Parliament there are close links. The Congress and the Labour Party conduct joint departments for publicity, information and research, international questions, etc. There is also, for purposes common to the whole movement, a National Joint Council, representing the Congress General Council, the Party Executive, and the Labour M.P.'s in equal numbers. Moreover, the two " national committees," that is, the General Council and the Party Executive, hold joint meetings whenever necessary for the decision of matters of common interest, including the control of the joint departments. National campaigns, such as the " Mines for the Nation " Campaign of 1920, have been run jointly by the Congress and the Labour Party.

The third body which makes some attempt to co-ordinate the Trade Union Movement as a whole is the General Federation of Trade Unions, which started amid a great flourish of trumpets with an attempt to combine all labour in 1899, and now exists mainly as a sort of strike insurance society into which a number of unions pay contributions at a regular rate per member, in return for the right to receive a regular rate of benefit when any of their members are on strike. The G.F.T.U. had before the War the distinction of being the only British association affiliated to the International Federation of Trade Unions, but since 1919 the Trades Union Congress has assumed its proper position as the representative of the British movement in international Trade Union affairs. Before the reorganisation of the Congress and the Labour Party, there existed between these bodies a Joint Board, as a loose sort of federal organisation. The G.F.T.U. formed at one time one of the constituent elements of this Joint Board. It was, however, excluded from the Joint Board in 1917 on the ground of overlapping, and has since remained an outside national body apart from the two great centralising Federations, and often in conflict with them, under its reactionary leadership, on questions of Trade Union policy. It includes most of the cotton operatives, the dockers, and a great number of the smaller craft societies, but outside it are not only the miners, railwaymen, and engineers, but the greater part of the general labour Unions. The position of

THE STRUCTURE OF TRADE UNIONISM 45

the G.F.T.U. may be summed up by saying that, save as an insurance society for certain Trade Union purposes, it no longer counts in the general life of the movement.

Of other federal organisations the most important is the independent Labour Research Department, to which many of the big Trade Unions, as well as Trades Councils and other Labour bodies belong. The L.R.D. is a specialist body, undertaking both independent research work likely to be of use to the movement, and particular investigations on behalf of this or that Trade Union. It has worked especially in research and publicity in connection with big national disputes, for the miners, railwaymen, cotton operatives, and engineers. Its relations with the Research and Information Department, maintained by the Congress and the Labour Party, are at present indeterminate.

It is impossible to dismiss the subject of general organisation in the Trade Union movement without some reference to a body, now no longer in being, on which at one time great hopes of solidarity were built. The Triple Industrial Alliance was formed by three of the largest Trade Union organisations—the Miners' Federation, the National Union of Railwaymen, and the Transport Workers' Federation. It was projected before the War, and formed in 1916, and the first attempts to employ it for industrial purposes were made in the years following the War. The purpose behind the Alliance was to avoid the waste and overlapping and disunity which result from the taking of separate action by the various industries which it included. A miners' dispute at once throws many railwaymen and transport workers out of work, and the reverse is the case in an equal degree. Accordingly these three industries saw the value of a general combination to secure joint action in the case of any industrial dispute of national extent. Mention was made from time to time of the possibility of bringing Trade Unions in other industries within the scope of the Triple Alliance, but no definite step was ever taken in this direction.

The intention of the founders of the Alliance was that each of the Unions included in it should simultaneously prepare a programme of demands, and that none should reach a settlement without the others. But in practice this proved very difficult to achieve. The three groups never managed to bring forward their demands simultaneously, or to take real joint action. Consequently, when the Alliance was called upon to act, it was in support, not of the demands of all three groups, but of one group alone, under conditions inconvenient to the other groups. In 1920 and again in 1921 the Miners' Federation called in the Alliance to strike in their support; in neither case was this done, though the threat was made. Finally, in the mining dispute of 1921, the

Triple Alliance dramatically broke down on "Black Friday," when the railwaymen and transport workers withdrew their threat to strike, and, with or without excuse, left the miners to fight on alone.[1]

The collapse of the Triple Alliance serves to bring home certain of the outstanding difficulties of Trade Union combination on a basis broader than that of a single industry. Sympathetic strike action, by large masses of workers not directly concerned in a dispute, is hard to secure save on the broadest and most fundamental issues ; and it is also difficult to expect joint action where, as in the Alliance, the control of policy is left in the hands of each separate Union. Real solidarity in action implies unified control of a kind which the separate Unions are not at present prepared to accept. This is why the Trades Union Congress is compelled to stop short of assuming any effective authority over the conduct of disputes. The Unions sometimes seem to want both freedom of separate action and effective co-ordination of control. In fact, they cannot have both.

Section 9.—INTERNATIONAL TRADE UNION ORGANISATION

The Trade Union Movement, abroad as in Great Britain, is organised on a national basis. In each country there are separate Trade Unions, of widely varying structure, linked up into a National Federation corresponding to the British Trades Union Congress. In some countries, however, as in France and Spain, there are rival Federations representing different policies and tendencies, each with its own rival set of affiliated Trade Unions.

Internationally, the Trade Unions from the various countries are linked up in two distinct ways—first by federation of the inclusive national federations of all trades, and, secondly, by special federation of the Unions in particular industries. The first form is exemplified in the International Federation of Trade Unions, with its headquarters at Amsterdam ; the second in the International Federations or Secretariats of Miners, Transport Workers, Textile Workers, and many other industrial or occupational groups.

British Trade Unions have not, on the whole, played an outstanding part in the International Trade Union Movement. The only British body affiliated to the International Federation of Trade Unions before the War was the General Federation of Trade Unions, with its three-quarters of a million members. The Trades

---

[1] I cannot discuss "Black Friday" here. For a full account, see my "Labour in the Coal-Mining Industry."

THE STRUCTURE OF TRADE UNIONISM 47

Union Congress had taken no part in international affairs, except by arrangement with the Labour Party in connection with international Socialist Conferences. British Trade Unions had a closer connection with some of the international Federations of workers in particular industries or groups of occupations. Thus, the Miners' Federation of Great Britain formed the most important unit of the International Miners' Federation, and the National Transport Workers' Federation was closely connected with the International Federation of Transport Workers. The International Textile Workers' Federation was also dominated by the British representatives, and, like the miners' organisation, had its headquarters in Great Britain. Many other international Federations also included British representatives (see p. 160).

These international Federations were for the most part very weak, and concerted action amongst them was not frequent or highly successful. They held periodical Conferences at which they debated matters of common importance : they occasionally supported one another in cases of serious dispute in a particular country ; but beyond this and occasional parallel agitations for industrial legislation they had not to any extent proceeded.

Nor was the I.F.T.U. itself much stronger. It was no more than a consultative and statistical bureau, hardly attempting to form any common policy for the workers in different countries.

In fact, such vigour as there was in the pre-War international working-class movement was largely concentrated in the International Socialist Bureau and the occasional Congresses held under its auspices. Upon this Bureau the British Labour Party, as well as the Socialist Societies, was represented, and by this means the Trade Union Movement played its part in international Socialist politics. It cannot, however, be said that the mass of the British workers, or even the leaders of the Trade Union Movement, had before the War paid any particular attention to the international aspirations of the Trade Union Movement. There were, of course, important and significant exceptions, but as a general rule British Labour had been somewhat insular in its outlook.

This is true even though British Labour has from the beginning played some part in the international movement. From its foundation in 1864 to 1872 the headquarters of the old International Working Men's Association were in London, and an International Socialist Congress was held in London in 1896, four years before the formation of the International Socialist Bureau.

Since the War there have been substantial changes for both good and evil. The old I.F.T.U., which was centred in Germany, was killed by the War, and in 1919 the whole movement had to be built afresh. The British Trades Union Congress replaced the

G.F.T.U. as the constituent British body in the re-formed International Federation, which thus represents the British movement as a whole. Unfortunately, the division between Communists and others, just as it has caused the creation of two rival Socialist Internationals (Second and Third Internationals), has split international Trade Unionism between the Amsterdam I.F.T.U. and the Moscow Red International of Labour Unions, to which the Russian and certain other Continental Unions belong. The affiliated membership of the I.F.T.U. was given as 18,248,000 in 1922. That of the R.I.L.U. is not available, but its largest element is the Russian membership of five millions.[1]

Under the auspices of the I.F.T.U., the Internationals of the various trades and industries have also been reconstituted and developed. There are now twenty-eight of these, with a total affiliated membership of 17,076,000 in 1922. Twenty-one include British representatives, with a total British membership of 4,750,000 in 1921, and probably about three millions to-day. These International Federations hold occasional Congresses, at which they attempt to develop common policies, communicate information between country and country, and to some extent organise financial aid, or even, very occasionally, sympathetic strike action, in trade disputes. But this last never goes beyond attempts to prevent blacklegging or the handling of blackleg goods, and seldom gets so far.

The I.F.T.U. itself is still predominantly a debating and statistical body, with very little co-ordinating power. It has, however, shown more enterprise than its pre-War equivalent. It has organised famine relief on a considerable scale, especially in Russia, has taken up the cause of international peace, and has helped to create an International Federation of Working-class Educational Organisations. But real Trade Union action on an international basis seems as far off as ever, though the creation of the International Labour Office, as part of the mechanism of the League of Nations, has provided a possible instrument for the creation of international standards in the conditions of employment and for labour legislation on an international basis. The I.L.O., however, is in its infancy; it cannot enforce its decrees until they are ratified by the national Parliaments of the various countries, and it has much ado to keep alive at all in face of the attacks of those who would fain prevent the development of any international regulation of labour conditions.

[1] For statistics of the I.F.T.U. and of Trade Union membership in various countries, see Appendix V., p. 158.

PART III

THE GOVERNMENT OF TRADE UNIONISM

Sect. 1. The Single-branch Union. Sect. 2. National Unions. Sect. 3. Workshop Organisation. Sect. 4. General Summary. Sect. 5. Trade Union Finance.

INTERNAL ORGANISATION : THE GOVERNMENT OF TRADE UNIONISM

FROM the structure of the various types of Trade Unions and the various forms of their inter-relation one with another, we now turn to their methods of internal administration and government.

On the whole there has been no great or sudden development in this sphere during recent years : rather there has been a gradual evolution corresponding to the growth in Trade Union membership, and a greatly increased complexity of organisation following necessarily upon an increased complexity of structure. The only startling recent development in Trade Union organisation has been the rapid growth in numbers and importance and the substantial change in character of the " shop stewards," and this, although it has left some lasting marks on Trade Union organisation in the engineering industry, has been so far mainly a war-time phenomenon. The shop stewards' movement, which rose so rapidly to influence in the munition shops during the War, withered no less rapidly under stress of trade depression and unemployment in the years following the War. We shall have to outline the story of its rise and fall, because it may yet have an important influence on the future of the movement. But in most of this Part we shall be concerned with forms of Trade Union government which have developed slowly and experimentally over a long period of years.

Section 1.—THE SINGLE-BRANCH UNION

Although the process of concentration in the Trade Union Movement has resulted in the disappearance of a large number of single-branch Unions by absorption into the larger national societies, there still remain, up and down the country, some hundreds of quite small Unions, ranging in size from a dozen members upwards, and consisting only of a single branch, with the simplest possible forms of internal government. Such Unions are usually governed in the last resort by a General Meeting of all the members, at which an Executive Committee is elected, probably by a show of hands. Their officers, who are also often elected at the General Meeting, are seldom full-time officials, and mostly continue to work at their trades, doing the work of the Union in their spare time. In return for this work they receive, as a rule, only small payments of a few shillings a week or a few pounds a year, although in some cases the larger single-branch Unions do maintain permanent officials and pay full-time salaries. Each Union of this type will have its book of Rules, its periodical Balance-sheets, Reports, and Statements, but beyond this it will probably issue no printed documents.

This position is sometimes modified where the local Union forms a part of some larger federal organisation, as in the case of the cotton trades and of a number of small Societies in other textile trades, and in the minor metal trades. In such cases the federal body often issues Reports of its own, which incorporate Reports from the various single-branch Unions of which it is composed; and in these cases, as we can see, it is often difficult to say exactly where a federal organisation of single-branch Unions passes into a national Union with its local branches.

Naturally these smaller Unions remain practically unchanged in structure, since their very small financial resources and their limitations of membership make it impossible for them to develop new methods of government or to strike out in new directions. They therefore present few special features, and, in fact, play very little part in the general life of the Trade Union Movement and contribute comparatively little to its effective fighting strength. This does not apply to a certain limited number of larger single-branch Unions in the big towns, which are more closely related to the national Trade Union Movement, and which, by virtue of their larger membership, are enabled to take a more effective part in negotiations with employers, and in the framing of Trade Union policy. To this type belong such Unions as the London Society of Compositors, with 15,000 members, the Birmingham Tinplate Workers with 2,500, and a few others. Unions of this character, of course, usually maintain a paid secretary and staff, and, apart from the fact that they are localised and have only a single branch, resemble the larger national Unions in their methods of government. It is also noticeable that single-branch Unions of this type exist mainly in trades in which some form of workshop organisation, such as the printers' " chapel," supplies in some measure the requisite element of branch life. This is true not only of the

London Society of Compositors, but also of the Tin-plate Workers, and in other cases. In such circumstances there may even be single-branch Unions whose membership is not localised in a particular district. Thus, the Amalgamated Society of Paper Makers has its 2,000 members scattered in paper mills over the whole country, but has no local organisation outside the workshops in which the members are employed. This, however, is an exceptional case. Apart from these exceptions, single-branch Unions can, to all intents and purposes, be ignored or dismissed with a mere mention in any account of the national Trade Union Movement as a whole. If they are to act effectively under modern industrial conditions, they are practically compelled, except in the largest centres, either to merge their individuality in larger organisations, or at least to surrender a great deal of their autonomy to national organisations of a federal type.

Section 2.—NATIONAL UNIONS.

Trade Unions extending over an area wider than a single locality have inevitably, from the first, developed a more complex system of internal government, since they have had, from the very beginning, to face the problem of co-ordination between the various districts and the framing of a more or less comprehensive policy for their whole membership. Such national Unions vary greatly in their internal structure and methods of government. It is, however, possible, by describing two or three of the main types, to indicate generally the nature of their organisation and the tendencies which are at present at work. Three typical Unions may be taken in order to illustrate the general character of internal government. Take first the direct successor of one of the oldest of the national Unions—the Amalgamated Engineering Union, formed by the fusion of the Amalgamated Society of Engineers with a number of smaller Unions in 1920.

(*a*) The Amalgamated Engineering Union consists to-day of about 1,700 branches. Of these some 200 are overseas branches, mainly in the Dominions. The home branches, some 1,500 in number, are grouped in a series of District Committees, which cover each a more or less homogeneous industrial area. The area covered by, and the number of branches included in, a district vary widely. Where there is only a single branch in any district the branch functions in the same way as the District Committee for the larger centres. The District Committee or the Branch Committee in single-branch districts enjoys a considerable amount of autonomy in relation to local questions. Its reports must receive the sanction and approval of the Executive Council which sits in London, but unless there is any violation of rule or national agreement, the District Committee can, to all intents and purposes, frame its own industrial policy locally.

This position is, however, modified by two conditions. In the first place, any action which involves expenditure from the central funds requires the sanction of the Executive, a sanction which is, in this case, effective. In the second place, the District Committee has purely industrial functions, and does not deal at all with friendly benefits, which are purely a matter for the branches and the national organisation.

The District Committee consists of delegates from the various branches in the district. In the larger centres only a limited number of branches are at any time represented on the District Committee, and the representation passes in turn from one branch to another. The district secretaries are elected by vote of the members of the district: in most cases they work at their own trade and do the work of the district in their spare time. In a few of the largest centres, however, there are full-time district secretaries, paid out of the national funds; and in certain others full-time local organisers have been appointed, and are paid by levy on the members in the district. The power to group the branches into suitable districts is vested in the Executive Council of the Union as a whole.

One of the functions of each District Committee is to provide for the appointment of shop stewards and shop committees in the various works in its area. The functions of these stewards and committees are discussed later in this book.[1] They work under the control of the District Committee, on which they are directly represented by at least one member in each district.

The districts, of which there are several hundreds, are grouped together in Organising Divisions, of which there are twenty-six in Great Britain and Ireland. For each Division there is a full-time officer, the Organising District Delegate, who works under the control of the National Executive. With this officer works a Divisional Committee, representing all the districts in the area. It is partly an organising body, and partly a co-ordinating authority for dealing with wages and conditions, often promoting joint action on such matters by all the districts in the division. The Divisional Committees are further important as the bodies authorised to elect from their own numbers the members of the National Committee of the Union.

Above the District Committees stands the national organisation. The national administrative body is the Executive Council, consisting of nine members, together with the Chairman and the

---

[1] See p. 59.

THE GOVERNMENT OF TRADE UNIONISM 53

General Secretary. The A.E.U. here differs in two respects from most other national Trade Unions. Its Executive consists of full-time officers, a practice which is found in only one other Society —the Boilermakers. Secondly, and as a consequence of the adoption of the full-time principle, the Executive is much smaller than is the case in most other Societies. The Chairman and the General Secretary are both elected by the vote of the whole membership, and there are, in addition, two assistant General Secretaries and three National Organisers, elected in the same way. The Executive Council, on the other hand, is elected over geographical areas specially constituted for the purpose. It sits permanently at the headquarters of the Union and is generally entrusted with the control of national policy and its execution in detail so far as national questions are concerned. It also deals with reports from the District and Divisional Committees on the "industrial" side of the Union's work and from Branch Committees on the "friendly" side of the work. Different members of the Executive naturally specialise in different parts of the administrative work. It is, in fact, the Cabinet of the Trade Union, and it conducts all national negotiations with the employers, with the assistance of the Organising District Delegates.

Under the orders of the Executive Council are the Organising District Delegates, who are elected by the vote of the members in the twenty-six divisions. The Organising District Delegate in the A.E.U. differs in certain material respects from the otherwise similar organisers who are maintained by most national Unions. His function is very largely that of co-operating with the various District Committees in his division in negotiations with employers, and only secondarily that of founding new branches, attracting new members, or organising in the ordinary sense of the term. The method by which he is elected gives him a considerable amount of independence, and in many cases he acquires a good deal of power in framing the policy of the Union within his own division. This, however, has become less since the institution, in 1920, of the Divisional Committees.

The Executive Council, while it has wide powers, is not the final authority in the government of the Union. As we have seen, the Divisional Committees elect a National Committee, which meets at least annually, and can be called together whenever it is required. This National Committee has two functions. It is empowered to lay down the lines of policy for the Union as a whole, and the Executive must work in matters of national policy within its instructions. It has power, where there is not time to take a ballot vote of the members, to call a national strike. And it is also, mainly at its special meeting held every four years, the supreme legislative authority, with power to alter the rules of the Union. It thus corresponds, not only to the " General Councils " maintained by some Unions for the declaration of policy, but also to the Conferences or Delegate Meetings, which are in most Unions the legislative authorities. But it does not, like most of these Conferences or Delegate Meetings, undertake also the judicial function of deciding disputes arising between members or local branches or districts and the Executive Council as to the interpretation of the rules or the exercise of their discretionary powers.

These judicial functions are assigned to a separate body, consisting of delegates elected from specially constituted areas. This judicial body, called the Final Appeal Court, sits annually to consider appeals by branches against the decisions of the Executive Council.

It should be noted that the A.E.U., despite the completeness of its representative machinery, makes frequent use of the referendum, and habitually refers important questions of industrial policy to a ballot vote of all the members. This practice, however, does not apply to the revision of rules, or to the formulation of new policies, as distinct from the settlement of agreements. The ballot vote is the method adopted for the choice of all officials and for the Executive Council and Final Appeal Court. It has, however, been discarded in favour of indirect election in the case of the Divisional and National Committees, which are the new features introduced into the rules since the War, and the merging of the old Amalgamated Society of Engineers into the Amalgamated Engineering Union. Apart from these new features, the rules of the A.E.U. are based mainly on the old rules of the A.S.E.

The constitution of the A.E.U. has been described thus at length because, despite the amalgamation of 1920, it is still the leading example in this country of the old type of Craft Union, and the developments which it has undergone are largely typical of the changes which other Craft Unions of similar type have experienced in recent years. We turn from the " new model " of 1851, as the A.S.E. has been often called, to the " new model " of 1913—the National Union of Railwaymen.

(*b*) The National Union of Railwaymen affords an instance of a constitution framed only eleven years ago, on the occasion of the amalgamation of three of the principal Railway Trade Unions, and represents, at any rate for a certain type of Union—the Union that is " industrial " in structure—the most modern type of government that has yet been developed. The N.U.R., like all other national Unions, is composed of a number of branches. Its branches are, however, far more variable in size than the branches of such Craft Unions as the A.E.U., and the membership of a single branch runs in some cases into thousands. The branches in their internal organisation reproduce many of the same features of those of the A.E.U., except that the machinery of the N.U.R. is more centralised in character. The outstanding point of difference between the two Societies is that there is, in the N.U.R., no organisation at all closely corresponding to the A.E.U. District Committee. Each branch deals with all matters that arise in the course of its business directly with the Head Office. This, no doubt, is due in part to the fact that the railway service lends itself more easily to national organisation than the engineering industry. But it is also, in some respects, a sign of the times. The N.U.R. has indeed a system of District Councils which, to the outsider, would seem to correspond to some extent to the District Committees of the A.E.U. They are, however, in fact, entirely different. The A.E.U. District Committees, as we have seen, are executive bodies possessing considerable power and local autonomy within their own areas. The District Councils of the N.U.R. on the other hand have practically no powers of industrial action or negotiation, and are principally propagandist and organising bodies consisting of delegates from the various branches, without any obligation being laid upon the branch to join its District Council unless it so desires. The effect of this status upon the District Councils has been somewhat curious. Being largely irresponsible propagandist organisations, without direct power, they have become to a great extent the centres of the advanced section in Railway Trade Unionism. At their meetings questions of Trade Union policy are freely discussed; but, when it is desired to place one of these matters before the Head Office, the District Council is compelled to refer the matter back to the branches, which, in their turn, approach the Head Office as independent bodies. The District Councils are thus at most semi-official, and the unofficial side of their character has been emphasised by their linking up into a National Conference of District Councils, and by their election of a National Committee drawn from the various Councils.

One curious effect of this system of half-recognition has been actually to increase the influence of the N.U.R. District Councils on the framing of policy.

In addition to the District Councils, there arise from time to time, either in a single district or in many, special Vigilance Committees, usually for particular grades in the railway service. There has also been since the War a growing tendency for the Union to recognise national grade movements, and to call representatives of the grades affected by a particular question into national conference in an advisory capacity. The final decision, however, even on a grade question, always rests with the Union as a whole.

Such movements as the National Conference of District Councils and the Vigilance Committees are purely unofficial, and find no place in the formal constitution of the Society. The N.U.R. is governed by an Executive Committee of twenty-four members drawn from various districts, and representing various grades of the membership. The Rule providing for this election is interesting enough to deserve full quotation. It runs as follows :

" RULE 4.—The twenty-four representatives on the Executive Committee shall be chosen by ballot on the single transferable vote system. The Union shall be formed into six electoral districts for this purpose. Within those districts the various grades shall be divided into four electoral departments. The electoral departments shall be classified as follows : (1) Locomotive department ; (2) traffic department ; (3) goods and cartage department ; (4) engineering shops and permanent way. The Executive Committee shall be chosen from each district triennially, one-third retiring each year ; but should two-thirds of the branches in any particular district be dissatisfied with their representative, they shall have power to demand a poll of the members of that district at the expiration of each year. The candidate receiving the largest number of votes shall hold office for the ensuing three years, and shall not be eligible for re-election for a period of three years, neither shall his branch be entitled to nominate for that period. Should a vacancy occur before the expiration of the term, it shall be filled for the remainder of the period by the candidate who obtained the next highest number of votes to the successful candidate at the election, provided he is employed on or in connection with any railway."

Thus it will be seen that the purpose is to give representation to both local and sectional groups, and that provision is made for separate sub-committees representing the various sections. In practice, however, these sub-committees do not seem to have acquired any considerable importance, though they might at any time become a big factor in the working of the Union.

The Executive Committee consists of members working at their trades, and meets in normal times quarterly, special meetings being held in addition as necessity arises. It is responsible for all negotiations with the Railway Companies, and is invested, under the Rules, with almost complete power in relation to industrial policy, strikes, etc. In practice, however, its power is limited by that of the General Meeting.

The N.U.R. General Meeting consists of delegates elected from specially constituted divisions. It meets at least annually; and special General Meetings can be held at any time to discuss points of national importance. The General Meeting alone can alter the Rules. It discusses and formulates the national policy of the Union, and, in addition, the practice has grown up that any agreement into which it is proposed to enter with the Railway Companies should be submitted to it by the Executive Committee for ratification. It is thus, in effect, the ultimate governing authority of the Union on all large questions of policy. The N.U.R. has two General Secretaries, industrial and political, and four Assistant Secretaries, elected by national ballot. The President is not a full-time officer, and the office is only held for short periods.

The centralised nature of the railway industry has combined with the personal ascendancy of Mr. J. H. Thomas to make the power of the full-time officials—and especially of the General Secretaries—very much greater than the power of the corresponding officials in such a Society as the A.E.U., where the existence of a full-time Executive Council greatly restricts the power of the officials.

(*c*) The Miners' Federation of Great Britain—the third body of which I propose to describe the constitution—is of a very different type, being a federal organisation consisting of a considerable number of largely independent associations. The structure of the Miners' Federation has been roughly described in the first part of this book. It consists, as we have seen, of over twenty separate units, some of which are themselves Federations of smaller units. It will be best to begin by describing briefly the government of a typical unit in the main Federation.

The branch unit of the mining industry is the Lodge, *i.e.*, the membership of the Union at a particular pit, or group of neighbouring pits. The Lodge possesses a certain amount of autonomy in dealing with domestic questions relating to the particular pit it represents, but this autonomy tends to decrease as more and more matters are dealt with by national or district agreements. Above the Lodge stands, in some of the larger Associations, the District, with its officer, the Miners' Agent, but not, as a rule, with any separate District Committee of its own. The next real unit of government is the Association itself, covering in most cases a county, but in some cases a very much wider area, *e.g.*, South Wales. The Association is virtually self-governing on all questions relating only to its own area; and can, on many questions, pursue an independent line of policy. On many matters, not covered by national agreements, it makes its own agreements with the District Colliery Owners' Association. Each Association has its own Executive Committee and officials, and usually a Council drawn from the various Lodges. In the larger Associations this

Council may be a delegate meeting of several hundred members. The larger issues of Association policy are generally decided by means of pit-head or lodge meetings, at which the Council delegates are instructed on the manner in which their votes should be cast. The referendum is also sometimes employed, but its use is, on the whole, on the decrease except on the largest questions.

The Miners' Federation of Great Britain, which includes practically all the organised collieries of Great Britain, is governed first by an Executive Committee, and secondly by a National Conference consisting of representatives from the various Associations. The National Conference meets annually, and, in addition, whenever it is specially summoned. It is the practice, moreover, to summon it whenever any important issue has to be decided, so that the Miners' Conference, consisting of delegates instructed by the various associations, which have, in turn, elicited the views of their members through Lodge and pit-head meetings, is the normal governing body of the Federation on all general issues. The great weakness of the Federation as at present organised lies in two things. In the first place it has no central financial resources, except such as it raises for special purposes by levies upon the affiliated Associations. This has proved a source of special weakness in the case of national disputes, since it tends to reduce the fighting strength of the whole body to that of the weakest Association. In the second place it has only a very small staff of its own. Its president is also a full-time officer of one of the affiliated Associations, and its secretary is its only full-time officer, though he has, of course, clerical assistance. The other officers draw the greater part of their salaries from the local Associations, and only receive *honoraria* and expenses in return for their services to the Federation itself. These weaknesses, however, do not prevent the miners' organisation from being extraordinarily strong and cohesive on most general issues of policy. Doubtless it has been more easy in the mining industry than in most others to administer a huge organisation with a comparatively simple form of government, owing to the fact that the membership is largely concentrated in certain districts, and that the pit forms a natural unit of government which serves as a basis for the whole organisation.

(*d*) These three industrial organisations, very dissimilar in some respects, yet serve, by the general similarity of their constitutional machinery, to indicate the general character of Trade Union government in this country. It will be seen that the national machinery presents in all three cases many of the same features. The National Executive has, in all three, many of the same powers, and these powers are checked and regulated, in every case, by the existence of some more representative form of organisation, such

THE GOVERNMENT OF TRADE UNIONISM 59

as the General Meeting or National Conference. District organisation presents greater dissimilarity, varying largely with the character of the industry in question. Branch organisation is, on the whole, much the same, except that in the case of the miners the pit, by forming a natural branch unit, gets rid of one of the most difficult problems of Trade Union organisation—that of creating a local unit corresponding to the realities of industrial life, and grouping the members in accordance with their community of economic interests. With this problem we shall deal in the next section.

Section 3.—WORKSHOP ORGANISATION.

The Trade Union branch, save in a few exceptional industries, such as mining, has no necessary connection with the members' place of employment. It groups them mainly round the places where they dwell, not round the places where they work. Of course, where a Trade Union has only one branch in a district, nearly all its members in the factories in that district will be in the same branch. But even this is not universally true; for a worker may get work in a new district without transferring from his old branch. Where, as in the case of the larger Unions in the important centres, there are several or many branches of the same Union in one town, the members of that Union employed in a single factory are often scattered at random among the various branches. Within a district, a man seldom shifts from one branch to another when he changes his employment.

This results in a lack of correspondence between the basis of the Trade Union organisation and the realities of industrial life. The Trade Union branch is often not a place where grievances or problems arising in particular factories or workshops can be profitably discussed. Hence, many Unions, notably in the engineering and printing industries, have sought to correct this defect by the institution, under various names, of shop stewards and Workshop and Works Committees.

The printers' "chapel" is, of course, a very old established body, and the effective basis of the strong Trade Union organisation in the printing trades. The "father of the chapel," the leader appointed by men in the shop, exerts a wide authority. There were printers' "chapels" before there were formal Trade Unions at all. They have supplied, throughout the history of Trade Unionism in the printing trades, a real need, and have been a great factor in ensuing stability of organisation.

The most significant single development in the Trade Union world during the War period was, undoubtedly, the growth of the shop stewards' movement, principally in the engineering and kindred industries. The shop steward, or his equivalent, as a minor semi-official of the Trade Union, existed under a variety of names long before the War, but his pre-War functions were, in most Unions, of little importance, as may readily be seen from the functions assigned to him under their rules ; for instance, the A.S.E. Rule-book before the War defined the function of the shop steward as follows :

" [District] Committees may also appoint shop-stewards in workshops or departments thereof in their respective districts, such stewards to be under the direction and control of the Committee, by whom their duties shall be defined. The stewards shall be empowered to examine periodically the contribution cards of all members, and to demand that alleged members shall show their contribution cards for examination when starting work. They shall report at least once each quarter on all matters affecting the trade, and keep the Committee posted with all events occurring in the various shops. . . . Should a shop steward be discharged through executing his duties he shall be entitled to full wage benefit."

It will be seen from this rule, which is typical, that the shop steward before the War was merely a minor agent of the District Committee, by which he was entrusted with the function of seeing that the members in his shop kept their contributions up to date, and that new workers who were taken on in the shop carried a Trade Union card. This minor official bears only a remote resemblance to the shop stewards who won celebrity during the War period. It is true that in some Unions and in some districts the shop steward, even before the War, had attained to a certain degree of importance, and had been allowed to assume certain functions in negotiating with employers, under the supervision and control of the District Committee. This was, however, quite exceptional, and the rapidity with which the new type of shop steward developed during the War years was therefore startling. It is worth while to refer briefly to the history of this development, which extended into all the principal engineering centres all over the country, and even made a beginning in certain other industries.

There is no doubt that war-time conditions were the main cause of the rapid growth in the power of the shop stewards. The Munitions Acts, by imposing a new type of discipline upon the worker, and still more a new type of restraint upon the officials and Executives of the various Trade Unions, played an important part in calling into being an unofficial movement based upon the workshops, through which the men expressed grievances which could otherwise have found no ready outlet. Secondly, the progress of dilution and the rapid change of workshop customs during the War imposed upon Trade Unionists the necessity of creating in the workshops an organisation capable of dealing with these questions from day to day as they arose, of making grievances articulate, and of formulating the men's point of view more quickly and more accurately than was possible or necessary under the slow-moving conditions of pre-War industry.

The new movement developed earliest upon the Clyde. Official shop stewards were appointed at an increasing pace, that is to say, the District Committees of the various Unions nominated increasing numbers of members to act under their authority in the workshops. But side by side with these official developments came an unofficial development. The workers themselves in many shops chose spokesmen without reference to any District Committee, and even without regard to the particular Union to which they belonged. There came thus to exist two types of shop stewards, one type ratified by the District Committee of a particular Union, and exercising power under its authority, and the other type chosen directly, without external sanction, by the workers in the shops, and responsible to no one except to those who chose them. The next step was not long in coming. Both official and unofficial shop stewards in many cases formed themselves into Works Committees, and elected chairmen, secretaries, conveners, etc. These conveners and the other shop stewards soon felt the need for a wider form of combination, and for contact between one shop and another, and the Clyde strike of February, 1915, provided the nucleus of an unofficial organisation which could be used for this purpose. The Strike Committee developed into the Clyde Workers' Committee, and as the shop stewards' movement on the Clyde grew and extended, the Clyde Workers' Committee developed itself into a central organisation representing unofficially all the various shops in the district. Official as well as unofficial stewards played their part in this development; but, of course, in relation to such movements the official stewards acted only in an unofficial capacity.

The Clyde organisation was soon imitated elsewhere. Shop stewards multiplied all over the country; Shop Committees, Works Committees, and Conveners sprang up, and in one town after another Workers' Committees or Shop Stewards' Committees on the Clyde model were created. Throughout, whatever the status of the individual stewards might be, this wider movement remained absolutely unofficial, if not definitely anti-official, and had no relation to the constitutional machinery of the Trade Union movement.

It would be a mistake to regard this movement as universally animated by the idea of any brand new policy. It would be still more a mistake to identify it absolutely with any new social doctrine. These mistakes have, however, been often made, and made the more readily because they possess an element of truth. The men who principally led the shop stewards' movement were mostly working-class theorists, and though their theories by no means always agreed, there was a certain community of view among them. They were for the most part of the younger generation, " Industrial Unionists " in the sense of desiring the organisation in a single Society of all workers in their industry; some of them, and these the most active, " Industrial Unionists " in the further sense of desiring the catastrophic overthrow of Capitalism, and its replacement by a system based on purely working-class industrial organisations exercising control both over industry and over Society as a whole. Some of them were Guild Socialists, that is to say, they desired the government of industry through self-governing associations of workers. Many of them became Communists after the War, when a Communist movement was organised in this country on the Moscow pattern. Far more of them, however, while they had a more or less clear view of immediate policy, had no dogmatic theories, but were content to face problems as they arose, using their organisation now to regulate the dilution of labour, now to oppose compulsory taking of men for the Army, and now to demand " peace by negotiation " instead of " the knock-out blow." But this at least can be said, the shop stewards' movement, wherever it appeared, stood for a greater element of control over industry by the workers through their industrial organisations, for a greater element of Trade Union intervention in workshop management, for a bigger say on the part of the rank and file workers in determining the conditions of their working lives. It stood, moreover, most clearly of all, for Trade Union organisation on a broader basis, for the solidarity of skilled and unskilled, and for a militant policy in industrial affairs.

It will be seen that these conceptions might very easily cut right across, not merely the old Craft Unionism, but equally Union by industry in the narrower sense. The left wing leaders of the shop stewards thought primarily of the union, not of all " plants " in an industry into a national Industrial Union, but of all " plants " in a district into a Workers' Committee, to which the industry was only incidental, and one big Union of all the workers the fundamental object. Moreover, the shop stewards' movement never defined at all clearly its attitude towards the existing Trade Unions. They often, and quite sincerely, repudiated the suggestion that they were out against the Trade Unions. Yet it is hard to see how the organisation which the leaders of the movement advocated could be either reconciled with present-day Trade Unionism, or conceivably developed out of it except by catastrophic methods. The line of division between the left-wing leaders and the comparatively few professed Union-smashers of the extreme " Industrial Workers of the World " school became at times perilously narrow.

It is interesting to place in relation to these theories of the principal spokesmen of the shop stewards' movement the actual steps that were officially taken by some of the Unions principally concerned with a view to constitutionalising the shop stewards' movement. In December, 1917, a serious dispute broke out in Coventry owing to the refusal of a particular firm to recognise the shop stewards chosen by its employees. This dispute resulted in a local strike, which soon threatened to become national in character. The employers and Trade Unions thereupon took action, and a national conference was held between the Engineering Employers' Federation and the engineering Trade Unions. At this conference national recognition of the shop stewards was discussed, and an agreement was actually drawn up and signed by a number of the Unions, the Amalgamated Society of Engineers, however, refusing to accept the terms offered. This agreement, which was afterwards accepted in a modified form by the A.S.E., provided for the recognition of individual shop stewards, and for their participation in the first stages of negotiation on questions arising in the workshops. It did not, however, provide in any way for any real recognition of Works Committees or give the shop stewards any considerable power.

Before the agreement was finally ratified, the War had ended and the vast organisation built up for War purposes in the metal industries was being reduced to normal dimensions. The shop stewards' movement, as an almost independent force challenging official Trade Unionism, decayed as rapidly as it had grown. The slump which began in 1920 and the national engineering lock-out of 1922 completed its dissolution. The shop stewards' movement is no more.

But it has left something behind. Shop stewards are now recognised as an essential element in engineering Trade Unionism, and officially represented, though only in a slight degree, on the District Committees of the A.E.U. The Shop Stewards' Agreement secures recognition of the stewards by the employers, and gives them certain limited powers. It is true, both that these gains seem insignificant beside the claims of the War years, and that the slump has made even these of little effect, because it is dangerous for a man to be active as a steward when there are many of his trade seeking work, and the " sack " may be the reward of energy. But the movement is likely to regain strength when the effects of the slump are no longer so keenly felt. The shop steward and the shop committee are really valuable additions to Trade Union machinery, the means to closer contact between the Unions and their membership. Workshop organisation has not yet been accorded its proper place in Trade Union organisation; but a beginning has been made, and from this in time big developments may follow.

To discuss in general, however, the possible future of the shop stewards' movement would be to go far beyond the province of this descriptive summary. It is worth mentioning that, although, apart from the special case of the printers, the shop steward has only become a permanent factor so far in the engineering industry, he has appeared also elsewhere, for example, in the boot and shoe and textile industries, and in certain wood-working trades. There seems no adequate reason why some form of workshop organisation should not become a permanent feature of Trade Unionism in almost every industry. There are some, indeed, who hold that the movement was purely a mushroom growth created by the War conditions, and that its present submergence is permanent. There are others who believe that it is in embryo a new form of Trade Union organisation, destined largely to revolutionise past methods of Trade Union action. Certainly, any plan of increased Trade Union " control " in industry seems necessarily to involve some effective form of workshop organisation.

Section 4.—General Summary

(a) *The Branch.*—With these considerations in mind, we can now proceed to summarise the main features of Trade Union government as it now exists. The smallest constitutional unit is in nearly all industries the branch, with its branch meetings, branch committee, and branch officers, and, in most cases, branch funds. The branch, in addition to its constitutional position inside the Union to which it belongs, is generally the body affiliated to local organisations of a federal character, such as the local Trades Council and Local Labour Party, and also in some cases the local Federation of Trade Unions in a particular industry. There is considerable difference between Unions in their attitude to the question of branch affiliations to such bodies. Where branches have local funds or some financial autonomy, no difficulty usually arises; but where finance is centralised, special provision has to be made nationally to enable branches to join Trades Councils and similar bodies. Some Unions actively encourage their branches to

THE GOVERNMENT OF TRADE UNIONISM 65

do this, some remain wholly neutral, and a few actually discourage affiliation.

Perhaps the greatest problem of branch life in Trade Unionism at the present time is one which we have discussed already in comparing the position of the miners and the engineers. In the case of the miners, as we have seen, the branch centres round a natural industrial unit—the coal-pit. In most other industries, however, the branch possesses no relation, or no very close relation, to any such industrial unit, and this is especially the case in the larger towns, in which a number of branches of the same Union exist. In these cases the branch is almost inevitably based rather on the place of habitation of its members than on their place of work, *i.e.*, in London most of the members who live in Chiswick will belong to the Chiswick Branch of the A.E.U. or the Woodworkers, although some of them may be working in Acton, and some of them in Poplar, right at the other end of London. Consisting thus of a number of members who have no close common industrial interest, apart from their general interest in the conditions of their craft or industry, the branch can hardly form an effective unit for many sorts of industrial activity, at any rate in the larger centres. There is no doubt that this fact—this detachment of the branch from industrial realities—has helped the centralising process in the Trade Union movement, and the removal of independent functions from the branch to the larger authorities.

(*b*) *The Workshop.*—We have seen that, save in the case of the printing trades and a few other Unions, the workshop is not recognised as a constitutional unit of Trade Union government. Even where there are shop stewards and shop committees, their functions and powers are, constitutionally, very limited, and they are recognised only as a subordinate part of the district machinery. During the War, the rise of the shop stewards' movement radically altered the situation; but, for the time at least, the shop stewards' movement has practically disappeared, and, while in some cases shop stewards have secured fuller recognition, workshop machinery is still weak and very imperfectly linked up with the larger organs of Trade Union administration.

(*c*) *The District.*—District Committees of the type described as existing in the A.E.U. are found principally in the larger Trade Unions which have a number of branches in the same district. They have, in many cases, wide industrial powers, and considerable local autonomy, including the right to negotiate with Employers' Associations, and to make agreements subject to the sanction of the National Executive but not, as a rule, the right to declare a strike, or, at any rate, to authorise the payment of strike pay without national sanction. In the more centralised Trade

Unions their powers are much more restricted, but in most Unions they retain the essential character of local executive bodies, enjoying, under the Rules of the various Unions, considerable power and prestige.

District Committees of this type must be sharply distinguished from the District Councils of such organisations as the N.U.R., Shop Assistants, or Union of Post Office Workers. These District Councils are purely organising and propagandist bodies, with no power of negotiation, and practically no authority under the constitutions of their Societies. They may, none the less, have considerable unrecognised powers, and this, as we have seen, is especially the case in such Unions as the N.U.R., in which a strong " ginger " movement exists among the rank and file.

(*d*) *Advisory Councils.*—In addition to District Councils, some of the larger Societies extending over the whole of the United Kingdom have special Scottish or Irish Advisory Councils. The Irish Council of the N.U.R. has been mentioned already; and to this may be added the Scottish Councils of the Shop Assistants and the Woodworkers. There are also in certain Unions with a diverse membership special Councils or Conferences for particular sections, either local or national. The Dockyard Conference of the A.E.U. is one example, and the Shop Assistants furnish others. The National Union of Clerks attempts to meet the same need by what it calls " Guild " organisation of the members employed in a particular industry or service. In other cases, as in that of the N.U.R. shopmen, no permanent machinery exists, but occasional advisory conferences are called as need arises.

(*e*) *National Executives and Officials.*—National Executive Councils are mostly bodies which meet periodically at fairly frequent intervals, and consist of members who are actually working at their trades. Such bodies naturally cannot superintend effectively the day-to-day work of their Societies, which falls more and more under the control of the Head Office officials. To the Executives, however, are referred matters of general importance and especially all matters which cannot be dealt with in accordance with precedents already laid down. They are, in a sense, the supreme executive bodies of their Societies; but their supremacy can usually be seriously threatened by a strong-minded General Secretary. This is not the case where the Executive Council is a full-time body, sitting as a permanent Cabinet of officers; but, as we have seen, there are only two Unions—the Boilermakers and the A.E.U.—in which such Executives exist. In these cases the Executive tends rather to reduce the General Secretary and the other officials to a secondary position, and to assume wide powers in the direction of the Union's policy. It is hard to say which of the two methods is really preferable, though the fact that the permanent Executive shows no signs of spreading may be taken as a strong argument against it. It is perhaps worthy of notice that in certain Continental countries an effective method has been found of combining the two ideas, and there has been, in this country, a certain amount of talk, which has not hitherto materialised, of experiments along the same lines. The German Metal-workers' Union is governed first by an Administrative Committee, consisting of a small number of full-time officers, and, secondly, by a larger Committee, including members of the Administrative Committee, but also including a considerably greater number of members drawn directly from the workshops. The larger Committee possesses the wider authority, and preserves the right to override the decisions of the small Committee of full-time officers. By this method an attempt is made to strike a balance between the two dangers which beset the rival British methods of organisation —the danger that a full-time Executive may get out of touch with the bulk of the membership, and the danger that a part-time Executive may not possess the experience or coherence of policy which is necessary for the government of a great national organisation, such as a modern Trade Union. Perhaps the institution by the A.E.U. of its National Committee of divisional representatives may be taken as an attempt to adapt this plan to British conditions.

In this account of National Executives no mention has been made of certain obsolete survivals of antiquated forms of government. There still remained, until a very few years ago, and perhaps there may remain even now, a few national Unions, which clung to the device of the governing branch, or governing district, *i.e.*, which drew their Executive Council, not from the whole body of members, but from a particular district in which their Head Office was situated. In most of these cases there was, in addition to such a governing District Executive, a wider body, often called a General Council, drawn from the whole country, but meeting at very infrequent intervals. This method of government is, however, practically obsolete, and only survives in a few badly organised Trade Unions, mostly of no considerable size.

(*f*) *Representative Meetings, National Conferences, and similar bodies* are intended to correct the attitude of the Executive Committees and full-time officers, by providing a better method of ascertaining, from time to time, the real will of the membership. There can be no doubt that their power in the Trade Union movement is on the increase, and that they are tending more and more to replace the referendum in the decision of a widening range of issues. The history of the N.U.R. since its formation, and the recent history of the A.E.U., both furnish clear indications of the growth of the powers of such Conferences and Representative Meetings.

(*g*) *Delegate Meetings.*—In most Societies the same body is entrusted with the duty of representing the will of the membership on important issues of current policy, and also with that of making and revising the Rules of the Society. The two functions are, however, clearly distinct, and they are occasionally separated. More often the same body has both functions, but the legislative function is only exercised at special meetings, held at comparatively long intervals. Between these meetings the rules cannot be altered. In some cases, the judicial function is combined with the legislative. In others, as in the A.E.U., the two are separated, and there is a distinctly chosen Final Appeal Court to deal with disputes arising within the Union. Such bodies, however, seem to be comparatively rare. In most Unions there is only one representative assembly which is at once legislature and judiciary, and lays down the general lines of policy for the Union as a whole.

(*h*) *The Referendum.*—The referendum, or ballot vote of all the members of the Union, while it shows no signs of dying out altogether, tends to be restricted to a narrower range of issues. Some old-fashioned Societies, particularly in the building industry, continue to take referenda of their whole membership month by month, often on quite insignificant issues. It is an ascertained fact that frequent balloting on small issues makes the members disinclined to vote, even where a really important question has to be decided. In the more modern Unions, although the referendum is retained, it is in most cases as an exceptional instrument of government to deal with broad, general issues. The improvement of the methods of representative government has made its use on small issues no longer necessary. It is preserved for its legitimate purposes of electing national leaders, of declaring for or against a national strike, and of accepting or rejecting agreements and settlements affecting the membership as a whole. But in some Unions even these vital issues are dealt with through the representative bodies, without any direct appeal to the membership as a whole.

Section 5.—Trade Union Finance

It is impossible at all completely to understand the internal government of the Trade Union movement without taking into account its financial aspect. A Trade Union draws by far the greatest part of its income from direct contributions from its members. Additional sources of income may exist, to a certain extent, and these possess considerable importance in the case of old-established Unions which have had time to build up con-

THE GOVERNMENT OF TRADE UNIONISM 69

siderable reserve funds, but even the richest and longest established of Trade Unions are still mainly dependent upon the weekly contributions of their members.

These contributions vary widely in amount from one Union to another.

Before the War, the highest regular rate of contribution was 1s. 6d. per week for Class A members of the Amalgamated Society of Engineers; but additional levies increased the actual amount paid by a few pence more each week. The A.S.E. had other scales for skilled men at 1s. 3d. and 1s. weekly, and lower rates for apprentices and less skilled men. About 1s. per week was the most usual rate of contribution to a Craft Union paying regular friendly benefits as well as dispute and unemployment pay.

In the case of the general labour Unions, whose members were for the most part in receipt of low rates of wages, the contribution was necessarily small, 3d. or 4d. a week being the most usual amount; while in most cases some provision was made for the admission of women at even lower rates, ranging from 1d. upwards. Even these low rates of contribution were not the lowest that were found in the Trade Union movement, for there were certain types of Unions which paid no benefits to members, and therefore needed only to raise a sufficient sum to cover their management expenses. Thus, in the Civil Service and in the Post Office contributions were, as a rule, exceedingly low, and were paid on a monthly, or even a quarterly, instead of a weekly, basis. For instance, the annual contribution to the Postmen's Federation was no more than 2s. 6d., while the Assistant Clerks' Association admitted members for 1s. per annum. On the railways, again, benefits do not form an important feature of Trade Union work, employment is for the most part continuous, and the Unions do not need to build up large funds for benefit purposes; we therefore find that in the National Union of Railwaymen scales of contributions ranged from 2d. to a maximum of 5d. per week. The Miners' Associations were, for the most part, in a similar position, and paid few, if any, Friendly Benefits. In South Wales the contribution was only 3d. a week, while in most of the other districts it was 6d.

If we turn from these Unions, consisting either of unskilled workers or of workers in a peculiar position in industry which makes them largely independent of Friendly Benefits, to the unions of skilled craftsmen, we find at once a great difference in the rate of contribution. The skilled Craft Unionist usually paid at least 1s. per week in ordinary contributions, and might frequently pay considerably more than this. In addition, many of the Craft Unions had regular levies upon their members, either for special purposes (contingent fund, superannuation fund, political fund, etc.), or were in the habit of supplementing their ordinary income by levies as a regular practice. Thus, in a Union of which the rate of contribution is 1s., a member may actually be called upon to pay something well over 1s. 6d. In one Union at least a percentage system had been adopted for securing a rate of contribution proportionate to the ability to pay of the member, the Steel Smelters having made the contribution payable dependent upon the rate of wages received. Thus, a member in receipt of 23s. per week paid 3d., while a member in receipt of 85s. paid 1s. 3d.

The changed value of money since the War, and the increased claims on the Unions for both benefits and administration, have in nearly all cases caused an upward revision of these scales. In the Post Office and Civil Service, the leading associations have reorganised themselves on more definite Trade Union lines, and contributions, while they remain low in comparison with other groups, have greatly increased. For example, the Union of Post Office Workers, which has absorbed the Postmen's Federation, has a contribution of 5d. a week, with lower rates for those receiving less than 30s. a week. The Unions of general workers have mostly been compelled to raise their rates to 6d. a week, still preserving lower rates for women members at about 3d. a week. The National Union of Railwaymen's scale now runs up from 5d. weekly. The Craft Unions have increased their rates less, or not at all, preferring to raise additional revenue by special levies, or even to suspend payment of certain benefits, instead of raising the regular contributions. Thus, the Amalgamated Engineering Union, successor to the A.S.E., has scales of 1s. 6d. and 1s. a week for its higher grades, and 6d. a week for the lower. The sixpenny scale, however, does not carry the right to the more important friendly benefits.

If we turn now to the question of benefits we shall find naturally that the Unions which have low rates of contribution pay only low rates of benefit, and further, pay benefit only for a much narrower range of purposes. A Craft Union with a high rate of contribution may pay benefit for strikes and lock-outs, unemployment, sickness, accident, superannuation, funeral, victimisation, legal aid, travelling, emigration, and various other purposes, while a Union of general workers, or any other Union with a very low rate of contributions, will probably confine itself to strike and lock-out, victimisation and legal aid, and will pay no Friendly Benefits at all, unless it makes arrangements for such of its members as choose to subscribe voluntarily at a higher rate of contribution, and receive extra benefits as above described. Unemployment benefit, however, is sometimes paid, though it has had to be suspended in

THE GOVERNMENT OF TRADE UNIONISM 71

most cases owing to the abnormal drain of the past few years. There is, indeed, a very wide range of difference between one Union and another in the benefits paid, and even in the amount of benefit assured in return for the same contribution. This arises largely from the fact that it is impossible to place Trade Union benefits, or the greater part of them, upon an actuarial basis. The cost of Sickness Benefit and Superannuation can to some extent be estimated in advance, but Unemployment Benefit and, still more, Strike and Lock-out Benefit, are dependent upon the condition of the labour market, and the amount of industrial unrest prevailing at any particular time. A period of industrial tranquillity means at once a greatly reduced demand upon the Trade Unions of all classes for benefits, while one big strike may easily sweep away the greatest part of the accumulated funds of even the strongest Union. Similarly, a period of acute industrial depression may eat up all the available funds in unemployment benefit. In 1913 all registered Trade Unions together spent half a million pounds on unemployed benefits. In 1919 they spent one million pounds, and in 1920 more than a million and a half. But in 1921, when the post-War slump became severe, the amount expended on this benefit alone rose to nearly fifteen million pounds, and the great majority of the Unions were compelled, first to resort to heavy levies, and then to suspend altogether the payment of unemployed benefits. Of this fifteen millions, about half came from the Ministry of Labour in the form of allowances under the Unemployment Insurance Acts, over two millions was drawn from the revenue of the year, while five millions was drawn from the reserve funds built up during the War, when, naturally, expenditure was low, as there were few strikes and hardly any unemployment. In one year nearly a third of the reserve funds of all registered Unions was swept away, and in 1922 further calls depleted them still more. Actuarial methods afford little help in dealing with such a situation.

While, however, it is not possible to place all Trade Union benefits upon an actuarial basis, there can be no doubt that some Unions have in the past promised benefits at a rate considerably higher than were really justified by their rates of contribution. Thus, some of the older Craft Unions in the building industry found themselves in considerable financial difficulties owing to the promise of too high rates of Superannuation Benefit, while the General Federation of Trade Unions, which, as we have seen, is a sort of Strike Insurance Society, to which Trade Unions pay contributions at a fixed rate, and from which they become entitled to a fixed rate of benefit in return, was forced, shortly before the War, to revise its scale of benefits, owing to the growing industrial unrest which had rendered it financially unsound. At least in the case of Superannuation, and Funeral, and other Friendly Benefits, it would be possible for the Trade Unions to show a greater regard to actuarial soundness in fixing the relation of the benefits and contributions, but there is obvious difficulty in this, particularly on account of the democratic forms of Trade Union government. It is not always easy to make the member, particularly the older member, see that the rate of, say, superannuation pay must be reduced if the Union is to remain financially sound, or to persuade the younger members to pay higher contributions in order to maintain the rate of benefit. There can be no doubt that in the majority of the old-fashioned Craft Unions Superannuation Benefit is to some extent a mortgage on the future, and is paid out of the contributions of the younger members. There is no necessary objection to this, provided a balance is maintained and the funds are not swallowed up to an undue extent. Where this happens the result is that young members cease to flock into the Union, and the old members find themselves faced with a dwindling reserve fund and the impossibility of maintaining benefits on the old scale. This, indeed, has actually occurred in some of the smaller Societies.

Tables given in the Appendices to this volume will provide some indication of the nature of Trade Union expenditure upon most types of benefit. It is, of course, very difficult to furnish figures which are a real indication of the proportions borne between the various benefits, since inevitably they vary very widely from year to year and from period to period. The industrial unrest in the years immediately preceding the War enormously increased the proportion of money spent upon Dispute Benefit of various kinds, while, as we have seen, the post-War slump was at once reflected in a big increase in Unemployment Benefit. A further difficulty in disentangling the amount spent for the various purposes arises from the fact that some Unions do not separate unemployment and strike pay, but prefer to pay unemployment pay in both cases with an extra allowance from the contingent fund in the case of strikes.

If we turn to the other considerable items on the expenditure side of the Trade Union balance-sheet, we shall find that much the largest of these is management expenses, that is to say, the upkeep of the general and district offices, salaries of officials, local and central, and administration of every sort. This, again, is an amount which fluctuates widely from Union to Union. A Union with low rates of contribution can afford to spend only a comparatively small sum per member on organising and managerial work, but its expenditure upon these things is likely to be a higher pro-

THE GOVERNMENT OF TRADE UNIONISM

portion of its total receipts than the proportion spent by a Craft Union with high benefits and rates of contribution.

The higher expenditure of such Unions results partly from the greater cost of administering a wide range of complicated benefits, and partly from the keeping of a larger staff of permanent officials, and from the undertaking by those officials of a large amount of expert work. For instance, many Craft Unions, *e.g.*, the Boilermakers, Shipwrights, Spinners, Weavers, maintain permanent officials in the various districts whose business it is to deal as experts with questions relating to the fixing and adjustment of piece-work prices, while, as a rule, a skilled membership requires, or at least receives, considerably closer attention than the members of less skilled organisations.

In the Appendices will be found certain Tables summarising the pre-War and post-War expenditure of important Trade Unions, both on the main types of benefit and on working expenses. It will be seen that, for all registered Unions, working and miscellaneous expenses, apart from benefits and political payments, accounted for $37\frac{1}{2}$ per cent. of total expenditure in 1913, and for $39\frac{1}{2}$ per cent. in 1922. In 1920, when demands for benefits were relatively low, working expenses rose to nearly 48 per cent. ; but in 1921, heavy unemployment benefit payments reduced them to $28\frac{1}{2}$ per cent. of the total. Apart from these abnormal fluctuations, there has been no great change in the relation of working costs to benefits taken together. On the other hand, total income and expenditure, both absolutely and per member, have greatly increased. In 1913, the average income per member was 28*s*. ; in 1922 it was nearly 68*s*. In 1913 average expenditure per member was about 14*s*. 6*d*. ; in 1922 it was 72*s*. 6*d*.

The figures referred to above are the average of registered Trade Unions of all types. In the following Table a distinction is drawn, and the Unions are arranged in occupational groups. The Table illustrates for the year 1921—the latest for which detailed figures are available—the difference explained above between Unions of different types. The registered Unions in the metal and textile groups are predominantly Craft Unions with high contributions and benefits. They show both the highest total expenditure per member and, in the metal group, the highest expenditure per member on management. But their expenditure on management is a much lower percentage of total expenditure than that of the other groups. The Public Services group at the other extreme pays few benefits, and, therefore, has both a low total expenditure and a very high proportion of management to total expenses. The Transport group pays few friendly benefits, but does pay industrial benefits, and therefore shows the same features in a less marked degree. The Building group includes both craftsmen's and labourers' societies, and therefore occupies a middle position. The Mining group, which would, in normal years, rank with the low benefit Unions, paid out in 1921 large sums in strike benefit, and therefore shifted from its usual position to the middle of the list. The General and Miscellaneous group is too diverse for classification.

Management Expenses of Registered Trade Unions, 1921.

Group.	(Thousands.) Membership at end of year.	(£ thousands.)		Total Expenditure per Member.		Management Expenditure per Member.		Percentage Proportion of Management to Total Expenditure.
		Total Expenditure.	Expenditure on Management.	s.	d.	s.	d.	
Metal	1,011	9,742	966	192	9	19	1	9
Textile	271	1,680	135	123	10	9	11	8
General and Miscellaneous	971	4,553	791	93	9	16	3	17
Mining and Quarrying	841	3,642	487	86	6	11	6	13
Building	456	1,673	365	73	4	16	0	21
Transport	869	2,450	852	56	4	19	7	35
Public Services	118	119	64	20	1	10	10	54

Every Union has a reserve fund, that is to say, a balance which it has built up by saving out of contributions over a period of years. This reserve fund may occasionally be swept away as a result of some great strike or long period of distress, but attempts are at once made to build it up again when normal times return. The amount of these reserve funds per member of the Society concerned again varies from Union to Union, and from group to group. Naturally, out of their smaller income per member the unskilled Unions cannot build up high reserve funds, although the years of the War, in which the number of disputes was small, furnished them with an opportunity for increasing their reserves considerably. The second Table printed in Appendix VIII shows, for all registered Unions, the total funds for a series of years. It should be noted that it refers, not to all Unions, but only to those registered under the Trade Union Acts.[1] At the end of 1922 the 514 registered Unions had total accumulated funds of nearly ten

See p. 163.

million pounds, or 39s. 4d. per member, as against six and half million pounds and 40s. a member in 1913.

Turn from these general averages to the averages of the groups dealt with above, as shown in the following Table for the year 1921.

Funds of Registered Trade Unions, 1921.

Group.	Amount of Funds (£ thousands).	Funds per Member. (shillings).
Metal	4,179	82
Textile	940	69
Transport	2,301	53
Building	985	43
Public Administration	114	20
General and Miscellaneous	918	19
Mining	7	0·2
All Trades	10,950	40

The Metal and Textile groups again head the list, while the miners, having spend all their money in the disastrous lock-out of 1921, sink to the very bottom. The transport workers, owing to freedom from strikes, stand rather high. Otherwise, the list corresponds roughly to the order of the Table given on p. 74.

It must be remembered, however, that the whole post-War period is in many respects abnormal from a financial point of view, owing both to rapid fluctuations in membership and to the extraordinarily high expenditure on unemployment benefits. It is therefore worth while to give, for purposes of comparison, a few pre-War figures, which probably illustrate more exactly the normal position of the Trade Union movement. In Appendix X the reader will find an analysis of the pre-War expenditure of certain important Trade Unions.[1]

As we shall see in dealing with the question of amalgamation, financial considerations often play an important part when amalgamation is under discussion. Differing rates of contributions and benefits, and differing management expenses, are often serious obstacles to the achievement of unity, even when the desirabilty of fusion is clearly recognised on both sides.

The financial administration of Trade Unions is, in the main, in the hands of the ordinary salaried officials, drawn directly from the ranks of the membership. The outside expert is called in very occasionally to deal with particular difficulties, but usually the Trade Unions train their own men for administrative work. On

[1] See p. 166.

the whole there is no doubt that this training has been a success, and that the funds of most Unions are administered with considerable skill and capacity. Branch work and district work furnish a useful training-ground for the members, and those who rise to positions of financial importance in the Union have usually served a considerable apprenticeship in branch or district organisation. On the whole the administration of Trade Union finance is conservative and cautious ; any departure from conservative methods results, as a rule, not from the action of the administration, but from pressure by the members. Cautious financial administration is perhaps less a feature of Trade Unionism to-day than it was thirty years ago, but it still persists to a very considerable extent, particularly in those Unions which have the highest contributions and benefits and reserve funds. Indeed, the charge has often been brought against particular Unions that they think more of their funds than of the need for industrial action. How far this charge is justified in particular cases it is not possible to argue here. As a general indictment, however, there seems little evidence behind it, except in the sense that those directly entrusted with the financial management of the Societies are apt to think primarily of finance, but to be checked in their action by rank and file pressure and the attitude of other officers and executive members who are not primarily concerned with the financial administration of the Union.

PART IV

INTERNAL TRADE UNION PROBLEMS

Sect. 1. Amalgamation and Federation. Sect. 2. Inter-Union Relations. Sect. 3. Women in Trade Unions. Sect. 4. Supervisors and Non-Manual Workers. Sect. 5. The Problem of Democratic Control. Sect. 6. Political Action. Sect. 7. Trade Unionism and the Co-operative Movement. Sect. 8. Trade Unions and Education.

Section 1.—AMALGAMATION AND FEDERATION

WE have seen, in earlier sections of this book, that there is a growing tendency for Trade Unions to combine into larger groups, both by federation of separate Societies, and by complete amalgamation. But we have hitherto discussed neither the forces at work behind such movements nor the obstacles which prevent consolidation from making more rapid progress. As we have observed, new Unions seem to be created as rapidly as old Unions become absorbed in larger bodies, though there is a constant tendency to form amalgamations of greater extent, and for a higher proportion of the workers in the key industries to become organised in a few big Unions.

There have been many " closer unity " movements in the history of Trade Unionism—in the years after 1830, when the Builders' Union and the Grand National Consolidated Trades Union were formed by fusion of many smaller Societies; in the 'fifties and 'sixties, when the great " Amalgamated " Societies of Engineers and Carpenters and Joiners became the " new model " of Trade Union organisation; in the 'eighties and 'nineties, when the great " federations " were mostly created; and again in the years immediately before 1914. These movements may be divided into two types—official movements, in which the Executive Councils and other governing bodies of various Unions meet for the purpose of achieving closer union of forces; and unofficial, or rank and file, movements, in which the rank and file members of different Unions meet for the purpose of propaganda on the subject of amalgamation and of stirring the official bodies to act more promptly and decisively.

In the years between 1910 and 1914 both these movements were in a state of considerable activity which the War only temporarily interrupted. The industrial unrest of 1911 and the following years brought once more to the surface the difficulties of Trade Union organisation, the enormous amount of sectionalism and overlapping which still existed, and the need for greater concentration of activity in face of the growing combination on the part of the employers, and the increasing State intervention in industrial affairs. Probably it would be true to say that at some time between 1911 and 1914 movements of this sort were on foot in every important industry. The Transport Workers' Federation was formed as the result of a big campaign in 1911, and had among its objects the promotion of amalgamation among the constituent Societies. The negotiations which culminated in the formation of the National Union of Railwaymen were in full swing during 1912. Abortive proposals for a general amalgamation of the Transport and general workers' Unions were the subject of many conferences during 1913 and 1914. Even during the War, though larger movements were for the most part suspended, the process of absorption of small Societies by large ones steadily continued, and the rank and file movement in favour of amalgamation gained considerably in force.

Despite this great activity on the part of the amalgamationists it is true that not a great deal was achieved. The National Union of Railwaymen stands out, as we have previously said, as the one great achievement of the amalgamationists in the years before the War. This, however, does not mean that the movement towards amalgamation was not making considerable headway, or that the state of feeling inside the various Unions remained as it was before. There can be no doubt that in almost all Unions a widespread sentiment in favour of amalgamation was created, or that this sentiment has borne fruit in the great amalgamations accomplished since 1918.

Official movements in the direction of amalgamation often begin as the result of pressure from the rank and file, but their greatest successes have been achieved in those instances in which officials and rank and file have been united. Where mere rank and file movements have been found without adequate support from officials and Executive Committees, although there may have been considerable activity on the part of the amalgamationists, the results have usually been meagre. The reason for this will appear more clearly when we have glanced at the difficulties that stand in the way of amalgamation.

Until 1917 the greatest single difficulty was without doubt the position of the law regarding amalgamation. Under the old Trade Union Acts two Trade Unions could not amalgamate unless each, in a ballot vote of its members, secured a majority of two-thirds, not merely of those voting, but of the whole membership. This barrier was proved not to be insuperable in the case of the N.U.R. It was none the less a very serious difficulty indeed, since the majority required represents a very much higher percentage of the membership of the Union than can usually be persuaded to vote, even on the most vital issues. There are many reasons which make it difficult for a Trade Union to poll the votes of anything like its complete membership. To begin with, there are at any time numbers of members out of work, working away from home or absent for other causes, whose votes it is exceedingly difficult to secure, even if it is possible to trace the members within the necessary time. The law, as it stood till 1917, was indeed an absurdity, and, although the position has been improved by the Trade Union (Amalgamation) Act of 1917, it is still by no means satisfactory. There seems to be no reason why two Trade Unions should not decide to amalgamate by a bare majority on either side, whereas the law still makes it necessary that 50 per cent. of the members should vote, and that the proposal for amalgamation should secure a 20 per cent. majority of those voting.

There are, indeed, certain ways in which this legal difficulty can sometimes be overcome. Often, where a small Society desires to amalgamate with a large one, instead of going to work under the Act of 1917 it dissolves altogether, first voting the whole of its funds to the larger body. The larger Union then accepts all its members into its own ranks on terms arranged before the dissolution. But this method, though it is often useful in the case of small Societies, is difficult to apply where two large Societies desire to come together, both because neither is willing to merge itself into the other and because there is the risk of a heavy loss of membership in the process. A further reform of the law is badly needed. Any two or more Societies should be allowed to amalgamate by a bare majority of those voting in each Union, and, in addition, any Society should be allowed to merge itself in another corporately, without the need for dissolution, or for a ballot of the Society into which it proposes to transfer its members. Until something like this is done, the legal difficulty will continue to be serious, and to prevent many useful amalgamations from taking place.

Besides the legal barriers there are many other difficulties in the way of Trade Unions which desire to amalgamate. The most important of these is probably the financial difficulty, and this is especially grave in the case of those Unions which pay high benefits for sickness, superannuation, unemployment, etc., and which therefore necessarily have large reserve funds to meet large potential liabilities. Where the two Unions which propose to amalgamate are of varying financial strength it may often be exceedingly difficult to secure a basis which is satisfactory to both parties. The weaker Union may find itself confronted with the possibility of reduced benefits, or of higher contributions for its members in the new amalgamation. The stronger Union may regard it as unfair to admit the members of the other Society on terms more favourable than their own members have secured by their accumulated contributions. To the militant Industrial Unionist, these may seem small matters; but they often, and almost of necessity, bulk large in the eyes of those who have to administer the financial affairs of the Societies concerned. They are not insuperable difficulties, but they demand considerable statesmanship before they can be overcome.

Next in importance comes the difficulty of officials. Amalgamation between two Societies means making one general secretary grow where two grew before, and even if the amalgamated body is likely to be far more powerful than either of the two Societies could be apart, there may be an unwillingness on the part of either of the general secretaries to give way to the other, particularly if the two Societies concerned are more or less equal in strength. In the case of the smaller Societies the difficulty often arises of absorbing the officials whom they have maintained, but it is usually found essential in order to achieve success in any project of amalgamation that all the full-time officials of the Societies concerned should be guaranteed posts at least at the same salaries under the new Society. Usually, officials thus taken over are guaranteed their new positions only for a limited period, after which they have to stand their chance of re-election by the members, unless the Union has a pension scheme, and they have by then reached the pensionable age. A general pension scheme for officials of all contributing Unions has recently been formulated by the General Council of the Trades Union Congress. The taking over of existing officials does not always meet all the objections, but usually, where there is a will, a way round the difficulty may be found.

The above difficulties exist often where the case for amalgamation between two or more Societies is perfectly clear, *i.e.*, where the Societies are rival Societies catering for the same class of members. Where this is not the case it is, of course, often open to question whether amalgamation is or is not the right policy, and at this point controversial opinions concerning the right form of Trade Union structure enter into the question. For instance, the Amalgamated Engineering Union is, as we have seen, a kindred craft Society, including workers in a large number of different engineering crafts. When amalgamation between this Society and one of the specialised Craft Unions, catering only for a single engineering craft, comes under discussion, it is clear that a distinct issue of policy is involved. The members of the Craft Union—say, the patternmakers [1]—will undoubtedly be divided on the issue. Some will say their best interests will be served by uniting with other classes of engineering workers; while some will maintain that the patternmaker's distinctive position renders it essential that he should maintain a separate craft organisation of his own, and should have, at the most, only federal connections with workers in allied crafts. This is the substance of the keen controversy between the National Union of Railwaymen and the Associated Society of Locomotive Engineers and Firemen. Still more is there room for difference of opinion when amalgamation is proposed on an even wider basis than that of kindred crafts; when, for instance, it is proposed that all the various Societies in the cotton industry—card-room operatives, spinners, weavers, overlookers, etc.—should form themselves into a single Cotton Industrial Union. The difference is most acute of all in those cases in which there is a wide gulf separating the skilled and unskilled workers, when it is proposed that skilled and unskilled alike, in whatever Unions they are now organised, should join together in a single Industrial Union covering all sections of workers employed in the industry.

Rank and file movements in the direction of amalgamation have almost always been of an Industrial Unionist character, that is to say, they have desired to bring about amalgamation into one Union of all workers employed in a particular industrial group. A number of these movements on Industrial Unionist lines sprang up in 1912 and the following years under the auspices of a rank and file Committee which set out with the object of " amalgamating all existing Trade Unions " and formed for this purpose separate Amalgamation Committees in a number of different industries, notably metal, building, printing, etc. Of these Committees the only one which showed vitality over a long period was the Metal, Engineering, and Shipbuilding Amalgamation Committee, which had a considerable following among the younger engineering workers of all trades, skilled and unskilled alike. But even in this industry amalgamation, when it came, took the form of a fusion of kindred Craft Unions, still leaving outside most of the less skilled workers.

This is largely because of the quite peculiar organisation of the

---

[1] The present Patternmakers' Society is actually the result of a secession from the A.S.E., the Patternmakers having been absorbed into the Amalgamated Society in 1851. Most, but not all, of them subsequently seceded on the ground that their special craft interests were not sufficiently considered in the amalgamation.

engineering industry. The engineering workers are divided between a number of important Craft Unions, mostly confined to skilled men, and the rival Unions of general workers, which endeavour to organise the less skilled grades. Official attempts at amalgamation have all been concentrated on the attempt to unite all, or some of, the Craft Unions in the industry, whereas the rank and file movement has gone steadily for amalgamation of all Unions, skilled and unskilled alike. This policy has brought it up against the very difficult situation created by the existence of the general workers' Unions stretching across many different industries and consisting mainly of less skilled workers. The official attitude in this case, as in others of the same sort, does not necessarily arise from any opposition to union by industry, but is also partly dictated by the desire to reduce the difficulties in the way of amalgamation.

It will be well before we leave this subject to say a little more with regard to the threatened differences of opinion that are at the back of the quarrels which often occur in connection with amalgamation. As we have seen, the rank and file movements are mostly of an " Industrial Unionist " character. This does not mean that they are necessarily animated by the tenets of strict Marxian Industrial Unionism, but they do desire a linking up on industrial lines of skilled and unskilled in the same Unions. One particular difficulty which arises in the interpretation of this conception of " Union by Industry " is the position of clerical workers. The advocates of Union by Industry have, as a rule, paid comparatively little attention to the position of clerks, who, in most industries, form only a small proportion of the total number employed. In the particular case of the railways, however, where the clerical element is both exceptionally numerous and unusually well organised, the question whether an Industrial Union should include clerks along with the other grades has recently been the subject of a great deal of discussion. The Railway Clerks' Association, while contemplating fusion as an ultimate possibility, has again and again declared against it for the present. This is due partly, no doubt, to clerical snobbishness, but also to the real doubt in the minds of many railway clerks whether the manual workers would be prepared to support the special demands which they would be likely to put forward. For instance, the working week of the clerk is, as a rule, shorter than that of the manual worker. Salaries are in many cases higher, and working conditions are considerably different. The clerks are not satisfied that railwaymen would fight in order to secure what they might regard as preferential treatment for the clerical grades. The railway clerks, moreover, have never so far taken part in a national railway strike, and, though they are willing to give guarantees against "blacklegging" in such a case, they do not relish the prospect of being called out, perhaps, in support of a claim directly concerning only the manual grades. They fear the loss of seniority and pension rights in case of defeat. In view of these doubts, the R.C.A. leaders hold that amalgamation is not possible at the present stage, or at all without very considerable guarantees of autonomy as well as of complete common action inside any composite organisation. The other problem which has raised difficulty in the case of the railway clerks is one which applies also in many other industries. The Railway Clerks' Association has achieved considerable success in the organisation of the higher grades of the railway services, particularly stationmasters, agents, and chief clerks. The N.U.R., although to some extent it does organise both clerks and supervisors in the operative grades of the service, and has indeed a substantial membership among them, has not progressed anything like so far as the Railway Clerks' Association in this direction. This clearly raises a problem which applies not simply to supervisory classes of clerical workers, but to supervisory workers of all kinds and in all industries. The problem of the relation of supervisors, foremen, etc., to rank and file Trade Unionists has long been acute in the Post Office, where the supervisory grades are organised in separate associations of their own. It has of late years shown signs of becoming acute in the engineering industry also. The achievement of Union by Industry in the narrower sense, by the union of skilled and unskilled manual workers in a single Society, would clearly raise up further problems of amalgamation and absorption in relation to such "higher" grades of workers.[1]

The War, as we have seen, for the time interrupted the amalgamation movement, mainly owing to the difficulty of taking ballot votes with many members away in the Army. By far the most solid achievement in the way of fusion during the War was the Iron and Steel Trades *Confederation*, which should be sharply distinguished from the *Federations* (without the "con") mentioned on the next pages. The Confederation embodied, in effect, a plan of complete amalgamation by instalments. The Societies which joined to form it undertook to enrol no new members. Directly under the Confederation they formed a new "Central Association," the British Iron, Steel, and Kindred Trades Association, in which all new members were enrolled. In addition, members of the older Societies could transfer to the new Association, or any of the constituent Societies could completely merge itself in this

---

[1] See p. 97.

new body. By lapses, deaths, and transfers, the membership of the older Societies thus continually dwindled, while the membership of the new Society, backed by the organising work of the whole Confederation, grew rapidly. All the negotiating work of the Central Association, and all such work affecting the members of more than one Society, was placed in the hands of the Confederation, which thus acted from the first as an effective industrial unit, even before the process of transference was complete. By the continuance of this process, the Confederation has already grown virtually into a single Union, and most of its constituent Societies have been dissolved.

There would seem to be no adequate reason why the very successful precedent set by those responsible for the formation of the Iron and Steel Trades Confederation should not be followed in other industries. It has the great advantage, first, that it avoids altogether the necessity for a ballot hampered by legal restrictions, and secondly, that, by leaving the existing Societies nominally in being, it makes easier a clean cut from obsolete traditions and the framing of an up-to-date constitution to suit the needs of the time. The Confederation, however, has so far found no imitators, possibly because it involves both very careful planning at the outset and complicated clerical work, both in the branches and at the head office, during the process of transition.

Before we dismiss the question of closer unity between the various Trade Unions it is necessary to say something of federation as well as of amalgamation. We have already analysed the various types of federation and given a list of the most important Federations in the principal industries. War-time developments, and more particularly the Whitley scheme for Standing Joint Industrial Councils, were responsible for considerable steps towards federal action by Trade Unions in the less organised industries. There grew up, for instance, in connection with wages applications during the war, a marked tendency towards common action amongst Trade Unions which had no basis for unity in pre-War times, and in some cases these extempore forms of combination have resulted in permanent federal bodies. Moreover, some Federations which existed before the War were considerably strengthened during the War period. The Transport Workers' Federation, for example, profited by the need for common action in regard to wages movements amongst the various Unions catering for dockers, vehicle workers, etc., and the basis of common action thus worked out subsequently led to the complete amalgamation of most of the constituent Unions, except the seafarers, into a single Society, the Transport and General Workers' Union. In this case, the T.W.F., by its very success, diminished its own

INTERNAL TRADE UNION PROBLEMS 85

importance, and fulfilled its destiny by handing over many of its functions to the new Union created largely through its work. It has since been reconstructed on a broader basis in the hope of inducing the railway Trade Unions to join.

The Engineering and Shipbuilding Trades Federation, on the other hand, lost ground, and with the secession of the Amalgamated Society of Engineers ceased to be representative of the engineering industry as a whole.

The building trade workers, who had only a very loose federal council before the War, formed in 1917 the powerful National Federation of Building Trades Operatives, which has been described in a previous section, and the Unions of general workers in the same year formed the National Federation of General Workers, in the first instance mainly for negotiating with the Ministry of Munitions on behalf of the less skilled grades in the munitions industries, but later with the wider purpose of promoting common action over the whole field of general workers' organisation.

Far more important, however, than the growth of Federations during the past few years is the steady progress of the amalgamation movement since the end of the War. Reference has been made already to several of the important fusions which have resulted in a much greater concentration of membership in several of the greatest Trade Union groups. Thus the Amalgamated Engineering Union, formed in 1920, absorbed the Amalgamated Society of Engineers, the Steam Engine Makers, Toolmakers, Machine Workers, Smiths and Strikers, Brassfinishers, and several smaller engineering Societies. The Transport and General Workers' Union absorbed the old Dockers' Union, the National Union of Dock Labourers, Scottish Union of Dock Labourers, National Union of Vehicle Workers, United Vehicle Workers (itself an amalgamation of the Tramway Workers and Licensed Vehicle Workers), and a number of other Unions. The National Union of General Workers has already absorbed the National Federation of Women Workers, the Gas, Municipal and General Workers, the British Labour Amalgamation, the Engine and Crane Drivers, and other Unions, and is on the point as I write (June, 1924) of amalgamating with two of the three other big Unions of general workers—the National Amalgamated Union of Labour and the Municipal Employees' Association. The National Union of Textile Workers was formed in 1922 by the fusion of the General Union of Textile Workers, the National Society of Dyers, and one or two other Unions in the woollen industry. The National Union of Distributive and Allied Workers is a fusion of the Amalgamated Union of Co-operative Employees and the Warehouse and

General Workers' Union. The National Union of Printing, Bookbinding and Paper Workers was formed in 1922 by the fusion of the Bookbinders and the Printing and Paper Workers, who had previously absorbed the Printers' Warehousemen and Cutters. Several Civil Service Unions have joined to form the Civil Service Clerical Association. The Union of Post Office Workers (1920) has absorbed the Postmen's Federation, the Postal and Telegraph Clerks' Association, and the Fawcett Association of postal sorters. The Musicians' Union was created in 1920 by fusion of the Amalgamated Musicians and the National Orchestral Association. The Garment Workers and the Scottish Tailors joined in 1920 to form the Tailors' and Garment Workers' Union. The Stonemasons and the two rival Unions of Bricklayers united in 1921 into the Amalgamated Union of Building Trade Workers, and the two Unions of Carpenters and Joiners formed in 1920 the Amalgamated Society of Woodworkers. A number of Unions of builders' labourers also united in 1920, forming the "Altogether" Builders' Labourers' and Constructional Workers' Society. The British Iron and Steel Trades Association, formed in 1917,[1] has continued to absorb the smaller Societies. The five local Unions of blastfurnacemen have developed their National Federation into a single National Union of Blastfurnacemen (1922), and the numerous small federated Societies of sheet metal workers and braziers have similarly joined up into the National Union of Sheet Metal Workers (1921). The Friendly Society of Ironfounders, the Scottish Ironmoulders, and the Coremakers have amalgamated into the National Union of Foundry Workers (1922). And these are only the most important of the large number of amalgamations accomplished during the past few years.[2]

Nevertheless, it is clear that a great deal remains to be done. There is still much overlapping in many industries, and much sectionalism even where there is not serious overlapping. Measured by the extent of the need, amalgamation does not make rapid progress. The cotton Trade Unions remain separated by crafts, and have recently, in 1923, rejected a scheme of closer federation. It still takes fifty Trade Unions of varying importance to negotiate a comprehensive agreement for the engineering industry, as appeared during the lock-out of 1922. Among the general workers, the N.U.G.W. and the Workers' Union are still rivals impairing each other's efficiency. The N.U.R. and the Locomotive Engineers keep the footplate grades on the railways in two rival camps. The Distributive Workers and the Shop Assistants,

---

[1] See p. 83.
[2] For a guide to recent amalgamations, see Appendix XII, and for the membership of the Unions here mentioned, see Appendix XIII.

the Sailors' and Firemen and the Marine Workers, the National Union of Clerks and the separate clerical Societies in various occupational groups, still maintain their unfortunate rivalries. Much has been done, but more remains to be done, in making Trade Union organisation scientific and orderly, and in thus laying firm foundations for general unity of the movement as a whole.

Section 2.—INTER-UNION RELATIONS

(a) *Demarcation*.—There is no problem that has caused a greater amount of heart-burning inside the Trade Union movement than that of demarcation between the various trades. For many years opinions have been widely expressed throughout the Trade Union movement that the continued existence of these problems is an absurdity, and yet it has so far proved impossible to find any satisfactory method of dealing with disputes as they arise. It is, however, true that recent amalgamations and federations have to some extent lessened both the number and the ferocity of these disputes, and that there is a growing tendency to settle them by agreement without making the employer a party to the settlement.

The general character of the problem is simple; each trade desires to have clearly marked out the type of work which it, and the other trades which are akin to it, are entitled to do; but each has usually a somewhat extensive conception of the class of work to which it is itself entitled. In the case of long-established processes custom may often settle the question in the long run, but new processes are continually being introduced, and changes in the method of manufacture, of course, make such changes inevitable. Whenever such a change takes place in connection with an organised group of trades there is serious danger that disputes will arise as to which of the trades is entitled to do the new work or use the new tool. Each trade fears that, if it loses control of a particular class of work or of a particular tool its work will be taken from it, and its members will have to walk the streets unemployed. Nor is this the only trouble. There is also a strong feeling of craftsmanship behind the objection to being ruled out of any class of work which a man feels that his training enables him to do efficiently. The fear of unemployment, however, if it is not the sole source of demarcation disputes, is no doubt their most serious cause, and while the problem of unemployment remains acute it is doubtful whether demarcation difficulties can be got fully under control. Amalgamation, indeed, does something towards this, but it is unlikely that amalgamation will go far enough to remove the difficulty altogether, or even that it would do so however far it went. It is obvious that it is often difficult from the very nature of the work to define accurately the lines of demarcation between crafts of a similar character. This would be so even if industry were purely static; for frequently one craft must co-operate with another in doing a single job, and there may be parts of the job which can be equally well done by either craft, but to which each craft is tempted to put forward an exclusive claim. Thus, in shipbuilding, the line between the shipwright and the joiner, or the shipwright and the upholsterer, or the shipwright and the boilermaker is by no means clear in numbers of marginal cases, and this is true even apart from changes in shipbuilding methods, although such changes often aggravate the problem.

Demarcation difficulties arising from changes in industrial practice can be easily illustrated by two particular examples. The coming of electricity has profoundly revolutionised many engineering processes. The electrical branch of industry is still growing and rapidly changing, and demarcation disputes between engineering fitters and electricians are continually arising. The second case is that of acetylene welding, where the welding tool introduced in recent years has been claimed in various shops by boilermakers, copper-smiths, sheet-metal workers, fitters, drillers, semi-skilled workers, and by several other classes of labour. Or, if we move outside the engineering industry to the other most fruitful field of demarcation disputes, we find that, in the building industry, fitters and plumbers, and plumbers and heating engineers, wage ceaseless warfare.

One or two brief but detailed instances of disputes will serve better than anything else to reveal the character of the problem.

Recent changes in shipbuilding practice have included a largely increased use of corticine for the surface of decks. The upholsterers have claimed that corticine is only a specially thick linoleum, and therefore belongs to them, while the shipwrights, in the words of their General Secretary, have asserted that it is " almost a deck." Or take a second case. For years plumbers and fitters on the north-east coast disputed concerning the fitting of certain classes of pipes. At last an award was secured; plumbers were to fit all pipes of less than $2\frac{1}{2}$ inches, and fitters all pipes of more than $2\frac{1}{2}$ inches. Two-and-a-half-inch pipes were unfortunately forgotten, and the dispute raged with undiminished violence for years afterwards. In another case, a long-standing dispute between plumbers and fitters was finally settled by the quite arbitrary decision that the same class of work should be done by the one trade on warships and by the other on merchant ships.

Lest we should seem by actual instances to turn the whole question of demarcation into ridicule, it must be stated that there is often an element of solid reason behind what seem the most absurd disputes. A process of nibbling at one trade by another does sometimes in fact result in throwing the members of the first trade out of work. Naturally their organisation must endeavour to protect them from such a danger. Clearly, then, as long as the unemployment problem exists, and lines of demarcation between skilled crafts continue to be recognised at all, nothing can possibly be effective in the last resort in solving the problem of demarcation, however much closer union between the various industries and crafts may help both by breaking down lines of craft demarcation in particular cases, and by providing for the better adjustment of difficulties as they arise.

The problem is considerably aggravated by the fact that the different trades which dispute over certain classes of work have often different rates of pay, so that there is an advantage for the employer in giving the work to the lower-paid trade. To meet this it has often been suggested that, where work is in dispute, it should be open to members of either trade at the higher rate, but the skilled trades have so far been unwilling to apply generally this apparently sensible solution, though it has been acted upon in certain cases with success. In any event, the settlement of difficulties relating to rates of pay does not remove the more important cause of demarcation disputes—the fear of unemployment.

We must turn now to the methods adopted by the Trade Unions in dealing with the problem. In both the shipbuilding and building industries there are special demarcation agreements covering a considerable proportion of the trades concerned. The principle of some of these agreements, unfortunately, virtually makes the employer the arbitrator. In one agreement, for instance, it is provided that where two trades are disputing over a particular class of work, the two trades shall each send representatives to a Demarcation Court, and the employer shall send a similar number of representatives. As each trade naturally votes in favour of itself this means in practice that the employers arbitrate. It does not always mean that the employer gives the work to the lower-paid grade of labour, since there are other things which he will take into account. He may, for instance, think there is more chance of peace and quietness if he gives it to the higher-paid class of worker, and this in such cases has sometimes occurred. The position, however, is exceedingly unsatisfactory, and certain Unions which are vitally concerned have refused to be parties to demarcation agreements in which the employers enter virtually as arbitrators.

Another method of dealing with the problem is for the Trade Unions to thrash the matter out among themselves. The Engineering and Shipbuilding Trades Federation, for instance, has throughout the whole period of its existence been very largely concerned with the question of demarcation. When two of the trades connected with it are in dispute the Federation appoints a small Board of representatives not including any representatives of either of the trades affected. This Court then issues its finding, which is supposed to bind the trades concerned, although in practice such awards are somewhat difficult to enforce. This method is obviously preferable on general grounds, although the difficulty, first, of finding a really impartial tribunal, and, secondly, of enforcement, makes it in some cases less satisfactory, because a binding decision is often not secured. Under either method the problem is usually dealt with solely with reference to specific cases which have arisen in practice, and the solutions arrived at may, and often do, vary from district to district. In a number of cases definite Apportionment Lists have resulted from a series of decisions, and these lists are issued in printed form for the information of the trades in the particular districts to which they apply. Where questions of interpreting such lists arise out of changes in processes they are generally dealt with as they arise. This method, however, has not yet been very widely extended, and it obviously presupposes in most cases a considerable amount of detailed work in advance by way of decisions on particular disputes.

(*b*) *Skilled and Less Skilled.*—Closely akin to the problem of demarcation is that of the relations between skilled, semi-skilled, and unskilled workers, so far as it is concerned with the types of work they are respectively entitled to undertake. The Craft Unions, however, do not recognise differences between skilled and less skilled workers as demarcation disputes, and do not recognise the right of the less skilled workers to raise such cases against skilled Unions. In fact, the skilled Unions virtually claim the right to do such work as they think fit, and, so far as they can enforce their claim, to exclude the less skilled where they think fit. This problem is principally of importance in the engineering industry, where the rapid development of machine processes has led to a growing encroachment by less skilled workers on jobs which were previously regarded as the province of the skilled tradesman. Occasionally, however, differences arise in most other industries as well, although in less acute forms. There is at present no recognised method of adjusting disputes of this character as between the various Unions involved, and this is likely to prove an increasing difficulty in view of the changed conditions which have resulted from " dilution "—that is to say, from the introduction of less skilled labour on work hitherto done by labour of a higher class. Such dilution, which, of course, made huge strides during the War, usually takes the form, not so much of the direct substitution of one worker for another on an identical operation, as of the introduction of simpler or more specialised machinery operated by a less skilled type of worker. It is thus only a continuation in an intensified form of the long-standing " Machine Question " in the engineering industry.

" The Machine Question," as it is often called, has perplexed the engineering industry and taxed the brains of engineering Trade Unionists ever since the Unions have been in existence. With the years it has only grown increasingly serious, and now it has reached the stage at which some form of agreement defining the relative spheres of the various grades of workers, and the methods of deciding upon the classes of work which are within the provinces of the various grades, is probably the most urgent problem which the industry has to face. The problem would largely disappear if the Unions of both types would accept the suggestion that all machines should be thrown open to all workers at standard rates based on a scientific grading of the machines themselves, instead of the men operating them, with the proviso that a skilled man working a machine of lower grade should still receive his own standard rate. But there is no sign that the skilled Trade Unions are prepared to accept or to consider any such solution of the problem. The most hopeful course for the moment seems to be some agreed system of rating the various machines, so that any worker operating a particular machine is entitled at least to the minimum rate laid down for the class of machine concerned. Such an agreement would probably enable all classes of machines, except the highest, to be thrown open to all workers at a standard rate, while still reserving the highest classes of machines to be operated wholly by fully skilled labour. It would also serve as a basis for regulating the rates to be paid to women machine operators as well as less skilled men.

(c) *Poaching.*—A very frequent cause of disputes between Trade Unions is the allegation of " poaching " by one Union on what another regards as its preserves. This takes two forms, actual inducing of men to leave one Union and join another, and the taking into a Union of non-unionists whom another Union regards as properly eligible for itself alone. For examples of the first, three cases will serve. During the unofficial dock strike of 1923, when the dockers in London and other ports struck against the advice of their Union, the Stevedores' Society, previously confined to that special grade, opened its ranks, and began to take in the revolting members of the Transport and General Workers' Union. The latter then appealed to the Trades Union Congress, which held an inquiry, and ordered the men to return to the Union they had left. Again, on the railways, the N.U.R. and the Locomotive Engineers, both of which try to organise the footplate grades, are constantly accusing each other of stealing members, and similar allegations are made by the engineering Craft Unions against the N.U.R., which, in seeking to organise all railway employees, tries to attract into its ranks the skilled workers in the railway locomotive shops. The two rival Unions of Seamen also make constant efforts to enrol each other's members.

The second type of " poaching " has already been partly illustrated in the mixed case of the stevedores. It is seen also in the constant allegations of the engineering Craft Unions that the Unions of general workers, particularly the Workers' Union, seek to enrol skilled men who ought to be in their Craft Societies. Or, again, the Distributive and Allied Workers' Union has had many disputes with the Bakers, Boot and Shoe Operatives, Garment Workers, and other Societies, when it has sought to organise productive workers, such as tailors or boot repairers employed in connection with Co-operative or other distributive undertakings. Some years before the War there was a furious dispute between the Miners' Federation and certain general workers' Unions which were organising colliery surfacemen.

The methods of dealing with disputes of these types are still by no means satisfactory, but they have greatly improved in recent years. The most usual course is to appeal either to a federation to which both the Unions concerned belong (*e.g.*, the Printing Trades Federation or the National Federation of Building Trades Operatives), or, where there is no such body, to the Trades Union Congress, which deals every year with a number of such appeals. Unfortunately, there is still no sure way of securing obedience to decisions of Congress, for an offending Union may even prefer expulsion to compliance. But the increased prestige of Congress has caused its decisions to be more readily obeyed during the past few years.

(*d*) *Entry to an Industry*.—A further type of inter-union dispute, which may grow more acute in future, especially if schemes of unemployment maintenance are started on an industrial basis, arises where there is a strong desire to close access to a particular industry in order to prevent a flood of casual labour from lowering the standard of life. The National Federation of Building Trades Operatives some time ago made an unsuccessful attempt to close access to the building industry to members of the general workers' Unions, urging that all builders' labourers should belong to the Builders' Labourers' Unions within the Federation. The general workers' Unions successfully resisted this attempt, and secured admission to the Federation. An exactly similar trouble has arisen, both before the War and again during the past year or two, in the waterside transport industry. The Transport Workers' Union complains, quite truly, that casual labour at the docks is greatly aggravated by the seeking of work by men from other occupations who are out of employment, but hold the card of one of the general workers' Unions. Registration of all dock workers, and admission to work at the ports only by the card of registration issued by the Transport Workers' Union, or the Transport Workers' Federation, is urged as a remedy; and it is clear that, if the plan of maintenance and decasualisation now under discussion, and already accepted in principle, is carried into effect, registration will be a necessary part of the scheme. This will not necessarily exclude all members of the general Unions, but it will mean that only a limited number of cards will be issued, and that only holders of these cards will be able to get employment at the docks. The building industry seems to be aiming at a similar solution. At the last Conference of the Building Operatives' Federation a resolution was carried, against the votes of the general workers' Unions and of the crafts concerned in other industries as well as building (*e.g.*, woodworkers), authorising the issue of a Federation Card as the sole claim to seek employment on building work.

The objection usually advanced against such plans of registration is that they tend to raise barriers against the mobility of labour, and to prevent the dovetailing of seasonal occupations. But both dock work and labouring in the building industry are at present occupations so cursed by casual labour that some remedy must be found. There seems to be no reason why the dovetailing of seasonal occupations should not be provided for by agreement under such schemes of decasualisation.

Section 3.—WOMEN IN TRADE UNIONS

We have already noted the great increase in the female membership of Trade Unions. There are now over three-quarters of a million women in Trade Unions, as against less than half a million before the War. During the War, when the number of women employed in industry rose fast, the number of women Trade Unionists rose to nearly a million and a quarter; and in 1920, despite the loss of many of the War-time recruits who had given up industrial work, it rose still further, to 1,340,000. It then fell, roughly at the same rate as the male membership, to 868,000 at the end of 1922.

Naturally, the female membership of Trade Unions is concentrated largely in certain groups. By far the largest single group is still that in the cotton industry, where women have long been employed in numbers considerably exceeding those of the men.

Next come the teachers, with 65,000 women members. Other industries in which women were organised to a considerable extent before 1914 included all the other textile industries, the boot and shoe industry, the clothing trades, printing and paper working, and distribution. In all these occupations, except the cotton industry, women were less strongly organised than men, and the number unorganised considerably exceeded the number in Trade Unions. The total female membership of Trade Unions in 1913 amounted to 433,000, of whom 214,000 were in the cotton industry, and 46,000 in the other textile industries; the next largest figures, apart from the teachers, being 25,000 in the public services, 23,000 in the general labour group, and 21,000 in commerce and finance.

By far the largest increase during the War was in the general labour group, which rose from 23,000 in 1913 to 199,000 in 1918, only to fall with startling rapidity to 49,000 in 1922. On the other hand, the teachers rose steadily to 143,000 in 1922. The big increase in other groups, such as printing and paper, textiles (except cotton), clothing, and the non-manual occupations can be seen in the Table printed in Appendix II.

The difficulties of organising women in Trade Unions have often been pointed out, and often exaggerated; for the experience of the past decade proves that women in most trades can be organised with success. There are, however, admittedly special problems to be faced. Women, in many cases, do not enter industry with a view to remaining in it permanently. Sooner or later the majority of them marry, and cease to be employed for wages. They tend, therefore, to regard the conditions under which they work with a less critical eye than the men who are likely to spend the whole of their lives in industry. This makes them more difficult to organise, because it makes them take less interest in attempts to improve their industrial position. Their eyes are fixed less on the factory, and more on things outside the factory. It is, however, easily possible to exaggerate this difficulty, and it is often very greatly exaggerated. A greater obstacle to the organisation of women is that presented by the low rates of pay which have always prevailed for women workers. It is probably more to the increase in women's wages than to any other cause that the rapid growth of Trade Unionism among women is due.

The incursion of women into industries and trades hitherto closed to them is too large a subject to be dealt with in this short book. Here I can only mention that during the War the substitution of women for men took place over a wide range of occupations. I can only give a few of the most significant instances. In the railway service, both in clerical and in the operative branches, on trams and buses, in metal, chemical and other classes of munition factories, in aircraft factories, in banks, and insurance companies, and in many other occupations women took up work hitherto closed to them. Moreover, the employment of women greatly extended in those occupations which were open to them in some measure before the War—in agriculture, in the smaller metal, wood-working trades, and in shops and offices.

The rates of pay secured in these new occupations varied very widely from case to case; and only in a comparatively small number of cases did the women secure equal rates with the men. This was the case on trams and buses in London and one or two big towns, whereas in other centres lower rates were paid to women substitutes. On the railways women received the minimum rates of the grades in which they were employed, but not the full advances granted to the men during the War. In the munitions trades women on skilled work were supposed to receive skilled rates, but here again, advances given during the War were not fully conceded; while women on semi-skilled and unskilled work received considerable lower rates than men on similar jobs. In the distributive trades equality was sometimes secured in the Co-operative movement, but almost everywhere in private employment women's rate were lower than men's. In offices women were, and are, almost always paid considerably less than men. These rates, however, while they did not realise the principle of equal pay for equality of work, were a considerable advance on the rates which were actually being paid to women before the War. They had, moreover, the effect of stirring up among women an interest in Trade Unionism and of making them far more likely to become, and to remain, good Trade Unionists, even when war conditions ceased to exist.

In many of the cases here mentioned, the employment of women ceased when the War ended, or was reduced to very small proportions. In agriculture, in the transport services, in the higher branches of the metal trades—women practically ceased to be employed. But in trades already partly open to women before the War, especially in clerical and in the less skilled factory occupations, there has been a permanent increase. And this has been more than reflected in Trade Union membership. Women now join Trade Unions much more readily than before the War.

It has often been complained that the men's Trade Unions have adopted towards women an exclusive policy. This attitude has indeed been maintained in many cases, and women are still not admitted into any of the Craft Unions in the engineering, shipbuilding, or building industries. The Transport Unions, on the other hand, including the National Union of Railwaymen, have adopted the policy of organising women, and endeavouring to secure for them full rates. Where the skilled Unions have not admitted women the general workers' Unions have naturally reaped their largest harvest, in some cases working in agreement with the skilled Unions, in a few cases almost in open opposition.

It was frequently pointed out before the War that, even in those Unions which had a strong female membership, women, as a rule, played an insignificant part in Trade Union administration. Indeed, wherever no special provision was made for the representation of women in mixed Unions, the tendency was for the management to fall almost entirely into the hands of the men. In the Weavers' Amalgamation, for instance, there are 130,000 women members out of a total membership of considerably less than 200,000; yet all the officials and, I think, all the members of the Executive Council of the Amalgamation are men, although there is a minority of women on many of the local Committees. What is true of the Weavers is true of many other Unions, and there are hardly any cases in which a mixed Union has elected a woman to a full-time office open to both sexes.

During and since the War, however, there has been a marked change in the status of women in Trade Unions. Many women took on important Trade Union work during the War, and the result has been a considerable permanent increase in the number of women elected to Trade Union Committees, or holding positions as branch secretaries. Women still play only a small part in comparison with their numerical strength in the movement, but sex exclusiveness is breaking down, and women are now more ready to take on responsible work, as well as men to accept their leadership. This applies especially in the Unions of non-manual workers. It will take a long time to break down all the barriers of custom and prejudice; but a beginning at least has been made.

This failure of women to take an adequate part in the management of mixed Unions has led a number of Societies to provide special methods of representation for women. For instance, the Tailors and Garment Workers and the Shop Assistants both have special Women's Councils of an advisory character. The National Union of Textile Workers, the Boot and Shoe Operatives, the Tailors and Garment Workers, the Printing and Paper Workers, the Distributive Workers and the Post Office Workers, all have special women organisers; while the Tailors and Garment Workers, Shop Assistants, Transport Workers, Printing and Paper Workers, Boot and Shoe Operatives, and other Unions maintain separate women's branches in certain cases. Women have seats on the Executive Councils of the Printing and Paper Workers, Shop Assistants, Boot and Shoe Operatives, Dundee Jute and Flax Workers, National Union of Textile Workers, and other Unions; but despite all this provision for sex representation the part played by women in framing the policy of the Trade Union Movement is still relatively small.

In the vast majority of cases women are now organised in the same Unions as men. The largest separate women's Society, the National Federation of Women Workers, became, by amalgamation shortly after the War, the Women's Section of the National Union of General Workers; and in other cases smaller Societies of women only have been absorbed into the mixed Unions. The Women's Trade Union League, which did good work as a propagandist body in days when the men's Unions still mostly regarded women as unorganisable, has merged itself in the Trades Union Congress, and the General Council of Congress now includes representatives of women Trade Unionists, and has a special Women's Sub-committee. The Standing Joint Committee of Women's Industrial Organisations, which works in close connection with the Labour Party, includes representatives of the women in mixed Unions, as well as of the Women's Co-operative Guild, the powerful organisation of the women in the Co-operative Movement, and of the Railway Women's Guild, a body organising chiefly the wives of working railwaymen, and an experiment worthy of imitation in other industries. The Labour Party, through its Local Labour Parties, has now strong Women's Sections in all parts of the country.

The aim of the Labour movement is, then, both politically and industrially, to make special provision for women's work within organisations open equally to both sexes. There are few women's Unions of any importance left in being, and the survivors are found mainly in non-manual occupations. The Association of Women Clerks and Secretaries and several Societies of women Civil Servants are the chief examples. In the teaching profession, the quarrel over the question of equal pay has led to the formation of a National Union of Women Teachers; but, even here, most of the women teachers are in the mixed National Union of Teachers, in which they outnumber the men. In the secondary schools, the Assistant Masters and Assistant Mistresses are organised in separate Associations, but work together through a joint committee. In the manual occupations, separate women's Unions are nearly extinct, except for a few small local Societies, usually the result of local quarrels or exclusiveness on the men's side.

Section 4.—SUPERVISORS AND NON-MANUAL WORKERS

One of the outstanding features of recent Trade Union development has been the growth of organisation among grades of workers hitherto regarded as incapable of effective organisation. This applies particularly to those who, receiving a salary instead of a wage, are in many cases inclined to think themselves too respectable for the adoption of Trade Union methods. Of course, many non-manual workers and salary-earners were already organised before the War; but not only has the number and scope of organisations among these classes greatly increased —there has also been a marked tendency for associations, which could not properly be called Trade Unions, to develop along Trade Union lines.

It is, indeed, very difficult to draw a hard and fast distinction between those Associations of non-manual workers which should, and those which should not, be regarded as Trade Unions. Some bodies which look like Trade Unions at first sight, such as the Scottish Clerks' Association, turn out, on examination, to be purely friendly societies; others, like the Commercial Travellers' Association and the National Association of Local Government Officers, are on the margin. They do not describe themselves as Trade Unions; but they do sometimes take action on Trade Union lines. Others, like the National Union of Teachers, are in process of developing into Trade Unions in the full sense of the term, and are already in effect Trade Unions for all practical purposes. Others, like the Union of Post Office Workers, and the Railway Clerks' Association, not only are Trade Unions in the full sense, but are definitely linked up as such with the Trades Union Congress and the Labour Party, to which the N.U.T. has not yet become affiliated. A most difficult case is that of the doctors, for the British Medical Association certainly acts as a most effective Trade Union on behalf of its members, yet it has neither contact, nor any desire for contact, nor collective sympathy with the general Labour Movement.

The British Medical Association, though it is an outstanding, is not an isolated case. It has been led to adopt Trade Union methods because of a change in the status of a large section of the medical profession. The National Insurance Act of 1911 made the panel doctor virtually an employee of the public, and set him bargaining with the State for better pay just like any wage-earner. Similarly, in other professions, the growth of salaried services under the State or the local authorities has placed a large number of professional men in the position of employees, and caused their associations to become bargaining bodies very like Trade Unions. Trade Unionism is found to be sauce for gander as well as goose.

These professional associations, however, even if they act like Trade Unions, form no part of the organised Labour Movement;

for most of their members are still essentially middle-class in sympathy and outlook. We have to go somewhat lower in the scale of incomes in order to find bodies that can properly be treated as Trade Unions in the ordinary sense of the term.

In this narrower sense the Trade Unions of non-manual workers can be classified in either of two ways, according to the type of service in which they work or according to their status and functions in that service. Under the first classification they fall roughly into four groups. First, there are numerous grades of salary-earners in the public services, of whom the largest groups are the Civil Servants, including the Post Office Workers and the Teachers. Elementary and secondary teachers are also strongly organised, and the former, at least, have adopted a definite Trade Union policy, and employ not only collective bargaining, but also, in case of need, the strike. Only recently the N.U.T. has conducted at Lowestoft a long and, on the whole, successful strike, and there have been numerous other instances in recent years.

Civil Servants and Post Office workers do not strike; but they undertake all other Trade Union functions, and their Associations are fully recognised for bargaining purposes by the Government. The " Burnham " Salary Scales were negotiated by the teachers' associations and representatives of the local authorities as employers, and the " Burnham " Committee is virtually a Conciliation Board for the teaching profession. The Civil Service is honeycombed by Associations of every kind of grade, from the higher administrative classes downwards. The Civil Service Confederation links up most of the Societies, including those in the Post Office, into a single body; and they also negotiate collectively through the Civil Service Whitley Council and its subordinate Departmental Councils. In the Civil Service, arbitration, instituted during the War but subsequently abolished, is now to be restored by the Labour Government.

The second group of non-manual Trade Unions includes the Societies organising non-manual workers in industry proper. In the engineering industry, for example, the Engineering and Shipbuilding Draughtsmen's Association is a powerful Union, now recognised by the employers, and also affiliated to the Trades Union Congress. Attempts have also been made to organise the supervisory grades in engineering, and the National Foremen's Association, which also belongs to the Trades Union Congress, has successfully enrolled 2,000 engineering foremen in face of the employers' opposition. In the mining industry the deputies' associations date back many years, and in some districts a majority of the deputies belongs to the Miners' Association. Of late, the Colliery Under-managers have also organised largely on Trade

Union lines, and have even linked up with the Trades Union Congress. In the transport services, the Railway Clerks' Association, and to a less extent the N.U.R., have organised supervisors together with rank and file workers, and the ordinary clerical grades are strongly combined. The Transport and General Workers' Union has a strong Clerical and Administrative Section, and there is also a weak Shipping Guild of clerks and others in the offices of the Shipping Companies. In the building industry, foremen are largely organised in the Unions of manual workers. A number of small foremen's Societies exist in the textile and clothing trades, and in both the cotton and the wool and worsted trades the overlookers are strongly organised in Associations of their own. In the distributive trades, both the Shop Assistants' Union and the Distributive Workers have a substantial membership in the supervisory grades, and there is a fairly strong National Union of Co-operative Officials. Other Societies exist among Supervising Electricians, Electrical Power Engineers, Scientific Workers, and Chemists; but the higher technical *personnel* of industry is for the most part unorganised, or organised only in Professional institutions which do not act at all as Trade Unions, though they exert in other ways a considerable influence on remuneration and conditions of employment.

The third group of non-manual Associations includes the commercial and financial occupations. The National Union of Clerks, which existed before the War, has made little permanent progress, despite its reorganisation into separate " Guilds," organising clerks in the various services. But there have sprung up several new Associations of importance, catering for particular groups of clerical workers. The Bank Officers' Guild and the Guild of Insurance Officials, the Law Clerks' Federation and the Architects' and Surveyors' Assistants' Professional Union, are all Trade Unions of a sort, though none of them has yet connected itself with the Trades Union Congress, and a good deal of snobbishness still persists among their members. The rank and file insurance workers, including both agents and inside employees in the industrial assurance companies, are fairly well organised, and are affiliated in most cases to either the Labour Party or the Trades Union Congress, or to both.

In a group rather apart from all these stand such bodies as the Musicians' Union, and the Actors' Association, which pursue a definitely Trade Union policy, and are connected with the Trades Union Congress. The two former, especially, have fought a long fight, and have often resorted to the strike in their efforts to secure standard conditions for their respective professions.

INTERNAL TRADE UNION PROBLEMS

In 1920 there was formed, for the purpose of uniting all these various types and grades of non-manual workers, a new body called the National Federation of Professional, Technical, Administrative and Supervisory Workers. This Federation, with an affiliated membership of about 300,000, aims both at improving organisation among these grades and at promoting better and more clearly defined relations between them and the Unions of manual workers. It has recently been discussing these points with the Trades Union Congress, which, in the reorganisation of 1920–21, set up a separate section for non-manual workers' Associations, and has already a substantial number of them in its ranks.

There are, we saw, two possible ways of classifying these Associations. So far we have classified them according to industry or service; now we must look at them for a moment from another point of view, according to the difference of the functions which their members exist to perform. Many of them clearly consist, for the most part, of workers who are just as much under orders as a mechanic or a miner. They are clerks, " pen-pushers," either in some branch of industry or commerce, or in a public service. Trade Unionism among such workers may be more difficult to promote, because of snobbishness and a false sense of respectability; but there is no reason why it should differ much in its working from Trade Unionism among manual workers.

A second group consists of supervisory workers, persons whose main job it is to oversee the work of others, and to act as go-betweens between them and the management. These foremen, deputies, superintendents, and the like are naturally for the most part promoted from the ranks of the manual or clerical wage-earners, and on promotion they have in the past usually left the ranks of the Trade Union Movement and come to regard themselves definitely as the servants of the employers, having no further concern with working-class movements. It is true that throughout the history of Trade Unionism a certain number of such promoted workmen have retained their connection with their Trade Unions in a more or less private manner, by being attached to Central Office Branches, and by other similar devices; but even where this has been the case they have upon promotion usually lost all share in the active government of their Societies.

Recently there has been a growing tendency both for these supervisors to form Associations of their own and for the ordinary Trade Unions to endeavour to organise them, or keep them as members after their promotion. This raises certain problems. Employers, as a rule, strongly dislike any form of association among supervisory workers, and, most of all, any that links them up with the manual workers. On the other hand, difficulties may arise where supervisors and supervised belong to the same Union, and the latter may claim to question the doings of the former in the branch meeting. Some Unions, such as the Railway Clerks, have tried to meet this difficulty by the organisation within the one Union of separate branches open only to the supervising grades. Others object to this as a denial of solidarity, or object to enrolling supervisors at all, on the ground that they act as a drag on the adoption of any advanced or militant policy.

Let us illustrate by a few examples.

(1) In the mines the deputy occupies a position largely corresponding to that of a foreman in a factory. In most of the districts of the Miners' Federation deputies are eligible for membership in the Miners' Association, and in some districts a majority of the deputies are actually enrolled in the Miners' Associations. In nearly all districts, however, there exist separate Deputies' Associations in which the majority of the deputies are organised independently both of the management and of the men. In a few districts there also exist Associations patronised by the employers in which deputies and under-managers are combined in a single Association.

The relations between the various Deputies' Associations and the Miners' Associations vary widely from one district to another. In one or two cases the deputies take joint action with the local Miners' Association, while in others the two are definitely hostile, and no working arrangement seems likely or possible. There is an increasing feeling in certain districts that it is important for the miners to pay more attention than hitherto to keeping control over those of their members who are promoted to supervisory positions.

(2) On the railways a rather different situation exists. The Railway Clerks' Association, as we have seen, has achieved very considerable success in organising the supervisory grades, including stationmasters, agents, and chief clerks. The success of the Railway Clerks' Association shows that there is no insurmountable obstacle to the organisation of these workers in a body which is quite definitely a Trade Union, pursuing a distinctly Labour policy, although there may be difficulty in organising them in an Industrial Union along with workers drawn from all sections, skilled and unskilled alike.

(3) In the Post Office the lower-paid grades of supervisory workers are already for the most part organised, having followed the example of the rank and file by forming Associations of their own, combined in a common Federation. The rank and file Associations do not attempt to represent the supervisory grades;

but promoted men can retain a nominal membership in the Union of Post Office Workers.

(4) In the engineering industry many foremen have long retained their membership of the Unions catering for the craft from which they have been promoted to foremanship. In many cases they have done this secretly by attaching themselves to the Central Office Branch of their Trade Union, and in very few cases have they continued to play any part in the government of their Society. Meanwhile the employers have used every endeavour to prevent any development of Trade Unions among foremen, and wherever possible have induced their foremen to join a body called the Foremen's Mutual Benefit Association, which is governed jointly by the employers and the foremen themselves, each employer having one vote for every foreman who is insured. This Society is certainly in no sense a Trade Union, and its rules explicitly prevent it from taking any form of collective action in regard to conditions of employment. It is a pure Benefit Society, designed to prevent Trade Unionism. Despite its existence, the foremen, as we have seen, have now a National Union of their own, free from dependence on the employers, and working usually in harmony with the manual workers' Unions, with which most of the members also retain their connection when they are promoted.

In these and other cases there is a marked tendency towards the growth of a common consciousness on the part of members of the *salariat* which is, at the same time, towards organisation along Trade Union lines. Considerable significance attaches to this movement. It is important that the attitude of rank and file Trade Unionists towards it should become more clearly defined. Many rank and file Trade Unionists are still apt to regard the professionals, and still more the foremen, as their natural enemies, and to refuse to have anything whatsoever to do with them or their organisations. If, however, the demand for some measure of control over industry is seriously meant by the rank and file Societies, it is evident that some new accommodation will have to be arrived at between them and the foremen and professional workers. The nature of this accommodation falls outside the scope of this book, which is concerned rather with facts and present tendencies than with the formulation of a policy for the future.

Section 5.—The Problem of Democratic Control

Trade Unions, like all other large-scale organisations, have to face difficult problems of constitutional machinery. As their size increases, and the members are scattered in more branches and over a wider area, contact becomes harder to maintain over the Union as a whole, and there is a growing danger that the Head Office may get out of touch with the feeling of the members. As, by industrial or kindred craft organisation, more different types of workers are included in a single Society, there is a danger that this or that section may feel its interests and point of view submerged in the wider unity of the whole, and may become discontented or even talk of secession. As routine work grows heavier, and negotiating and administrative work more complex, there is danger that officials may have less time to get among the rank and file and may develop bureaucratic tendencies. As more skill is demanded in administration, and higher salaries have to be paid to officials, there is danger that the officials, promoted in a sense into the middle class, may lose their working-class contact and outlook.

On the other hand, if a particular Union is punctilious in preserving democratic methods, there are other dangers. Local autonomy may lead to the muddling of complicated accounts, or the unconscious rupture of some vital understanding with the employers. Too frequent recourse to a ballot vote of all the members breeds apathy, and produces decisions carried by the voices of a small minority. A Delegate Meeting or Conference large enough to represent directly all the branches is far too large and unwieldy for any useful discussion, and reduces itself to a machine for registering votes determined in advance. Popular election over a wide area weights the scales in favour of any candidate who has achieved either fame or notoriety, and has been at least heard of by the largest number of members. Anger against the distant, and seemingly inaccessible, officials is easily stirred up, even if they have done no wrong. But a man who can once establish a personal ascendency is likely to become nearly omnipotent, because he makes himself into a sort of personal symbol of the Union and its power. In short, all the troubles of democracy beset Trade Unionism.

There is no panacea for these ills, which are, to some extent, inherent in all forms of large-scale organisation. Nor is there any one way for all Unions of diminishing their effect. Each Union has to think out its problems for itself, trying to strike a balance between efficient central organisation and local freedom and initiative, between reasonable authority to officials and delegates and the exercise of sovereign authority by the rank and file.

The left wing in the Trade Unions usually maintains, quite truly, that officials have too much power, and goes on to propose drastic, but largely mistaken, remedies. It is often suggested, for example, that all power should reside in the rank and file, and that, if this power must be exercised largely through delegates, these delegates should be bound at all points by instructions received directly from the rank and file. But to adopt this remedy would be to expel reason and common-sense from Trade Union assemblies. In practice, in Trade Union meetings, as elsewhere, the " delegate," even if he receives instructions, must be left a wide discretionary power in the exercise of his vote. New suggestions may emerge at a Conference, or old ones be put in a new light. It is merely folly to bind the delegate in advance to act in a particular way, even if the conditions of action are changed.

The remedy, then, for the undemocratic element in present Trade Union practice cannot lie in any automatic system of voting under instructions. It is rather to be sought in making the constitutional machinery more readily responsive to changes of opinion and outlook, and in providing for an easier flow of sentiments and ideas from the rank and file to the responsible leaders. It is for this purpose that workshop organisation is so important, and that the linking up of the workshop machinery of Trade Unionism—shop stewards and shop committees—directly with the district and national organisation is indispensable. What is most needed is, first, a national unit round which the members can group themselves for discussion of their problems, and, secondly, direct contact between these workshop units and the delegates and officers who are responsible for the framing of national and local policy.

If the problem of democratic government demands a constant flow of ideas throughout all sections of the Union, it demands also special facilities for the group life and the representation in the wider body of each distinct section that has problems of its own. An Industrial or kindred Craft Union can hardly be fully successful unless it accords representation to the main grades or trades included within its ranks. The skilled worker may be ready to link his interests with the interests of other sections in his industry, but he will not sink them altogether, or be content with a Union which denies him any form of special representation. The forms of such representation, however, will differ widely from case to case. Sometimes special organisers or separate branches will be needed, sometimes the allocation of special seats on the Executive, sometimes the right to formulate a special sectional programme. In one form or another, distinct provision must be made if several clearly marked sections are to be successfully combined into a single Society.

These problems, acute enough inside the larger Unions, become still more acute in wider bodies like the big Federations of Trade

Unions or the Trades Union Congress, and most acute of all in international Trade Union organisation. Take the Congress as an example. It consists of representatives of its affiliated Societies, and among these representatives full-time officials form a very large element. The Congress elects annually a General Council, which in practice consists entirely of full-time officials. We have mentioned already the movement in favour of handing over increased powers from the separate Unions to the Congress and the General Council. One reason why this is opposed is that it involves, in practice, a transfer of power from the rank and file, or from delegates directly responsible to the rank and file, to a body of officials who are much more difficult to advise, instruct, or control, or to a body of delegates, in which officials predominate, largely open to the same objection. Each Union has its own democratic machinery, and frames its own policy more or less on democratic lines. But the Congress has no democratic machinery of its own, and control over the separate Unions by it, therefore, seems to involve an oligarchic *régime* and the risk of a further loss of contact between leaders and led. Internationally the position is a stage worse, for the International Federation of Trade Unions consists of delegates from a number of national Congresses, each open to the criticism of being undemocratic and overweighted by officials. It is a stage—and a long stage—further off the ordinary workers in the shops. In other words, international Trade Unionism suffers from just the same weakness as the League of Nations—it has no direct responsibility to an international rank and file.

It is clear that, if even in national Trade Union affairs really effective co-ordination is to be secured, democratic machinery must be improved and broadened so as to bring the central body more directly in touch with the rank and file. The most important aspect of the relations between the Trades Union Congress and the Trades Councils, mentioned in a previous section, is that it may help in developing this contact. But clearly the solution of the problem can only be found gradually and by experimental means, and even so it can never be solved completely. Democracy cannot be a perfect system, in Trade Unions or in political affairs.

Section 6.—POLITICAL ACTION

This book does not profess to deal with the work of the Labour Party, or with the political aspects of the Labour Movement as a whole. A treatment of that subject would demand a book to itself. Here I am concerned only to describe very briefly the participation of the Trade Unions in politics, without discussing

INTERNAL TRADE UNION PROBLEMS

either the policy or the work of the Labour Party in or out of Parliament.

Political action by Trade Unions now takes place chiefly through the Labour Party, nationally and locally; but it did not, of course, begin with the Labour Party. The Trades Union Congress itself was created largely as the instrument of the Trade Unions in the political struggle for recognition by the law,[1] and it has always, even since the creation of the Labour Party as a separate body, taken certain kinds of political action, such as pressing for industrial legislation and sending deputations to Ministers on any matter raised at Congress on which a mandate was given. Long before there was a Labour Party, or even an independent Labour group in the House of Commons, there were members sitting in Parliament as the representatives of Trade Unions, but attached usually to the Liberal Party. The Labour Representation Committee, out of which the Labour Party grew, was originally created by a resolution passed at the Trades Union Congress. But for some years it grew but slowly, and many of the big Trade Unions held aloof.[2] Not until 1909 did the Miners' Federation, the most active group in sending the early Trade Union members to Parliament, throw off its traditional Liberalism and join the Labour Party.

Since that time the Labour Party has become almost as representative of the Trade Union Movement as the Congress itself. At its last Conference, in 1923, it had an affiliated Trade Union membership of 3,277,000, about a million less than the membership of Congress in the same year; 127 Unions or Trade Union Federations belonged to it. These figures, however, somewhat underrate its representative character, for a number of Unions pay to the Labour Party on a smaller membership than to Congress,[3] and very few important national Trade Unions, except among the non-manual workers, are now outside its ranks.

While the national Trade Unions join the Labour Party, their local branches in many cases affiliate to the Local Labour Parties in the various constituencies. Since the reorganisation of the Party Constitution in 1918, Local Labour Parties have been established practically throughout the country, and have taken over most of the electoral work in both national and local politics that used to be done by the Trades Councils in centres where no separate Labour Party was in existence. Now, in some cases the

[1] See Introduction, p. 6.
[2] See statistics in Appendix VII.
[3] Only a very small part of this disparity is accounted for by Trade Unionists securing exemption from political contributions under the Trade Union Act of 1913.

Trades Council is affiliated to the Local Labour Party, and in others the two form practically a single body, with separate sections for industrial and political work. In yet others there is no Trades Council, the Local Labour Party undertaking to work through an Industrial Committee.

Each Trade Union affiliated to the Labour Party has its separate political fund, kept apart from the general fund, which cannot be used for any of the main political purposes. This restriction was established under the Trade Union Act of 1913, which virtually removed, with certain limitations, the notorious Osborne Judgment preventing Trade Unions from undertaking any political action at all.[1] This Political Fund is spent in a variety of ways. Some of it is paid over to the National Labour Party in the form of affiliation fees; some goes through the Union branches in fees to the Local Labour Parties; and a substantial amount is retained by the Union which raises it, and used to finance the candidates whom the Union nominates to stand for Parliament in the Labour interest.

This system has its drawbacks. It means that a large number of the Labour Party candidates have Union money behind them, whereas any candidate who is not backed by his Union, or by one of the Socialist Societies affiliated to the Labour Party, such as the I.L.P., must either himself find the money to finance his candidature or raise it locally among his supporters—a very hard task in these days of large electorates and expensive contests. A Local Labour Party which wants to run a candidate at little expense to itself must therefore choose either a rich man or the nominee of a Trade Union prepared to find the money. In the past this has given Trade Union candidates a preferential position, and has resulted in the election of " twicers," men who try to combine membership of Parliament with regular official work in their Unions—to the nearly inevitable detriment of both functions. Of late, however, with the growth of the Party, the number of " twicers " has decreased, both because of the activity of the leading Socialist body—the Independent Labour Party—in promoting and financing candidates, and because a number of Unions, conscious of the evil, have relieved their officials of their duties on their election to Parliament, retaining them temporarily in an honorary or advisory capacity.

The Labour Party is thus becoming less and less a purely Trade Union party. A large majority of its members are still Trade Unionists who have been actively associated with their Unions in some official capacity. But side by side with the

---

[1] For the law relating to Trade Unions, see p. 140.

actual Trade Union representatives sit more and more members of the I.L.P. with a growing body of men, not in a position to be Trade Unionists, who have directly joined the Labour Party under its new constitution. In voting strength at Party Conferences, these groups count for nothing in comparison with the massed votes of the Trade Unions; but their influence both in Parliament and in the Party itself is very considerable. A large share of posts in the first Labour Government went either to I.L.P. members or to other "intellectual" recruits to the ranks of the Party.

There is in the House an Industrial Committee, consisting of Trade Union Members of Parliament, created for the purpose of pressing Trade Union matters in the House and the Government; but this body is of too recent creation for any account of its working to be possible. It was one of the first fruits of a Labour Government.

The Local Labour Parties, of course, are concerned with municipal as well as national elections, and the Trade Unions also play their part in this work, and have many hundreds of nominees sitting on local governing bodies of the various types. There is now an organised Labour Party on most local governing authorities of any importance, except in certain of the rural districts.

The political action of Trade Unions is thus organised mainly apart from the other activities through the federal structure of the Labour Party, in which they join with the Socialist Societies and the individual members admitted to the Local Labour Parties under the new constitution of 1918. But at the centre the political and industrial wings of the movement are again co-ordinated in the joint organisation already described in the first part of this book.[1] Since the great growth of the Labour Party, and more especially since the formation of the first Labour Government, there has been some uneasiness lest this joint machinery should acquire too exclusively political a character, or its action come to be dominated by considerations of parliamentary strategy; and this has led to some renewed emphasis on the distinct industrial functions of Congress. But there has been so far no serious clash, and the political and industrial sections now work very closely together.

Section 7.—TRADE UNIONISM AND THE CO-OPERATIVE MOVEMENT

There is still no close or coherent relationship between Trade Unionism and the Co-operative movement. Co-operators and

[1] See p. 44.

Trade Unionists do, indeed, exchange fraternal delegates at their Annual Congresses, and there exists a standing Joint Committee of Trade Unionists and Co-operators for dealing with some of the problems arising out of the position of Trade Unionist employees of Co-operative Societies. But, although there have been attempts from time to time to promote closer unity between the two movements, and, since the entry of the Co-operators into politics, the members of the Co-operative Party in Parliament have acted as part of the Labour Party in all but name, no real unity of the two movements has yet been achieved.

This does not mean that they have not been of considerable mutual assistance. The Co-operative Stores have often aided the Trade Unions greatly in time of strikes, and the Co-operative Wholesale Society's Bank has more than once come to the aid of a Trade Union with a highly opportune advance. The C.W.S. was the instrument used by the British Trade Union movement for sending supplies to Dublin during the famous dispute of 1913–14, and the miners in 1921 held out largely with aid from the Co-operative Societies. Moreover, the part which the Co-operative movement might play in connection with industrial disputes has often been suggested and discussed.

Pre-war discussions generally dealt mainly with the industrial relations that might be established between Trade Unionism and Co-operation, though the question of the entry of the Co-operative movement into politics was a " hardy annual " among Co-operative Congress resolutions. There would, however, have been comparatively little prospect of an early entry of Co-operation into closer relations with the other sections of the Labour movement had it not been for the War. The attempts of War-time Governments to tax Co-operative surpluses as profits did in a few years what half a century of agitation might hardly have accomplished. The Co-operative Movement entered the political field—somewhat half-heartedly indeed, but in breach of a long-standing tradition of political neutrality.

It is true that this development has taken place independently, and that the Co-operative Party is nominally quite distinct from the Labour Party. The Co-operative candidates stand, not as Labour candidates, but as Co-operators, with Labour support. Nevertheless, the entry of Co-operation into politics does mean a much closer approach to the other wings of the Labour movement, and already, in a number of centres, Co-operative Societies are affiliated to local Labour Parties in preference to forming local Co-operative Parties of their own. In others Joint Labour and Co-operative Associations have been called into being. This does not mean that the whole of the Co-operative movement is flocking into an alliance with political Trade Unionism, or even that the Co-operative Parliamentary candidates will necessarily be, in all cases, Labour men, though all have been hitherto ; but it does mean that the current is setting steadily in the direction of closer political unity between the two movements. The really separate existence of two working-class parties, with the prospect of fighting each other in the industrial constituencies, would be, indeed, an obvious absurdity.

But, while there has been this approach to unity, far more remains to be done. A substantial body of Co-operators is opposed to either Labour or Co-operative political action, and many Co-operative Societies still stand aloof from both the Co-operative and the Labour Party. Moreover, on the industrial side far less has been accomplished. The majority of the Trade Unions now bank with the Co-operative Wholesale Bank, and a good many joint meetings are held with the slogan " Every Co-operator a Trade Unionist, and every Trade Unionist a Co-operator " ; but there is no organic link between the Trade Unions or the Trades Union Congress and either the Co-operative Union, the federal organ of the Co-operative Movement as a whole, or the English and Scottish Co-operative Wholesale Societies. The Co-operators do not, as in Belgium, form part of the Joint Labour Council, and there is no general plan of mutual assistance between the two movements. There are, moreover, certain causes of conflict which may at any time create strained relations.

Co-operative Societies, while they are slightly above the average of private employers in most of the trades with which they are concerned, are by no means model employers. The Trade Unions which have members employed by them, so far from finding agitation unnecessary, have quite often to take up an aggressive industrial attitude in order to secure a remedy for grievances. Strikes occur, not so frequently as in private employment, but more frequently than ought to be necessary under a democratic employer, and the relations between the Societies and their employees differ very little from those which exist in private employment. Closer union with the other wings of the Labour Movement would perhaps do something to improve the attitude of Co-operators as employers ; but the fact that matters stand where they do stand is not reassuring. There are still some Co-operative Societies which pay definitely bad wages, even according to current standards, and the Co-operative member, even if he is also a Trade Unionist, is often unwilling to concede to his own employees the concessions which he demands from his own employer. Of course, working in a hostile environment, the

Co-operative Movement has largely to adopt capitalist standards in order to compete with its rivals; but this is not the whole explanation of a position which is often very unsatisfactory. One of the biggest problems facing the Trade Unions is that of establishing with the Co-operative Movement such relations as will really link up the two in an effective unity for the struggle against Capitalism, in which both are equally concerned.

Section 8.—Trade Unions and Education

Among the most notable developments of recent years is the increased interest of the Trade Unions in educational work. This is not, indeed, altogether a new thing. Ruskin College, Oxford, was founded in 1899, though at first it had few direct Trade Union connections. The Workers' Educational Association, the first serious attempt to interest the Trade Unions in educational work, held its twenty-first birthday in 1924. But the big development of direct Trade Union participation in such work has taken place in comparatively recent years, and to a large extent since the War.

The Trade Union movement has always professed enlightened views on general educational questions. Year after year Trades Union Congresses and Labour Party Conferences have declared in favour of thorough-going reform of our educational system, and, although a dissentient voice has sometimes arisen from the Trade Unions in the cotton and wool industries when questions of half-time and continued education have come under discussion, the leaders of the Trade Unions, even in this industry, have usually taken an enlightened view. Labour, then, has a clean record so far as its general educational demands are concerned, and Labour members upon public bodies, notably upon Local Education Authorities, have usually assumed an advanced attitude both with regard to such questions as higher education, school feeding, medical and dental treatment, etc., and with regard to the status and emoluments of the teaching profession. We are here concerned, however, not so much with Labour's attitude to the wider questions of general education as with the work that has been done in the sphere of adult education among Trade Unionists themselves.

The Workers' Educational Association, formed in 1903, has been for many years the largest working-class educational body. It has district and branch organisations throughout Great Britain, and organises a very large number of classes of many different types. In 1923–24 it had about 30,000 students in these classes, and of these the great majority were Trade Unionists.

The W.E.A. is in form a Federation, open to working-class and

INTERNAL TRADE UNION PROBLEMS

educational bodies as well as to individual members. Many of the big national Trade Unions, including the Trades Union Congress, are affiliated to it, and many Trades Councils and Trade Union branches are affiliated to its branches and districts. Its policy is one of fostering co-operation between the working-class bodies (including Co-operative bodies) which belong to it and the educational organisations. Its classes receive, in many cases, grant aid from the Board of Education and from Local Education Authorities, and it has established with each University a Joint Committee, equally representative of University and working-class elements, through which it organises Tutorial Classes of a more advanced type than its ordinary classes. In its educational methods it aims at avoiding propaganda, and at leaving the student, with the fullest freedom of discussion to guide him, to make up his own mind in the light of a clear presentation of the facts. The W.E.A. is represented on the Education Committee of the Trades Union Congress, and is connected with the " International " of Working-class Educational Bodies.

Its most notable achievement in the last few years has been the creation of a subsidiary body—the Workers' Educational Trade Union Committee—for the purpose of organising schemes of educational work directly for Trade Unions. The W.E.A. is represented on this body, and does the organising work; but the Committee consists predominantly of representatives of the contributing Trade Unions, which now number six or seven, including the Iron and Steel Trades Confederation, the Railway Clerks, and the Union of Post Office Workers. The Committee is free to spend its funds on any type of educational work. Its chief activities are the organising of winter evening classes and of Week-end Schools for Trade Union members, and the provision of Scholarships to Summer Schools and Colleges.

Ruskin College, Oxford, which has been since 1910 under the control of Trade Union and Co-operative representatives, is a residential College providing full-time teaching for working-class students, most of whom are helped to attend by scholarships from their various organisations. It also conducts a large Correspondence Department, and organises a few outside classes through the Ruskin College Fellowship of ex-students. It is affiliated to the W.E.A., and the Trades Union Congress is one of the bodies controlling it.

In 1909, before Ruskin College had passed under full working-class control, there took place a strike of the students against the victimisation and dismissal of the then Principal. The strikers seceded and formed a rival College which, after a hard struggle, was taken over by two big Trade Unions, the National Union of

Railwaymen and the South Wales Miners' Federation. Known originally as the Central Labour College, this body is now called the Labour College (London). It is also residential, giving full-time education, and drawing its students mainly from the two Trade Unions which control it, and from other Unions, which provide scholarships for their members. It is definitely Marxian in policy and outlook, and still pursues its old feud with Ruskin College.

The seceders from Ruskin founded not only a new College, but also a very successful monthly paper, *The Plebs Magazine*, and a Society, The Plebs League, which became, some years later, the nucleus of a national movement for working-class education on left-wing Marxian lines, under the inspiration of the Plebs League, which took for its motto, " I can promise to be candid, but not impartial," and conducted a violent campaign against Ruskin College and the W.E.A. Classes were started in many parts of the country, and in time organisations were formed calling themselves " Labour Colleges," though most of them had no premises, and they were, in fact, federations of local classes and of working-class bodies which affiliated to them. Next, these local " Colleges," with the parent College in London and the Plebs League, formed the National Council of Labour Colleges, as a militant left-wing rival to the W.E.A. Finally, they imitated the W.E.A. by forming a scheme of their own on the lines of the W.E.T.U.C., jointly with two big Unions—the Building Trade Workers and the Distributive Workers. The Labour Colleges have received no aid from the Government or Universities, standing for what they term " independent working-class education " on militant, propagandist, Marxian lines.

In the various ways mentioned above, a considerable number of Trade Unions have undertaken definite educational provision for their members, and many more have given some sort of support to one or another of the working-class educational bodies. A further step was taken when, in 1922, as a result of action taken by the W.E.T.U.C., the Trades Union Congress General Council itself established an Education Committee, with the object of co-ordinating and developing the work on behalf of the whole movement. This action, taken at a time when Trade Union funds were very low, did not lead at once to any big developments. Indeed, up to the time of writing,[1] much of the time on this committee has been spent in fruitless disputation between the protagonists of the Labour Colleges and the W.E.A. But a beginning has been made of recognising definite educational work as a vital

[1] June, 1924.

INTERNAL TRADE UNION PROBLEMS

function of the Trade Union Movement as a whole, and considerable developments are likely to take place under Congress auspices in the near future. The dispute between the rival schools of thought has too long been made an excuse for inaction by many Trade Unions ; but there are now signs that the Unions are no longer prepared to see the educational pitch queered by a quarrel which has long been largely unreal.

Into the merits of this quarrel the present writer, who has been for years closely associated with the W.E.A. and the Tutorial Class Movement organised by it throughout the country, has no intention of entering. It need only be pointed out that the total educational facilities available for adult workers are miserably inadequate to meet the needs of the case. The Trade Union movement, while it has given a measure of support both to the W.E.A. and Ruskin College, on the one hand, and to the Labour Colleges, on the other, has, on the whole, not yet realised the paramount importance of education to the workers. Where educational bodies have been at work the difference has soon made itself manifest. Classes in industrial and political history, economics, current social problems, and many other subjects, have served to awaken keen interest among local leaders of Labour in many centres, and the students who have been equipped in such classes have, in a vast number of cases, been able to play an important part in shaping the subsequent policy of Labour in their districts. If the power of the Trade Unions is to be increased and wisely used, there can be no doubt that one of the most important of the tasks before them is the task of educating their own members. It is necessary not merely to increase the number of subscribing members of Trade Unions, but also to create inside every organisation a larger nucleus of keen members with a clear understanding of the problems both of Society as a whole and of the industry with which they are concerned—an understanding which alone can make them capable of winning in industry and in Society the power which they are increasingly disposed to claim.

The machinery of Trade Unionism could be used for the building up of a far more effective and inclusive working-class educational movement than independent educational bodies of any complexion can ever hope to create without the full co-operation of the Trade Unions themselves. All National Unions could afford to spend some of their resources upon education—indeed, it would most handsomely pay them to do so. And other Unions might well follow the example of the Building Trade Workers, who finance their educational scheme by means of a small special levy on all their members. Trade Councils, Trade Union branches and District Committees could, to a far greater extent than now, undertake the organisation of classes and circles, and endeavour to make ordinary Trade Union meetings far more educational in character than they are to-day. There is practically no limit to what could be done if only there existed among the national and local leaders of Labour a clear idea of the part which education must play in making the working-class movement more efficient, both for the work of to-day and for the fresh tasks which its growing power will certainly soon force it to assume.

PART V

TRADE UNIONS AT WORK

Sect. 1. Collective Bargaining. Sect. 2. Negotiation and Arbitration. Sect. 3. Strikes and Lock-outs. Sect. 4. Standard Rates and "Payment by Results." Sect. 5. Hours of Labour. Sect. 6. The Question of Control.

Section 1.—COLLECTIVE BARGAINING

AN association of workmen is not a Trade Union unless it attempts by collective bargaining to regulate the conditions of its members' employment. It may adopt different methods of doing this, but in every case some form of negotiation with the employers is involved. Nowadays, in nearly every case, the employers are organised in an association of their own, so that in the normal instance collective bargaining takes place between two associations, each speaking for a large proportion of the trade or industry to which the negotiations refer. There are still, of course, non-federated employers, though they are less numerous proportionately than unorganised workers; but non-federated firms in most cases follow the conditions established by bargaining between the employers' and workers' associations.

The earlier struggles of Trade Unionism centred largely round the establishment of this right of collective bargaining, which employers used to denounce as an unwarrantable interference with freedom of contract and the individual worker's liberty to dispose of his labour at his will. This argument, of course, ignores the fact that employer and worker are not equal parties to the wage bargain. The worker must sell his labour in order to live; the employer has usually resources of his own, and can hold out and pick and choose. Moreover, each employer is virtually an organisation in himself, in that he employs, especially under modern conditions, many workers. These facts are so obvious, and Trade Unionism has so definitely established its right of collective bargaining, that the old arguments are now seldom seriously advanced. But it is only during the last few years—since 1914—that Trade Unionism has been fully recognised by such great bodies of employers as the railway companies and the shipowners; and the right is still often denied to particular types of workers, such as supervisors and administrative workers, and even clerks and technical employees. There are also left many individual firms which refuse to employ Trade Unionists, and insist on the " open shop "; but these are now found mainly in small centres and badly-organised industries. Speaking generally, the right of collective bargaining has now been established over almost the whole area of industry.

Collective bargaining does not, of course, automatically settle the conditions of employment; for the two sides may fail to agree. In some cases they resort, on failure, to mediation or arbitration, which is discussed in the next section; in others the Union or the employers' association seeks to enforce acceptance of its terms by means of a strike or a lock-out. Trade Unions among the manual workers in practically all cases make provision for such an emergency by including dispute pay among the benefits which they provide. This is also increasingly true of the Unions of non-manual workers. The Teachers, for example, have recently conducted several strikes, and so have the Draughtsmen, the Insurance Workers, and the Electrical Power Engineers. But there are Trade Unions which, without declaring explicitly against strike action, seldom or never use the strike weapon. The Railway Clerks seldom strike, though they have conducted small strikes and even threatened a national stoppage. The Union of Post Office Workers does not strike; for, after deciding some years ago to build up a Strike Fund, it reversed its decision and repaid the money. The Postal Workers and Civil Servants both use the machinery of conciliation to the full, and, if that fails, resort to political pressure and arbitration in preference to the strike. It is more difficult to strike against the State, which was slow to recognise Trade Unions at all, than against a private employer. State employees, moreover, have usually pension and seniority rights which they fear to forfeit by strike action.

In general, however, the right to strike is an essential part of Trade Union policy, though the Unions always try to avoid strikes where they can get what they want, or an acceptable compromise, by negotiation. Strikes are expensive, and it is usually easier for the employer to hold out than for the men, save in those few industries in which a strike rapidly deranges the life of the community (*e.g.*, railways). The provision of dispute pay is regarded, in most cases, as the most essential Trade Union function, for negotiation is likely to be ineffective unless it is backed by the power to declare a strike and to pay dispute benefit in order to enable the workers to hold out while they are receiving no wages. Dispute pay is thus more essential than the many other benefits which some Trade Unions provide. Friendly Society activities—sick pay, funeral benefit, superannuation, etc.—are often added in

TRADE UNIONS AT WORK

order to increase the stability of organisation by binding the members more firmly to the Union; but these, and even unemployment benefits, are supplementary activities. The essential marks of Trade Union action are collective bargaining and the strike.

Since organisation has become the rule, and non-unionism the exception, among both workers and employers, there has been a growing tendency to regularise the methods of bargaining by establishing formal machinery. At first, meetings are held between the representatives of the two sides only to deal with disputes as they arise. Then the procedure at these meetings is formalised, and a regular Joint Conference or Joint Committee or Conciliation Board is organised, often with several distinct Trade Unions represented on the men's side, but usually with only one Association on that of the employers. At the outset such machinery is often local; but before long national machinery of negotiation is developed. Local questions are still dealt with by the local bodies, but the general regulation of wages and conditions becomes increasingly a national matter, and national conditions are laid down within which the local machinery must work. Even if the national machinery is constructed at first only to deal with appeals from the local bodies, it often develops into an authority laying down general conditions for the whole trade.

This does not mean that the right to declare a strike or lock-out is given up, but that resort is not had to a stoppage of work until every attempt to settle matters by negotiation has failed. In a few cases, but only in a few, there is regular provision for referring differences to impartial arbitration where agreement cannot be secured. But such provision lasts only as long as the agreement establishing it, and this is usually concluded either for a definite period or subject to a fixed period of notice on either side. Of course, where there is no regular provision for arbitration, any particular dispute may always be referred to arbitration by consent of both sides.

Negotiation is usually carried out mainly by officials, and it is one of the chief functions of the Trade Union official to be an expert negotiator. The negotiators may be given freedom to settle disputes without reference to those whom they represent; but more often proposed settlements have to be referred for confirmation or rejection either to a ballot vote of the members or to a Delegate Conference of the Union or Unions concerned.

The growth of national machinery of negotiation has been a marked feature of recent Trade Union development. Such machinery existed before the War in most of the well-organised industries. It was extended considerably during the War, when the enforcement by the State of compulsory arbitration in the munitions industries made it indispensable in many trades. After the War, it was extended still further, largely under the Whitley Reports. The Whitley Committee was a war-time body, established to foster better relations between employers and workers. It recommended for all organised industries the establishment of Joint Industrial Councils, equally representing Trade Unions and employers. These bodies were intended to have much wider functions than mere boards of negotiation on wages and conditions, and were put forward as a means of satisfying the demand for "workers' control." But, in fact, they have become mere negotiating boards, hardly differing at all from the Conciliation Boards and Joint Committees which existed in many trades before the War. The well-organised industries, with very few exceptions, have established no machinery under the Whitley scheme.[1] Its only important effect has been the setting up of formal negotiating machinery on a national scale in many of the less organised industries which lacked such machinery before the War and in the public services. Its larger aspirations have come to nothing.

Section 2.—Negotiation and Arbitration

In practically all organised industries there exist, as we have seen, regular methods of dealing with differences by means of negotiation. In most cases such negotiation takes the form of some sort of Conference or Joint Committee representing, on the one side, the District Committees or National Executives of the Trade Unions, and on the other side, the local Associations of Employers or their National Federation. The constitution and scope of these joint bodies differ very widely, both on account of the different circumstances of the various industries, and of variation in the strength and policy of organised Capital and Labour. It is, however, possible, without going into the details of particular schemes, to pass certain general comments upon them.

(a) The scope of conciliation machinery may be more or less restricted, in the sense that it may deal with a wider or with a narrower range of questions ; thus, some Boards are confined purely to general wage adjustments ; others (e.g., in building and engineering) deal also with working conditions, hours, overtime, and all other questions which ordinarily form the subject of dispute between Capital and Labour. There has been a certain tendency for the scope of Conciliation Boards to be extended for the purpose of bringing a wider range of questions under review ;

[1] A Whitley Council was set up in the building industry, but was later destroyed by the secession of the employers.

thus disputes have arisen concerning the right of the negotiating bodies to deal with questions of " discipline " and " management," which employers often claim to be matters for themselves alone.

(b) Negotiating bodies are now nearly always based upon organisations of employers, on the one hand, and Trade Unions on the other. There are, however, a few bodies in badly organised trades chosen by a direct vote of the whole body of workmen concerned, whether they belong to a Trade Union or not. Such a position used to exist on the railways, where the Conciliation Boards set up for each important railway after the 1907 and 1911 disputes were in both cases based upon the vote of the whole body of railwaymen included within the terms of reference of the Boards. The National Union of Railwaymen, from a constitutional point of view, had nothing to do with the choice of the representatives, although naturally in most cases it got its own men elected. This position arose only because, up to 1914, the railway companies still refused to recognise the Trade Unions, which had not yet become strong enough to enforce fully the right of Trade Union bargaining. Since the War, full recognition has been secured, and the old Conciliation machinery has been swept away.

(c) Agreements constituting machinery for negotiation usually contain provisions for the postponement of any drastic action, such as a strike or lock-out, until the case has been fully considered. This being so, clearly one of the most important questions in setting up such machinery is how long the procedure laid down will take to operate. On some questions, common to all districts, negotiation is in most cases wholly national ; but in others it begins locally, either in a particular factory or with a local meeting between the Employers' Association and the Trade Union District Committee, or Joint Committee of several Unions. Failing a settlement locally, a national meeting follows, after a certain interval. In some cases an additional stage is interposed in the form of a divisional Board, covering a wider area than a single district. The general tendency on the Trade Union side has been to speed up the procedure of conciliation to the greatest possible extent. The employers, on the other hand, often desire to make it work as slowly as possible, especially when wage advances are in question.

(d) Agreements concerning the methods of negotiation may or may not contain provisions for Arbitration. That is to say, the Board may be an instrument of pure negotiation on which the two parties meet and endeavour to thrash out their difficulties and reach a common agreement without outside intervention, or there may be special provision for the calling in of outsiders to deal with a question which cannot be settled by direct negotiation. The former is the case with the local and central conferences in the engineering industry, into which no element of arbitration, or so-called " impartiality," enters. Where an element of arbitration is introduced, it may be present in very varying degrees. Thus, in the mining industry an independent chairman is sometimes called in when the two parties fail to reach an agreement, with or without power to give a binding decision. In one or two cases there is a provision that all disputes not settled by direct negotiation must be referred to arbitration. In most cases the element of " impartiality " is only introduced, if at all, after an attempt has been made to arrive at a direct settlement.

(*e*) During the War large sections of industry were working under the system of Compulsory State Arbitration imposed by the Munitions Act of 1915. At the end of the War Compulsory Arbitration was swept away; but it left certain marks of its presence behind. The Committee on Production, established during the War as a compulsory tribunal of arbitration, became, after a series of changes, a permanent body as a voluntary tribunal of arbitration under the name of the Industrial Court. It consists of full-time arbitrators, some originally lawyers, some employers, and some workers, but now all acting as " impartial " State officials. Disputes are referred to it only by consent of both parties.

This permanent body was set up under the Industrial Courts Act of 1920. At the same time, power was given to the Minister of Labour, with or without the consent of the parties, to set up a Court of Inquiry into any industrial dispute. A Court of Inquiry is constituted specially to deal with a single dispute. Sometimes it consists of a single person, but usually it includes a chairman who is a lawyer or judge and one or more representatives of employers and Trade Unions not directly concerned in the dispute. The Court can give no binding decision; its function is to elucidate and publish the facts and to make recommendations for a settlement. Either party can reject its recommendations. In fact, it serves often rather as a court of mediation for bringing the parties together again with a view to compromise.

The Ministry of Labour had before the War, under the Conciliation Act of 1896, power to intervene in any dispute with a view to promoting an agreed settlement by mediation. Since the War this power, confirmed under the Industrial Courts Act, has been used more often. Even if no formal Court of Inquiry is set up, the Ministry of Labour now, in most cases, intervenes in important disputes before a strike or lock-out is declared. There is, however, no power to compel the parties to accept a settlement or to refrain from strike action while mediation is in progress or a Court of Inquiry in session.

There is one other matter in connection with the relations between employers and Trade Unions which must be touched upon here. In most organised skilled trades the Unions have built up, both locally and nationally, codes of working rules and conditions under which alone their members are allowed or willing to work. These codes or bye-laws, as they are sometimes called, are in most cases agreed to by the organised employers, in which case they become incorporated in agreements, national or local. In some cases, however, there is no formal agreement, and the observance of the bye-laws is enforced by the Trade Unions without any formal assent on the part of the employers. In addition to these written codes and rules, which are usually printed for the use of members, there is, of course, a mass of workshop customs, written and unwritten, agreed and not agreed, which are no less rigidly enforced by Trade Unionists as the essential conditions on which they are prepared to work. These unwritten customs and regulations, which the Unions are, naturally, able to enforce more effectively in times of good trade than when unemployment is prevalent, are an important element in the control which the workers exercise over the conditions of employment. Many matters which are not, or could not be, effectively dealt with in written agreements are controlled through trade custom and etiquette. Petty workshop tyranny and attempts at undue " speeding up " of labour have largely to be combated by this means, in which Trade Unionism approaches more nearly than at any other point to securing a real voice in the control of industry. In the printing trades, for example, there are important workshop customs which no employer, in an organised shop, could hope to transgress with impunity. And this is true in varying degrees of practically all skilled crafts.

Section 3.—STRIKES AND LOCK-OUTS

The machinery of conciliation and negotiation described in the last section does not cover the whole of industry, and, where it exists, is not always successful in preventing disputes. Where no machinery for conciliation or negotiation exists, this does not mean that the workers, in the event of a grievance arising, proceed at once to the drastic remedy of a strike. In the majority of cases a Trade Union is called in, and an attempt is made to settle the matter by direct negotiation with the firm or firms concerned. It is only where an employer or group of employers refuses to recognise Trade Unions, or to negotiate with the accredited representatives of the men, that strikes commonly occur without previous pourparlers between the parties.

Even where the machinery of negotiation exists, strikes may occur in either of two cases : in the first place, the two sides may fail to effect a settlement, and in this case, unless arbitration is invoked by both parties, the workers may resort to a strike, or the employers to a lock-out, at any time after the breakdown of negotiations. Secondly, unofficial strikes, and, to a less extent, unofficial lock-outs, may occur before the negotiating machinery has been fully operated. It is often made a complaint against Trade Unions that failure to operate such machinery is more frequent in their cases than in that of the employers, and that breaches of agreement on the part of Trade Unions are unduly frequent. This, however, is a misunderstanding of the real situation. The employer controls industry and gives his orders as to the way in which industry is to be carried on. If the workmen desire an alteration, they must either persuade the employer to agree to it, or else come out on strike. On the other hand, if the employer desires an alteration, he does not, as a rule, declare a lock-out—he makes the alteration and leaves it to his workmen to strike against it or give in. This is less true in proportion as an industry is highly organised ; but even in the best-organised industries this is the method by which the employers all too often bring about changes in particular workshop conditions. Thus the employer can, merely by altering conditions, compel his workers either to accept the change or to strike, and so give them the appearance of being the aggressors, even when their action is of a purely defensive character. Moreover, on the whole, the employer's desire is to preserve the *status quo*, whereas the workmen usually desire to alter it. This is a further difference between the position of workmen in relation to strikes and that of the employers in relation to lock-outs. The lock-out is a far less necessary weapon to the employer than the strike is to the workmen.

In Appendix XI to this book statistics are given which show the number of strikes and lock-outs in the years before, during, and after the War. The number and extent of strikes had enormously increased during the years immediately preceding the War, and, whereas the first years of the twentieth century were, on the whole, years of industrial tranquillity, from 1911 onwards there was a growing industrial unrest. Even the figures of strikes do not convey an adequate idea of the change which came over the attitude of Trade Unionists during these years ; for the number of concessions secured without recourse to strikes probably increased in quite as great proportion as the number of strikes. The prevalence of strikes during these years did not indicate necessarily any breakdown of the machinery of negotiation: it showed that the workmen were in a state of greater unrest, and that a larger number of demands for improved conditions was being brought forward. The proportion of settlements without recourse to a stoppage probably remained just as high during the years of unrest as during the preceding period.

The question is often asked whether the strike weapon is, on the whole, a success or a failure. This question is really unanswerable, since any attempt to measure the actual results of strikes and lock-outs gives an entirely misleading result. A strike may fail in attaining its object immediately; but that object may be attained shortly afterwards, perhaps by negotiation, as an indirect result of the strike, but without recourse to a further stoppage. This does not really mean that the strike has failed, and that peaceful methods have succeeded: it means that the strength and organisation among the workers is such that the concession has been gained. The question of the method employed is secondary: the real determining factor is the strength of organisation.

There is a further difficulty in answering the question whether strikes succeed or fail. An enormous proportion of strikes end, not in complete success or failure on either side, but in a compromise. The workers secure something, but not the whole of their demands. Employers give up some things and retain others. Thus, where attempts are made to tabulate the results of strikes according to their success or failure, it is usually found that the majority fall into a middle group, and this middle group really includes a considerable proportion of compromises which are equivalent to successes for the one side or the other.

The strike is undoubtedly an inconvenient, and in many cases a brutal, weapon. It entails often much suffering upon the striker, and, where a great industry is concerned, it often has the effect of throwing out of work large numbers of persons who are not directly concerned in the question at issue. In addition, the strike, particularly in the greater industries, may entail considerable hardship on the public. Nevertheless there is no prospect at all that the organised Labour movement will be induced to give up the right to strike, or to accept any limitation of it. Nor, indeed, even if limitations or restrictions were imposed, could they be really effective. The power to strike exists whether it is legalised or not, and as long as the workers remain in a position in which they have unsatisfied grievances, strikes will continue, and the right to strike will not be willingly surrendered. Machinery of negotiation and full recognition of Trade Unions undoubtedly have the effect of diminishing the number of strikes, and of securing settlements in many cases without recourse to the strike; but they achieve these results, as we saw in the last section, because the right to strike is present in the background. Abandonment or limitation of the right to strike would be likely to result, not in a decrease in the number or severity of strikes, but in the breakdown of the machinery of direct negotiation between employers and Trade Unions.

The most usual type of strike is, of course, that in which a body of workers leave work in support of demands made on their own behalf; but there have always been cases in which large bodies of men have struck, on grounds of solidarity, in support of demands which do not affect them directly. Such action is called " sympathetic " strike action. It occurs not only when both bodies of men belong to the same Union or Federation of Unions, though this is the commonest case, but also between quite independent groups. Moreover, while most strikes centre round direct economic demands, there may be strikes arising out of political issues. The Council of Action threatened a " general strike " when there was a threat in 1920 of war between Great Britain and Russia, and in 1919 and 1920 a general strike on the mixed politico-industrial issue of mines nationalisation was seriously debated. The policy of striking on political, as distinct from purely industrial, issues, is usually called " Direct Action." It has so far, in this country, not passed beyond the stage of threatening and discussion, though it may at any time come again to the front. The German Trade Unions employed it against the " Kapp Putsch " in 1920.

Section 4.—Standard Rates and " Payment by Results "

Wherever Trade Unionism achieves any strength or measure of recognition we find it endeavouring to enforce by means of collective bargaining some sort of standard rates or methods of remuneration for its members. In most trades of a skilled character the Trade Unions enforce, at least locally, standard time rates of wages, at less than which no member of the Union is allowed to work in the district concerned. In Unions covering several distinct classes of labour there may be, of course, distinct standard rates fixed for various classes of the members, as when, in some districts, different day rates are fixed by the Amalgamated Engineering Union for pattern-makers, turners, fitters, machinists, etc. The principle, however, is in all cases the same—that of securing a standard rate of remuneration which is regarded as a minimum by all the members of the Union in the district. These standard rates are not in any sense maxima, and in many industries, especially those that work mainly on a time-work system, many members may be in receipt of wages in excess of the standard rates

TRADE UNIONS AT WORK

laid down by the Union. They are, in fact, minima, which may apply to a greater or less proportion of the members of the trade. Where an industry is conducted successfully under time-work conditions, that is, where the worker is paid simply so much per hour, or per week, or per month, the standard time-rate is the main item in wage bargaining between employers and Trade Unions. It may, however, have certain complications of its own. Thus, instead of fixing a flat minimum rate for all members of a particular trade, the Unions may elect to fix incremental scales ranging upwards from an agreed minimum, and varying either with the quality or nature of the work done, or with the years of service, or the qualifications of the worker concerned. Such incremental scales, as opposed to flat rates, exist principally in occupations in which employment is of a continuous character, *i.e.*, principally among clerks and in the Government, Local Government, and Railway services. They are, in any case, not essentially different from standard rates of the ordinary type, since in every case the object of the Trade Union is to fix a minimum standard rate below which no member of the craft is allowed to work.

The problem of wages is far more complicated in those industries which adopt, in whole or in part, a system of " payment by results," that is to say, in which the worker is paid, not so much per hour or per day or per week, but so much per unit of production, or at any rate an amount dependent in one way or another upon the amount produced. Systems of payment by results are seldom entirely disconnected from time-rates; for the Unions usually demand that, even where the worker is paid on a piece-work or bonus system, a standard day wage shall still be guaranteed, irrespective of output. This insistence on the day rate is of greater or less importance according to the character of the occupation. Where the conditions of the trade are such that a given amount of effort can be relied upon under normal conditions to produce a given output, it is not so necessary for the Union to insist upon a guaranteed day wage, because if piece-work prices are fixed at a reasonable level a reasonable day wage follows almost as a matter of course. Thus, in the textile industries, wage negotiations centre almost entirely round piece-work prices, and advances or reductions are calculated by way of a percentage on or off the piece-work prices. The same conditions apply in certain other trades, notably in some branches of the iron and steel trades, and of shipbuilding.

Apart from the special complication of the " abnormal place," [1]

---

[1] The " abnormal place " is a position in which, owing to difficulties presented by the conformation of the coal seam, the coal-hewer is not able, in a

the mining industry belongs to the same group. These conditions, however, do not prevail in all industries, and there are many cases in which a system of payment by results is adopted although there is no sufficient assurance that a given amount of effort will regularly result in a given output. This is particularly the case in the engineering and kindred trades, and the greatest pains have been taken by the Trade Unions, where payment by results has been accepted, to secure a full guarantee that day-work rates will be maintained irrespective of output or piece-work earnings. This is secured by permitting the introduction of payment by results only on condition that the employer guarantees in advance the day-work rate to all piece-workers, whether their output is above or below what is regarded as the standard quantity. The Trade Unions in organised trades are able as a rule to make this point good, and the guaranteed day rate has been incorporated in the various agreements dealing with piece-work and bonus systems in the engineering industry. In trades which are less well organised this has not been secured, even where the conditions of a trade make it exceedingly important. Thus, in some of the occupations covered by the Transport Workers' Federation, as well as in sections of the boot and shoe and clothing trades, and in other important occupations, piece-work systems are in operation without any guarantee of day rates to the piece-worker.

The policy of the Trade Unions in different trades in relation to payment by results varies very widely indeed. Broadly speaking, we may say that piece-work is generally either welcomed or accepted with equanimity where an increase of effort normally results in a uniform increase in output, whereas it is usually rejected or makes its way only with considerable difficulty in trades to which these conditions do not apply. This is exactly what might be expected, since it is clear that where output in normal cases closely corresponds to effort, it is usually possible to adjust piece-work prices with almost as great ease and accuracy as it is possible to lay down the day-work rate of wages, or a series of day-work rates.

The storm centre of the battle which has raged between employers and employed on the question of payment by results has been the engineering industry. In engineering before the War the great bulk of the work was of a non-repetitive character, and exceedingly difficult to measure in terms of output alone. The employers, however, were exceedingly desirous in many cases of securing the widest possible extension of payment by results as a means of stimulating output, and the system was considerably

given time, to extract the amount of coal necessary in order to secure the average, or something approaching the average, piece-work earnings.

extended during the War. The Trade Unions, on the other hand, have usually opposed, or accepted only with extreme reluctance, any extension of payment by results in connection with which they have not been able to foresee quite clearly the exact results upon the wages and conditions of their members.

The case put forward in favour of payment by results as against time work is twofold. It is urged, in the first place, that under a system of payment by results the workman is rewarded in accordance with the energy, efficiency, and initiative which he puts into his work, and that thereby production is stimulated, machines and other plant utilised to the fullest possible extent, cost of production lowered, and the consumer benefited in the form of lower prices, the employer in the form of higher profits, and the workman in higher earnings : at the same time it is suggested that payment by results is in itself a juster system, since it secures more nearly to each man the reward of his own labour, and does not, like time-work, mean the granting of the same reward to efficient and inefficient alike. In reply to these arguments Trade Unionists usually retort in the first place that most of the systems actually suggested involve a reduced labour cost per unit of product, as well as a higher production per worker, with the result that an increasing output under the wage system may well mean unemployment for some of their members, and that, even if higher wages are given at first, as soon as the employer has discovered the highest output of which his workers are capable prices are cut, so that the remuneration to the worker returns almost, if not quite, to the previous level. Moreover, it is urged that many systems of payment by results are bad for Trade Union action, because they result, not in that collective solidarity which inspires the workers who are out for a common standard rate, but in setting one man against another, and in forgetfulness of the loyalty which is owed to the Trade Union. The case on both sides of the argument is, no doubt, to some extent fallacious, and includes arguments which could not be finally sustained. There is, however, much to be said for the workman's case, at any rate as against the prevailing systems of payment by results, just as there is undoubtedly a considerable element of truth in the employer's case, if the only thing to consider is that of stimulating profits and lowering the labour cost of production. We shall be better able to see the arguments in their proper perspective as we look rather more closely at the various methods of payment adopted.

The simplest method is straight piece-work, that is, the system under which the worker is paid so much for every unit produced, whether it be payment per ton or per article, or per dozen or per hundred of output. This system prevails over a wide range of industry. The coal hewer is paid so much per ton hewed, the coal trimmer so much per ton trimmed, the cotton weaver so much per yard woven, the smelter so much per ton produced. Under this system the labour cost of the article to the employer remains constant, and any increase in the output of the workers means a corresponding increase in wages. At the same time the employer saves by securing a higher output, because overhead charges are reduced and machines more fully utilised. A piece-work system clearly may be good or bad from the workman's point of view very largely according to the methods by which piece-work prices are fixed. If the employer is able to fix piece-work prices arbitrarily at his own valuation, and to vary them thereafter, it will clearly mean that the wages of the operative remain absolutely under his control, except in so far as the Trade Unions successfully insist on a payment of a guaranteed time-rate, irrespective of output. The adoption of the piece-work system, therefore, so far from making collective bargaining by the Trade Union unnecessary, leaves the need for it altogether unaltered, and merely results in making conditions of bargaining more complicated, and thereby in laying greater responsibility upon the Union for the maintenance of fair conditions.

It is not surprising to find that piece-work is most universally in operation, and is working most smoothly in those industries in which the work is capable of being measured in terms of a simple unit of production, and in which processes are fairly uniform. In these cases the workers often work under price lists agreed upon between the Trade Unions and Employers' Associations, and little scope, apart from such questions as " bad material " or defective machinery, is left for bargaining with regard to individual piece-work prices. This is usually possible in the textile, and in the main in the iron and steel industry, and in other cases. Where the unit of output is not so easily measurable, systems of payment by results are often found, as in engineering, but in these cases it has been necessary for the Unions to adopt more elaborate measures for the regulation of piece-work prices. Where they have not done so, they have found the system liable to very grave abuses.

Piece-work is undoubtedly the most widely prevalent of the various systems of payment by results, although it is not the system which has attracted the greatest attention in this country in recent years. Where Trade Union conditions compel the employer to agree to reasonable piece-work prices he is often dissatisfied because there is no direct reduction in the labour cost of the article in addition to the reduction in overhead charges secured by greater output. To meet this point several systems have been devised, under which, while the workman's earnings rise with any increase in output, they do not rise so fast as the output, so that the employer not only saves on his overhead charges, but also pays a lower price to the worker for each unit of output. The most notable example of a system based on this idea is the Premium Bonus System. This system has two main forms, and a very much larger number of subordinate varieties. Under it, instead of a piece-work price being fixed for each job, a standard time is fixed within which each job ought to be completed. The workman is guaranteed his time-rate ; and if he does the job in less than the standard time he receives payment at time-rates for the time actually taken, *plus* a premium on any time saved out of the standard time allowed. Under one variety of the system the worker is paid for one-half (or some other fraction) of the time saved out of the standard time allowed, the firm reaping the benefit of the remaining fraction of the time saved (Halsey System, Weir System, etc.). Under another the employee is paid a bonus of 10 per cent. for every 10 per cent. saved out of the time allowed (Rowan System). It will be seen that under the former of these systems earnings are theoretically unlimited, whereas under the second system, however much the man may produce, he cannot possibly earn twice his time-rate, because he cannot conceivably save 100 per cent. of the time allowed.

In addition to the Premium Bonus System there are numerous other systems of payment by results of a more or less " fancy " character. Many of these have been imported from America, and are closely connected with the doctrine of scientific management. They mostly aim at securing a lower labour cost for each article produced, and at the same time an increase in hourly earnings to the worker in return for his increased production. The increase in earnings is not, however, under these systems equivalent to the increase in output.[1]

A further important fact in connection with payment by results is the distinction between individual and collective payment under these various systems. In some cases payment by results is worked on a purely individual basis, and each individual worker is paid in proportion to his or her individual output. In others the system adopted is collective, and a bonus is paid on the total output of a shop or group of workers without reference to the output of any particular individual. Trade Unions in many cases strongly advocate the adoption of a collective system wherever this is made possible by the conditions of the work.

Under any system of payment by results everything depends in

---

[1] For a study of these systems, see my book, " The Payment of Wages."

the last resort upon the level at which prices or standard times are fixed. In many cases the employers have claimed and still claim the right to fix and adjust prices and times without reference to or consultation with the workmen directly concerned, or their Trade Unions. In others the Trade Unions have been able to enforce more or less complete systems of collective bargaining with regard to payment by results.

In some cases, Trade Unions insist on preliminary price lists applying over the whole country or a whole district, and covering a wide range of different operations. In other cases, where there is no standard list applicable generally, shop lists have been devised, or there are regular methods in a particular establishment of both fixing and adjusting prices and times whenever a new job is introduced, or an old job recast.

The perennial complaint of Trade Unionists is that the employers " cut prices." This complaint is not heard, or is not heard so much, where established price lists exist, but wherever the system of collective bargaining is defective, or the wide variety and non-repetitive character of the operations performed make price lists impossible, disputes on this point are continually arising.

Employers of the more sagacious type often point out that it is bad policy to cut prices, and guarantees have been introduced into many piece-work agreements that prices will only be reduced when the method of manufacture of the article concerned is altered. It is, however, exceedingly difficult to make these guarantees effective, and the complaints, so far from ceasing, continually increase in volume. In some of the better-managed shops, and in some shops in which prices are fixed with an approach to scientific accuracy, price-cutting has been largely eliminated ; in others, and especially wherever the method of fixing prices is unscientific, price-cutting flourishes exceedingly. Indeed, one of the arguments put forward by employers in favour of the Rowan Premium Bonus System is that, by rigidly limiting earnings in any case to less than double time, it makes it unnecessary for the employer to cut prices, however unscientific the method of fixing them may be. Such a method of making the workmen pay for the employers' inefficiency hardly requires comment.

It will have been seen, from what has been said above, that the reception accorded to payment by results by Trade Unions in the group of industries round which controversy has principally raged is easily explicable. Payment by results may satisfy a Trade Union where (1) the nature of the operations performed is such that effort is easily measured in terms of output, and (2) where a full and complete system of collective bargaining exists. Where either of these conditions is wanting payment by results will usually be applied, if at all, only in the teeth of Trade Union opposition, although when it has once been introduced, if prices and times are fixed on a liberal scale, Trade Unionists who have strongly opposed its introduction may subsequently be unwilling to face the substantial reduction in earnings which might be involved in a return to day-work conditions.

There are obviously certain industries, including notably the greater part of the industries of transport and distribution, which are unsuited to payment by results; and there are others in which the opposition has so far been largely successful, notably the building industry, in which climatic conditions and the state of the materials used conspire to make adequate measurement of effort in relation to output exceedingly difficult. In other industries payment by results continues to make headway in the face of opposition, but there is no sign that the Trade Unions which have so far opposed it are prepared to withdraw their antagonism. There have even been signs in certain industries in which piece-work has been long established—notably mining—of a desire among a considerable section of the workers to return to day-work conditions, and to demand enhanced day-work rates as a substitute for piece-work conditions.

Section 5.—HOURS OF LABOUR

As important as the question of wages is that of the hours of labour. Indeed, it is in a sense more important, for a change in wages may be neutralised by a change in prices, whereas a reduction in the hours of labour is clear gain. The Trade Unions, therefore, attempt everywhere to enforce not only standard rates of wages, but also a standard working week. Before the War there was great variety in the hours worked in different industries. The underground colliery workers had secured a nominal eight hours day in 1909,[1] and there was a shorter working day in some non-manual occupations. But among the well-organised manual workers fifty-three or fifty-four hours a week was the commonest standard, and some occupations had a much longer working time. Large sections even of the iron and steel industry still worked on twelve-hour shifts.

After the War, the majority of industries in which the workers were fairly well organised secured, not indeed the eight hours day, but the forty-eight hours working week. The engineering trades secured a forty-seven hours week, and the builders forty-four,

---

[1] Actually, at least, eight and a half hours on the average, including winding time. It became seven (or seven and a half) in 1919.

with less in winter. Forty-eight hours a week came to be recognised for most industries as the maximum standard. At the National Industrial Conference in 1919 the employers agreed to the legal enforcement of a nearly universal maximum of forty-eight hours, and the International Labour Conference at Washington, with the support of the British Government, agreed to an International Convention for making forty-eight hours the maximum for all industrial countries. But, when it came to the point, the Government would not redeem its pledges by giving legal effect to this maximum.[1] The Trade Unions were left to get and hold the forty-eight hours week unaided.

Despite the trade slump which began in 1921, they have done this successfully in most cases, and forty-eight hours remains the maximum in all properly-organised trades. This is, indeed, the one really substantial gain which has been retained through the bad times following the post-War boom.

This does not mean that no more than forty-eight hours' work can be done by any worker in a single week, but that any extra work done above the daily or weekly standard must be paid for at special rates. Overtime rates are in all organised trades higher than the ordinary rates. There is no regular proportion. Sometimes all overtime is paid for at a fixed rate (*e.g.*, time and a third, or standard rate *plus* one-third of such rate) ; sometimes the first hour or two hours at one rate, and further hours at a higher rate. Usually Sunday and holiday work are paid for at still higher rates (*e.g.*, double time), but this is not universal in trades which have to run continuously on Sundays as well as weekdays. Many Trade Unions not only fix overtime rates by bargaining with the employers, but also limit the amount of overtime which any member may work, or even prohibit overtime altogether (save in breakdowns and special emergencies) when unemployment is prevalent. Special rates are often fixed for work done at night by night-shift workers, as well as for overtime.

The fixing of the hours of labour is, of course, closely involved with the fixing of standard rates of wages. The standard weekly rate is payable for the standard number of hours' work. Where hours are reduced, rates of wages have often to be increased in order to prevent diminution of the workers' earnings. This arises not where the wage is fixed for time-work on a weekly basis, but where hourly rates are in force, as in the building industry, or where the workers are employed on some system of payment by results (*e.g.*, miners, engineers, cotton operatives). In these cases the workers usually demand and secure a proportionate advance

---

[1] The Labour Government is shortly to introduce a Bill doing this (June, 1924).

in hourly or piece-work rates when the standard working week is shortened.

Section 6.—THE QUESTION OF CONTROL

Trade Unionism does not limit itself to the regulation of hours and wages. It attempts also to deal with a wide variety of matters which affect the status or working conditions of its members. Many of these raise no question of principle; but every now and then, on a demand by some Union to regulate some particular condition or to introduce a new factor into the process of collective bargaining, the employers raise the alarm, and accuse the Unions of trespassing on matters which fall outside their legitimate sphere, and of attempting to " interfere with the management " in the discharge of their exclusive functions. How such conflicts are actually resolved depends on the determination and organised power present on either side; for there can, in fact, be no sharp marking off of " questions of management " from matters about which collective bargaining is constantly taking place. But behind the determined effort to limit the sphere of Trade Union action lies the real fear of the employers that Trade Unions will seriously press their often-expressed claim for a share in the " control of industry."

How far do the Trade Unions control industry already? It is clear that, in so far as they exercise control at all, this control is mainly negative. They do, to a great extent, impose conditions upon employers with regard to the terms under which industry is to be conducted, but they do not themselves actually prescribe the methods of industrial administration. Every collective bargain that is made by a Trade Union with an employer or Association of Employers embodies certain restrictions upon the manner in which the employer is to run " his own business." Every working rule or bye-law which the Trade Union lays down for the observance of its members is an instance of interference and restriction.

Thus, when employers speak of Trade Unions as " restrictive organisations " they are saying what is to a great extent true; but when they go on to conclude from this that the influence of Trade Unions upon the organisation of industry is malign they draw a false deduction. Any body which is excluded from the giving of direct commands can operate only by way of restriction. If I cannot say how industry is to be carried on by giving orders directly in the workshop or office, my only means of action is to say to those who have the authority to give orders that, in giving them, they must conform to certain conditions. The Trade Union, excluded from power over management, can only make its voice felt by prescribing indirectly conditions which limit the power of the management.

In this indirect sense Trade Unions do exercise considerable control. In the great industries there exists a mass of what we may term "Trade Union legislation," that is to say, of direct agreements between employers and Trade Unions which bind the organisers of industry often as firmly as statute law. There exist also many rules laid down by Trade Unions, but not formally endorsed by the employers, which are hardly less effective in fixing conditions of industrial management. A few examples of such rules will serve to drive home the point.

When a Trade Union makes a rule that none of its members shall work at less than a certain wage, or for more than a certain number of hours in a week, or that for all overtime its members shall receive at least time and a quarter or time and a half, it is legislating for the industry and controlling the industry quite as fully as the State when it passes a Factory or Minimum Wage Act, and is taking away from the employers sole jurisdiction and transferring in part to itself a certain sphere of industrial control. In laying down such general conditions of industrial organisation the Trade Union creates a precedent for further types of interference. It confines itself in the early stages of its operations to endeavouring to establish certain generalised conditions applicable to a whole industry or occupation, and to enforcing these as minima upon the employers concerned. A further step is taken when, in addition to laying down general minima, the Trade Union proceeds to lay down more specialised rules for the administration, not of the whole industry, but of particular factories or groups of factories.

To this class belong most of the Trade Union regulations to which employers take the greatest exception. In the organised industries they have learnt by experience to accept the principle of collective bargaining with the Trade Unions on general questions affecting the industry as a whole, *i.e.*, wages, hours, and general conditions of labour; but it seems to them a monstrous invasion of their rights when the Trade Unions claim, in addition, to prescribe regulations for workshop organisation, or to dictate the manner in which the employer shall deal with particular employees, or groups of employees, in *his* factory. The employer then accuses the Unions of " restriction of output," and very often in industries in which the precedent has not been clearly established, refuses to negotiate upon such questions. Gradually, however, the Trade Unions make headway in face of the employers' opposition. Agreements regulating workshop organisation, made perhaps between the workmen in the shop and the employer, but ratified by the Trade Union or its District Committee, become more and more frequent. The employer is compelled to realise that collective bargaining cannot be made to stop short absolutely at general principles, and to recognise the right of the Unions to deal also with these further questions. In addition, a great deal of similar detailed regulation takes place, not under the formal authority of the Trade Unions, but under agreement of an informal character between groups of Trade Unionists in particular workshops. One of the most important forms of Trade Union control over industry, especially in those Unions in which the skilled craftsmen are strong, consists in the enforcement of workshop customs, often unwritten, but recognised generally as proceeding from the Trade Union, and as forming a part of the collective action of organised Labour. An instance of such workshop customs can be easily found in almost any industry. Printing " chapels " have their strongly established customs in particular shops. The engineering Trade Unionists lay down strict regulations with regard to the " manning " of particular classes of machines, or the rates to be paid for doing particular jobs. The textile workers, the miners, and many other classes of workers have similar regulations applying to individual mills, pits, etc.

One of the most important forms of this collective intervention in industrial control centres round the question of " discipline." More and more in recent years the Trade Unionists in a works, and, following their lead, the Trade Unions themselves, have claimed the right to question and criticise actively the disciplinary methods employed by foremen and managers. This applies not only to codes of rules prescribed by establishments for their employees ; it applies also to the treatment meted out to particular workers for supposed breaches of discipline. Many strikes, both authorised and unauthorised, have centred round this question in recent years.

I am concerned here, not so much with the wisdom or unwisdom of the actual regulations and customs enforced by Trade Unions, as with the fact that in the aggregate these customs represent a considerable control by the Trade Unions over the management of industry. The negative character of this control does not alter the fact that it is a real form of control, and that by this negative interference the Trade Unions are playing an increasing part in the administration of industry. Moreover, the line is sometimes hard to draw between negative and positive control, and it is easy to see that by a greater extension of their power of intervention and of laying down conditions by which employers have to abide the Trade Unions might pass to more positive forms of control. A parallel that is sometimes used in this connection is worth citing.

Parliament, it is sometimes pointed out, did not begin as a controlling or governing body. It began as an advisory body which prescribed to the Crown conditions under which alone it was prepared to render service to the Crown. But from this negative and critical position Parliament passed, by a series of stages, into a position of positive control over government. In the same way, it is suggested, the indirect control at present exercised by Trade Unions is capable of an expansion which would not merely increase its amount, but change its character fundamentally, until it developed into a system of positive control and industrial management by the workers.

Clearly there are many obstacles in the way of any such complete development, and even of any great extension of the control at present exercised by the Trade Unions. Some of these obstacles will have appeared very clearly in the course of this survey of the present position of Trade Unionism. For instance, it will have been clearly seen that the present state of organisation in the Trade Union Movement is far from adequate even to the tasks which Trade Unions have to perform at the present time, and that it would be still less adequate to the task of positive control over industry. The overlapping between Union and Union, the rivalries and differences of policy between Trade Unions representing different sections of workers within a single industry, the lack of effective co-ordination between the Unions in the various industries: all these things and many others make the Trade Unions of to-day incapable of exercising much positive control over the management of industry. As we have seen, movements towards the amalgamation and federation of Trade Unions, and more conscious movements in the direction of securing an organisation which would unite in a single Union all the workers employed in each industry, while they are active, have not yet achieved any result which is considerable in comparison with the work that remains to be done. Before we can imagine the Trade Unions exercising positive industrial control we have to imagine a drastic reconstruction of the Trade Union Movement.

But even union by industry, as it is generally understood, would not provide bodies capable of completely controlling industry. The bodies which are called Industrial Unions to-day do not include, or even aim at including, the whole personnel of an industry. They include perhaps, or aim at including, all manual workers in an industry, and even some sections among the clerical workers; but the higher grades of management, and still more the professional grades which play an important part in most industries to-day, are left at present almost entirely untouched by organisation, or at best are organised apart in associations of their own. If the Trade Unions sought to control industry in any complete sense, they would be confronted with the necessity of bringing into their ranks the professionals and managers who perform essential industrial functions, or else of training up within their own ranks men capable of taking their places—a task which would be further complicated by the necessity of retaining these men within the Labour Movement when, after they had been trained by the Unions, the employers tried to entice them away with tempting offers of salaried positions.

I dwelt, in an earlier section of this book, upon the relations between the Trade Unions of to-day and the various classes of supervisory and professional workers, and it will be seen from what was said there that, although a process of assimilation is undoubtedly beginning, it has still a very long way to go.

If we suppose the enormous obstacles outlined in the preceding paragraphs to have been overcome, that is to say, if we suppose the Trade Unions to have reorganised themselves upon " industrial " lines, and to have brought within their ranks a sufficient proportion of the professional and managerial personnel of industry to be able to exercise effective control of industrial processes, how far, then, would the road be clear for the complete control of industry by Trade Unions so metamorphosed and enlarged ? There would still remain clearly the great problems of " finance," which, under modern conditions, more and more dominates the industrial situation. It is conceivable that the Trade Unions might succeed in supplanting the producing employer, and in taking over direct control of mines, factories, workshops, and railways, but how far could they hope to supplant the banker, who employs comparatively little labour, but has industry firmly in his grasp through the working of the credit system ?

To treat of this problem would take me far beyond the limits of this study. It may be true that, as some schools of social theorists maintain, it is the province of the Trade Union to supplant the employers and to assume control of factories and other places of work, whereas it is the function of the workers, organised politically, to supplant the traders and financiers, and to assume control of all the raw materials of industry. In any case, financial as well as industrial control is inevitably involved in any scheme for the positive control of industry by the workers.

PART VI

TRADE UNIONISM AND THE STATE

Sect. 1. The Legal Position of Trade Unions.   Sect. 2. Industrial Legislation.
Sect. 3. Conclusion.

Section 1.—THE LEGAL POSITION OF TRADE UNIONS

FROM the first, the relations between Trade Unionism and the law have been close, if not usually cordial. According to the common law, a Trade Union, if it is not in itself illegal, at least comes into conflict with the law as soon as it takes any action for the regulation of the conditions of the employment of its members. Hence it has come about that the whole of the rights of Trade Unions are dependent upon Statute Law, and that the Trade Unions, in the course of their career, have suffered several setbacks as a result of judgments delivered by reactionary judges in the Courts.

The present position of the law relating to Trade Unionism is exceedingly confused. The legal position of the Trade Unions themselves is regulated directly by five Acts of Parliament—the Trade Union Acts of 1871 and 1876, the Trade Disputes Act of 1906, the Trade Union Act of 1913, and the Trade Union (Amalgamation) Act of 1917. As this last has already been described in a previous section,[1] we need say nothing more about it here.

It is not possible in a short summary of this character to enter fully into the history of the two famous judgments which have so profoundly influenced the recent history of Trade Unions in this country. Both the Taff Vale case of 1902 and the Osborne Judgment of 1909 have had a profound effect upon the working of modern Trade Unionism, and have led to amendments of the law in order to bring it more into harmony with justice and with economic realities. The Trade Disputes Act of 1906, the first and greatest achievement of the new Labour Party which was returned to the House of Commons in that year, did secure to the Trade Unions immunity for their funds from the consequences of " tortious " acts committed by their members, and did to this extent place the Trade Unions and their officials in a privileged

---
[1] See p. 79.

position as regards the committing of certain types of " tort." This privileged position, however, is more apparent than real, since it is rather a special privilege given in order to redress a general disability. Under the Trade Union Acts the Trade Unions are subject to forms of regulation which are not extended to other types of voluntary association. It was this special form of regulation which made the Taff Vale Judgment possible, and thereby necessitated the granting of special privileges by the Trade Disputes Act. Both the Taff Vale Judgment and the Osborne Judgment are evidences of the tendency of the lawyers in this country to impose upon Trade Unions all the obligations of " incorporation " without therewith conferring upon them any of the advantages which " incorporation " carries with it. This has led to an anomalous position which undoubtedly ought to be remedied ; but it is impossible to remedy the present position of the law relating to Trade Unions by any piecemeal action, and it seems very doubtful whether any Government for some time to come will be likely to embark upon the highly controversial legislation which would be involved in any attempt to amend the Trade Union Acts as a whole. The employers are continually calling for the repeal of the Trade Disputes Act, which they regard as a one-sided piece of preferential legislation ; but the repeal of this Act, not accompanied by the remedying of the legal disabilities of Trade Unions, and the placing of them to the full extent in as good a position as other forms of association, would be a far greater injustice than any that is involved in the continuance of the present muddle.

The attitude of the law to Trade Unions has, as we have seen, been on the whole exceedingly reactionary, and any attempt by the Trade Unions to extend the scope of their powers has been resented and, if possible, declared illegal ; but along with this willingness to interfere with the free development of Trade Unions in their relations to other bodies—employers, the State, etc.—there is a considerable reluctance on the part of the law to interfere with the internal management of the Unions, or with the relation of their members one with another. This applies not merely to the definite exclusion of certain forms of interference under Section 4 of the Trade Union Act, 1871, but also to a general attitude on the part of the Courts, which has been evidenced on many occasions, notably during the constitutional crisis in the Amalgamated Society of Engineers in 1912. Moreover, Section 4 of the Trade Disputes Act has to some extent precluded the Courts from interference in the internal relations of Trade Unions.

The present position of the law affecting Trade Unions is exceedingly complicated, and can only be clearly defined by reference, both to the leading principles of British law, and to a number of statutes which regulate not only Trade Unions, but also other forms of association. It is, however, necessary to attempt a brief summary of the position, even though it is evident that such a summary cannot but be inadequate and may be even, in some respects, misleading.

(*a*) The legal position of Trade Unions in civil matters is principally governed by the Trade Union Acts of 1871, 1876, and 1913. The Act of 1871 in the main removed the common law illegality of Trade Unions by providing that a Trade Union shall not be held to be unlawful merely because its objects are " in restraint of trade." This carried with it the legal recognition of contracts made by Trade Unions.

The Act of 1871, however, also contained a descriptive clause, inserted presumably for the purpose of identifying the types of association included under the term " Trade Unions." This clause (as modified by the Act of 1876) defined a Trade Union as an association existing for the regulation of the relations between workmen and masters, or between workmen and workmen, or between masters and masters, or the imposing of restrictive conditions on the conduct of any trade or business, *and* the provision of benefit to members. This may have been a substantially true description of the scope of Trade Union action in the 'seventies ; but, as the movement grew, the scope of its activities expanded, and, in particular, it began to take part in political action.

Out of this expansion grew the famous Osborne case. Mr. Osborne, a member of the Amalgamated Society of Railway Servants, claimed an injunction against the expenditure of the funds of the Society on political objects. The case, which went from court to court, right up to the House of Lords, was finally decided against the Society, mainly on the ground that the objects of a Trade Union, as defined in the Trade Union Acts, must be regarded as inclusive. No mention being made of political action, such action by a Trade Union was declared illegal, and a further case extended the same principle to local as well as national politics.

Legislative action to put matters right was at once demanded by the Labour movement, and at last, in 1913, a new Trade Union Act, partially destroying the effect of the Osborne Judgment, was passed. This Act in the first place made it lawful for a Trade Union to engage in any lawful activity sanctioned by its rules. Certain specified political activities, including electoral work and (by a decision of 1915) subscription to a political newspaper, were specially excluded from this general enabling power, and it was provided that, in order to engage in these activities, a Trade Union must (*a*) take a ballot of its members, (*b*) provide for the exemption from contributions to be used for this purpose of any members desiring to be exempted, and (*c*) pay for such activities only out of a special fund to be kept separate from the general funds of the Union. It is under these conditions that Trade Unions now participate in political activities.

(*b*) The position of Trade Unions in relation to the criminal law is governed by a different body of statutes, of which the most important are the Conspiracy and Protection of Property Act of 1875 and the Trade Disputes Act of 1906. The Act of 1875 provides that " no combination to do any act in furtherance of a trade dispute shall be indictable as a conspiracy unless such act, if committed by one person, would be punishable as a crime." It also imposes penalties for violence, intimidation, watching, besetting, following, and various other offences—provisions which were used in order to make effective Trade Union action largely ineffective, especially in cases of picketing, etc. The position as regards picketing, however, has been more favourably re-defined in the Trade Disputes Act.

The Act of 1906 arose out of a case which has had even more far-reaching effects upon the Labour movement than the Osborne Judgment. A person who procures a breach of contract is liable to an action for damages by any of the contracting parties unless adequate justification exists. Under this common law principle the Taff Vale Railway Company in 1902 proceeded against the Amalgamated Society of Railway Servants for damages sustained in connection with a strike involving a breach of contract. The case went finally to the House of Lords, and the Union was mulcted in damages to the tune of £23,000. Here again, legislation at once became necessary, if Trade Union action was not to be utterly crippled. A great outcry ran through the Labour movement, and there is no doubt that the return of 30 Labour members to the House of Commons in 1906 was very largely a result of the Taff Vale case. The Liberal Government introduced an unsatisfactory Bill, only half remedying the grievance. The Trade Unions, however, demanded complete redress, and ultimately the Labour demands were accepted in substance, and the Trade Disputes Act of 1906 became law.

This Act provides, *inter alia*, that a " tortious " act done by a Trade Union is not actionable if it is done in contemplation or furtherance of a trade dispute, on the ground that it has induced a breach of a contract of employment, or that it is an interference with a person's trade or business. It also lays down that no action can be brought against a Trade Union or its members acting on their own and the Union's behalf in respect of a "tortious" act committed on behalf of the Union. This provision holds good whether or not a trade dispute exists.

This very brief summary of the legal position is not intended to do more than convey a general impression of the relations at present subsisting between Trade Unions and the law. For the most part the Judges are out of sympathy with the Trade Union movement, which they still tend to regard as an unwarrantable interference with the "liberty of the subject." This being so, Trade Unions must always expect under present conditions to have statute law illiberally interpreted, and "case" law accordingly weighted heavily against them. Their only redress in such circumstances is to wring fresh legislation from Parliament every time the Courts perpetrate a new injustice.

The Trade Union Acts, it should be noted, impose no form of compulsory registration on Trade Unions; but they do make provision for a voluntary registration, of which many Unions avail themselves. Registered Unions have to make to the Chief Registrar of Friendly Societies certain annual returns of membership and finance which unregistered bodies are under no obligation to make. They also have to get changes of rule passed by the Chief Registrar, who has also special powers under the Act of 1913 for the approval and formulation of Trade Union Political Rules. In return, registered Unions get a few minor privileges, but not enough to make registration in any sense compulsory. A body can claim the protection of the Trade Union Acts without being registered, if it can prove that it is in fact a Trade Union; and it is now possible without registration to obtain from the Chief Registrar a certificate declaring that a body is a Trade Union. Societies which are unwilling to register sometimes find such a certificate useful in defending actions in the courts. In fact, however, the majority of the big Unions are registered.

Section 2.—INDUSTRIAL LEGISLATION

I now come to those types of legislation in which the State interferes for the purpose of regulating the relations between employers and workmen. Before the War there had been for some time a marked tendency towards an increase in the scope of such legislation. The Factory Acts, indeed, had not recently been amended or extended to any considerable extent; but after 1906 there had been a considerable number of Acts of Parliament regulating wages and conditions of labour in various industries. Notable among these were the Trade Boards Act of 1909, which provided for the fixing of minimum rates of wages in certain

TRADE UNIONISM AND THE STATE

sweated occupations by Trade Boards, partly chosen from Employers' Associations and Trade Unions, and partly appointed by the Government Department concerned; the Shops Act regulating the conditions of employment of shop assistants and making provision for weekly holidays; the various Acts dealing with coal mines, including the revised Coal Mines Act of 1911, the Coal Mines Regulation (Eight Hours) Act of 1908, and the Coal Mines (Minimum Wage) Act of 1912. This last Act established as a temporary measure a new principle by laying down for a period of years minimum rates of wages for a class of labour which was at the same time highly organised and comparatively well paid according to current standards. This, however, was definitely a piece of emergency legislation passed as a direct result of the Miners' Strike of 1912, and not the result of deliberate or considered industrial policy.

The Trade Boards Act calls for somewhat longer explanation. It was modelled upon similar legislation which, first in Victoria and other States of Australia, and subsequently in many other countries, had been passed with a view to the elimination of the "sweating" system. Under it, Boards partly representative of employers and workers, and partly consisting of "appointed members" nominated by the State, were set up in a number of "sweated" trades, with power to fix minimum rates of wages for the various grades of workers employed. Although the procedure for the fixing and enforcement of minimum rates was exceedingly slow and cumbrous, although the inspection provided was quite inadequate, and although the policy pursued by the Boards was conservative in the extreme, the Act did good work, both in raising the wages of some of the worst-paid workers, especially women, and in stimulating Trade Union organisation. The Act was first applied to four trades—tailoring (of certain kinds only), paper-box making, lace-finishing, and certain kinds of chain-making. Its scope was slightly extended by Provisional Order procedure, and in 1918 a far more comprehensive measure became law, with a view to after-War conditions. The Trade Board principle was extended to a much larger number of badly organised or ill-paid trades, and the powers of the Trade Boards were also made more comprehensive and the procedure more expeditious. The Corn Production Act of 1917, it may be noted, already extended to agriculture a principle essentially the same as that of the Trade Boards Act; but the Agricultural Wages Board was subsequently destroyed by the Conservative Government, and is only now being restored by the Labour Government (June, 1924).

The employers during the post-War slump made many attempts to get the Trade Boards Acts either repealed or drastically restricted, and for a long time the starting of new Boards was stopped. But the Acts have survived these assaults and remain fully in operation to-day.

It would take us too far afield to deal with many other types of legislation which have affected Trade Unionism, and which have served to bring the Trade Unions into much closer relation to the State. Amongst them I can only mention the Workmen's Compensation Act and the Health Insurance Act, while I must say rather more about the development of Unemployment Insurance during the last few years.

Following upon the establishment of Employment Exchanges under the Labour Exchanges Act of 1909 the State, in 1911, applied the principle of compulsory insurance against unemployment to a group of industries of which the principal were engineering, shipbuilding, and building. The fund from which employment benefits were dispensed was a fund contributed in part by the State, in part by the employer, and in part by the workman through deductions from his wages made by the employer. Provision was made whereby this fund might be administered in certain cases through the Trade Unions themselves, and there was a further provision enabling a Trade Union which paid unemployment benefit on complying with certain conditions to secure from the State a refund of a certain proportion of the total sum spent on unemployment benefit, *i.e.*, the so-called " Ghent " system. In practice, the unemployment insurance provisions of the Act were largely worked through the Trade Unions, and a considerable number of Trade Unions in non-insured trades availed themselves of the rebates on their expenditure on unemployment benefit. Clearly the tendency of this Act was in the direction of making the Trade Union to some extent the administrative agent of the State, and the same tendency appeared also in the Health Section of the Insurance Act of 1911, under which most Trade Unions become Approved Societies for the purpose of administering State Benefits in case of sickness, etc.

During the War, Unemployment Insurance was extended to a number of fresh groups of munition workers, and in 1920 a comprehensive Act was passed, making the system nearly universal except for agricultural workers and domestic servants. The refund under the " Ghent " system was swept away; but the scheme, as a whole, continues to be administered largely through the Trade Unions. During the past few years of abnormal slump there has been a bewildering succession of Unemployment Insurance Acts altering contributions, benefits and methods of administration. These follow one another so fast that I shall attempt no summary of the position here. An important Bill, designed to put the system on a more permanent basis, is before Parliament at the present time.[1]

Section 3.—CONCLUSION

In the preceding parts of this book I have surveyed briefly the structure, the government, the internal problems, and the relations with employers and with the State, of the Trade Union movement. It now remains to say something of the wider ideals behind the movement, whether in the minds of its leaders or members, or in those of particular groups which, although numerically small, exercise an influence upon the framing of policy. I have already had occasion to mention, in passing, a few of those movements, because immediate Trade Union policy is naturally affected in a greater or less degree by the more distant ideals which animate the members of the great Trade Unions.

It cannot be said that the Trade Union movement in Great Britain is anything like so inclined to theorise about its beliefs as most of the Continental movements. It has grown up gradually, and in response to immediate necessities, and it bears all the marks of this growth and upbringing. It has adjusted itself slowly and painfully to most changing conditions, and has accumulated a vast mass of conservative tradition which is a source at once of strength and of weakness. It finds idealism and revolutionary theory difficult and largely alien to its temper, because its organisation has been so largely determined by purely utilitarian circumstances. Nevertheless, there is a growing mass of idealism and of theory in the Trade Union movement itself, even apart from those tendencies which affect Trade Unionism, though they do not arise directly out of it.

It is true that there was, in the middle of the last century, a body of theorists closely connected with the Trade Union movement, who had a definite, if a narrow, conception of the function of Trade Unionism. Mr. Frederic Harrison and the Positivist group, as well as Thomas Hughes and the Christian Socialists, fought hard for the freeing of Trade Unionism from artificial legal restrictions at a time when Labour combination was still commonly regarded as a crime, at least as soon as it produced any fruits in overt action. These men did great service to the Trade Unions in the fight for free combination from 1867 to 1876; but after 1880 their influence gradually waned. Christian Socialism died out, and the Positivists lost hold and interest, as their fundamental individualism made them less and less in harmony with the growing demands of Labour for legislative action. Indeed, from the time when the Trade Unions first began to turn their

[1] June, 1924.

attention to politics, this demand was made with increasing vigour. The coal miners, led by Alexander MacDonald, and the cotton operatives were foremost in the new movement; but on occasion they had most of the Trade Union world behind them. Even at the time when the influence of Mr. Harrison and his friends was at its height, the Trade Union leaders who relied so largely upon their help still remained opportunists, and supported or opposed State or industrial action without much conscious reference to any comprehensive theory of the function of Trade Unionism or of the State. Their administration of the Trade Union Movement was cautious and conservative in the extreme; but it did not acquire this caution from any constructive theory.

From the time of the Dock Strike of 1889 onwards the Trade Unions were to a considerable extent captured by the Socialists, and resolutions at Trade Union Congresses reflected clearly the aspirations of Fabianism and the Independent Labour Party. This process of permeation of the Trade Unions by I.L.P. Socialism continued almost unchallenged up to the beginning of the years of serious industrial unrest which date from 1911; but with the coming of industrial unrest, whatever its cause, new theories of social organisation and industrial action began to make themselves heard. In 1911 and 1912 it was of Syndicalism that we were told, and a considerable propaganda, based partly upon French Syndicalism and partly upon American Industrial Unionism, sprang up under the energetic leadership of Mr. Tom Mann. The wave of Sydnicalism, however, soon passed, and when it receded there were left two policies which seemed to show signs of greater vitality upon the soil of Great Britain. The first of these was Marxian Industrial Unionism, the second, Guild Socialism, or National Guilds.

Marxian Industrial Unionism had been in the field before the wave of Syndicalism came to this country, but it failed to make any considerable headway until the industrial conditions became favourable to it. When the wave of Syndicalism receded, Industrial Unionism of this type did not recede with it. The new situation in the Trade Union world caused the Industrial Unionists, or many of them, to modify their outlook, and their propaganda in its new form began to attract many adherents. The earlier Industrial Unionists had begun with the assumption that the old Trade Unionism was of no use, and ought to be scrapped completely and absolutely, and that the only way to salvation was the foundation of a new Unionism on a definite class-war basis. They looked for " One Big Union," divided into " Locals " by districts and into industrial sections according to the various industries, and forming a part of a world-wide movement—the Industrial Workers of the World. The Syndicalists, on the other hand, were for the most part amalgamationists, and urged, not the scrapping of the old Unions, but their amalgamation along industrial lines, with a view ultimately to the formation of a great class organisation for Labour as a whole. The Industrial Unionism which was left behind when Syndicalism disappeared had largely adopted these tenets, or was at least prepared to work inside the existing Unions for amalgamation as a step towards the completer industrial structure which it desired.

Broadly speaking, the theory of the Industrial Unionists was this. They regarded the State in all its forms as the expression of Capitalism and as existing for the protection of property, and accordingly they desired its complete destruction. They looked forward instead to a Society administered by the workers through their industrial organisations. On the purely industrial side they demanded the complete control of industry for the working-class organisations, and were not prepared either for any accommodation with Capitalism or for any sharing of control with the State. On the methods of the transition to the new system of Society they held varying views. They agreed, indeed, that industrial organisation and industrial action were the principal things; but some of them believed that working-class political action was necessary for the purpose of hampering and of ultimately abolishing the Capitalist State, while others held that political action should be shunned completely by the working class, which should confine itself entirely to the industrial weapon. Throughout, Industrial Unionists of both schools based their doctrine upon Marxian economics, upon the materialist conception of history above all else. They were few, but their indirect influence was considerable, particularly inside the National Union of Railwaymen, in the shop stewards' movement, and among the South Wales miners.

National Guildsmen, or Guild Socialists, agreed in many respects with the Marxian Industrial Unionists, but had also important points of disagreement. Whereas the Industrial Unionists put their main emphasis on the need for revolutionary action to destroy the State, and to make the Unions the sole organs of administration, the Guild Socialists were concerned less with the political aspects of revolution and more with the problem of building up the Trade Union movement into an organisation capable of winning and exercising real and positive control over industry. They agreed with the Industrial Unionists in preaching solidarity, to be attained partly through union by industry instead of by craft. But they stressed also the need for the Unions by experiment and participation to learn how to exercise control and prepare for the assumption of full responsibility in advance of the day of its attainment. Their propaganda was largely directed to pressing the need and devising schemes for amalgamation on " industrial " lines, and to pointing out possible next steps for the Trade Unions in connection with the winning of control, particularly in the workshops. There were differences of opinion and policy among them, just as among the Industrial Unionists. Generally they tended, without sacrificing their idealism, to a possibilist outlook, and to pay most attention to the " next steps," while keeping the ultimate goal in view. Their influence in the Trade Union movement was less direct and concentrated than that of the Industrial Unionists, but their propaganda had a considerable effect, particularly in the railway and engineering industries and in the Post Office. They also considerably influenced the policy of the Socialist Societies, especially the I.L.P.

These two tendencies between them never commanded the conscious adherence of more than an infinitesimal fraction of the workers in the Trade Unions, most of whom are always content to face immediate problems as they arise, without considering more ultimate issues. On points of immediate policy, however, both tendencies came to represent a good deal of what the younger active Trade Unionists were thinking. Trade Unionists, without diminishing their attention to questions of wages, hours, and general conditions of labour, were already, before the War, coming to think more of wider questions of policy, and endeavouring to secure a share in the control of industry and industrial policy. This was particularly marked in the industries principally affected by the tendency to union by industry. During the War the shop stewards' movement embodied a marked expression of it, while similar rank and file movements appeared on the railways, in the mines, and in other industries.

After the Russian Revolution, or at least when the events in Russia came to be widely studied, the left-wing movements entered on a new phase. Industrial Unionism and the left wings of the shop stewards and of the Guild Socialists went over to a Communism based on Russian precept and example. The slump, by making the conditions unfavourable for industrial action, helped to give this movement a predominantly political tendency, and to divorce it from industrial realities. The political quarrels between the Labour Party and the new Communist Party found their way into the Trade Unions, and prevented the birth there of an industrial policy based on post-War conditions and backed unitedly by the keener elements.

TRADE UNIONISM AND THE STATE

Guild Socialism meanwhile, having lost its left wing to the Communists, launched out into the experiments of the producing Guilds in the building and other industries, usually with the more or less keen backing of the Trade Unions concerned. But the economic conditions were as unfavourable to Trade Union action in the productive field as to strike action, and while many of these Guilds have survived and done excellent work within a limited sphere, none of them has reached, or is likely to reach, dimensions which in any way menace capitalist supremacy or control. The whole Guild movement, while it retains its separate identity and has secured the endorsement of the Trades Union Congress, is now making its contribution less directly as a separate school of thought than through its action on many different schools of thought and on the policies and programmes of the Trade Unions. It is largely the fruit of Guild activity that the Labour demand for nationalisation of industry has changed its character and come to connote not bureaucratic administration by the State, but democratic control as well as public ownership. The Bill presented by the Miners' Federation to the Coal Commission in 1919, embodying a definite scheme of workers' control, was the outward sign of this changed objective.[1]

It is impossible for me in this book to enter further into this big subject of workers' control. I have written much about it elsewhere; it is, to my mind, the idea that gives inspiration to the forward movement of Trade Unionism. But that is a personal view, and I am trying to keep this book to its limited purpose of describing the movement as it exists without entering at large into any views of what it might be. Here, then, I leave the whole matter, only giving the readers, in my notes on books,[2] the means of following up for themselves the wider questions of policy for which this volume only professes to supply the indispensable groundwork of fact and circumstance.

[1] This Bill, brought forward again by the Labour Party, was rejected in Parliament in May, 1924, by the united votes of Conservatives and Liberals.
[2] See p. xiii.

STATISTICAL APPENDICES

I. *Membership of All Trade Unions and of Trade Unions Affiliated to the Trades Union Congress.*

Year	Total Number of Societies.		Number of Societies represented at Congress.		Total Membership of All (in thousands).		Membership of Trade Unions represented at Congress (in thousands).	Membership of Trades Councils represented at Congress (in thousands).
	Trade Unions.	Trades Councils.	Trade Unions.	Trades Councils.	Trade Unions.	Trades Councils.		
1866	—	—	81	13	—	—	110	89
1867	—	—	104	11	—	—	155	38
1868	—	—	18	11	—	—	50	64
1869	—	—	25	12	—	—	250	—
1871	—	—	34	11	—	—	289	—
1872	—	—	44	8	—	—	270	—
1873	—	—	88	20	—	—	509	226
1875 (Jan.)	—	—	83	24	—	—	594	101
1875 (Oct.)	—	—	87	22	—	—	414	117
1876	—	—	91	22	—	—	455	122
1877	—	—	93	19	—	—	565	130
1878	—	—	92	22	—	—	486	136
1879	—	—	73	19	—	—	412	110
1880	—	—	89	16	—	—	381	95
1882	—	—	103	23	—	—	404	103
1883	—	—	114	21	—	—	467	94
1884	—	—	95	21	—	—	488	110
1885	—	—	110	27	—	—	500	131
1886	—	—	98	23	—	—	515	123
1887	—	—	104	27	—	—	561	135
1888	—	—	109	29	—	—	568	159
1889	—	—	145	26	—	—	687	176
1890	—	—	268	37	—	—	1,593	334
1891	—	—	274	36	—	—	1,094	260
1892	1,208	—	251	37	1,501	—	1,155	496
1893	1,255	—	198	28	1,479	—	721	150
1894	1,295	150	165	27[1]	1,439	698	1,015	66[1]
1895	1,311	154	170	—	1,407	691	1,000	—
1896	1,317	151	178	—	1,493	701	1,076	—
1897	1,337	169	180	—	1,669	708	1,093	—
1898	1,309	173	188	—	1,702	714	1,184	—
1899	1,304	179	181	—	1,861	706	1,200	—
1900	1,302	184	184	—	1,972	753	1,250	—

[1] Trades Councils were excluded from the Trades Union Congress after 1894.

STATISTICAL APPENDICES

Membership of All Trade Unions and of Trade Unions Affiliated to the Trades Union Congress—continued.

Year.	Total Number of Societies.		Number of Societies represented at Congress.		Total Membership of All		Membership of Trade Unions represented at Congress	Membership of Trades Councils represented at Congress
	Trade Unions.	Trades Councils.	Trade Unions.	Trades Councils.	Trade Unions.	Trades Councils.	(in thousands).	(in thousands).
					(in thousands).			
1901	1,297	189	191	—	1,979	794	1,200	—
1902	1,267	195	198	—	1,966	812	1,400	—
1903	1,255	212	204	—	1,942	847	1,500	—
1904	1,229	233	212	—	1,911	873	1,423	—
1905	1,228	239	205	—	1,934	902	1,541	—
1906	1,250	247	226	—	2,129	943	1,555	—
1907	1,243	253	236	—	2,425	987	1,700	—
1908	1,218	258	214	—	2,389	1,021	1,777	—
1909	1,199	258	219	—	2,369	996	1,705	—
1910	1,195	252	212	—	2,446	1,010	1,648	—
1911	1,204	247	202	—	3,019	1,176	1,662	—
1912	1,149	—	201	—	3,288	—	2,002	—
1913	1,135	326[1]	207	—	4,189	1,490[1]	2,232	—
1914	1,123	—	—	—	4,192	—	—	—
1915	1,106	—	215	—	4,405	—	2,682	—
1916	1,115	—	227	—	4,687	—	2,851	—
1917	1,234	—	235	—	5,553	—	3,082	—
1918	1,254	—	262	—	6,664	—	4,532	—
1919	1,346	—	266	—	8,081	—	5,284	—
1920	1,425	—	215	—	8,493	—	6,505	—
1921	1,296	520[1]	213	—	6,793	2,870[1]	6,418	—
1922	1,190[1]	496[1]	206	—	5,580[1]	2,481[1]	5,129	—
1923	—	—	—	—	—	—	4,369	—

[1] Excluding societies with headquarters in the Irish Free State. Trade Unions thus excluded had 180,000 members in 1920.

II. Membership of Trade Unions by Industries at Various Dates.

Group.	1892.	1900.	1910.	1913.	1918.	1920.	1921.	1922.
Agriculture	34	—	4	22	125	211	149	93
Mining and Quarrying	315	524	730	920	998	1,155	949	844
Pottery and Glass	14	21	16	—	—	55	47	40
Metal, Engineering and Shipbuilding	278	342	369	547	962	1,148	1,004	839
Cotton	156	190	275	372	403	457	429	398
Other Textiles	48	57	104	152	306	365	293	256
Leather	6	7	5	—	—	25	15	12
Clothing	83	67	67	107	213	238	180	164
Food, Drink and Tobacco	15	17	19	—	—	40	34	30
Woodworking and Furnishing	32	40	39	61	86	122	103	83
Paper and Printing	45	57	74	85	144	221	194	180
Building and Contracting	160	254	156	250	326	572	470	377
Railways	46	81	116	327	524	618	507	443
Other Transport	107	105	126	369	475	645	493	446
Banking and Insurance	} 6	15	56	} 98	—	97	89	82
Distribution, Clerks, etc.					—	375	195	155
Public Administration	22	46	98	239	361	457	397	364
Teaching	—	—	—	122	172	207	200	206
Entertainment and Sports	—	—	—	—	—	52	45	36
Miscellaneous	—	—	—	—	—	79	59	49
General Labour	101	111	118	375	1,081	1,354	760	483
TOTALS	1,501	1,971	2,446	4,189	6,664	8,493	6,612	5,579

III. Federations of Trade Unions.

Group.	Approximate Membership of All Trade Unions in Group.[1]	Approximate Membership represented by Federation.	Name of Federation and Date of Formation.	Remarks.
Coal Mining	850	800	Miners' Fed. of G. B. (1889).	Virtually a single union.
Iron and Steel	120	100	Iron and Steel Trades Confed. (1917).	Virtually a single union.
Engineering and Shipbuilding.	650	—	Engineering and Shipbuilding Trades Fed. (1889).	Unrepresentative and ineffective.
Cotton	400	300	United Textile Factory Workers' Ass. (1883).	Mainly for political purposes; does not negotiate.
Wool and Worsted.	100	80	N. Ass. of Unions in the Textile Trades (1917).	Loose, but negotiates for the whole industry.
Paper and Printing.	180	180	N. Printing and Kindred Trades Fed. (1891).	Rather loose.
Building	350	300	N. Fed. of Building Trades Operatives (1917).	Strong and effective as a negotiating body.
Transport	450	360	N. Transport Workers' Fed. (1911)	Now being reconstructed.
Professional and Administrative.	650	300	N. Fed. of Professional, Technical, Administrative and Supervisory Workers (1920).	Largely propagandist.
Civil Service	300	200	Civil Service Confed.	Now being reconstructed.
General Labour.	700	700	N. Fed. of General Workers (1917)	Fairly effective in matters of common concern.

[1] In some cases Federations include Unions, or sections of Unions, classified under another group. The two columns of figures are not always fully comparable.

IV. Women in Trade Unions at Various Dates.

	1900.	1910.	1913.	1918.	1920.	1922.
Cotton	98	156	214	261	293	254
Other Textiles	13	27	46	169	202	119
Clothing	4	8	25	117	127	70
Commerce and Finance	2	6	21	105	131	50
Public Administration	—	6	23	87	94	—
Printing and Paper	1	3	6	41	72	49
Teaching	—	—	65	115	134	143
General Labour	—	7	23	199	166	49
Miscellaneous	—	—	—	—	—	—
Total (including other occupations)	123[1]	221[1]	433	1,228	1,340	868

[1] Not including teachers.

V. International Trade Union Organisation.

Country.	International Federation of Trade Unions. Affiliated Membership.			Other Trade Unions Abroad. Membership.		
	1912.	1921.	1922.	1912.	1921.	1922.
Argentine	—	75	—	—	248	—
Australia	—	—	—	—	684	700
Austria	428	1,080	1,050	—	50	—
Belgium	116	698	619	—	220	—
Bulgaria	—	15	15	—	20	—
Canada	—	165	118	—	100	150
Chile	—	—	—	65	18	—
China	—	—	—	—	300	—
Czecho-Slovakia	—	828	400	—	1,000	400
Denmark	107	243	233	—	110	—
Esthonia	—	—	—	—	30	—
Finland	21	—	—	—	50	—
France	387	756	758	—	300	350
Germany	2,553	8,417	8,576	500	4,000	—
Great Britain	874	6,560	4,369	2,414	—	—
Greece	—	170	—	40	—	—

STATISTICAL APPENDICES

International Trade Union Organisation—continued.

Country.	International Federation of Trade Unions. Affiliated Membership.			Other Trade Unions Abroad. Membership.		
	1912.	1921.	1922.	1912.	1921.	1922.
Holland	62	224	201	—	440	—
Hungary	112	153	203	—	190	—
India	—	—	—	—	500	—
Ireland	—	—	—	50	—	250
Italy	321	1,200	401	—	900	1,000
Japan	—	—	—	—	110	—
Latvia	—	23	12	—	28	—
Luxembourg	—	21	12	—	5	—
Mexico	—	—	—	—	710	—
New Zealand	—	—	—	—	83	—
Norway	61	96	—	—	—	96
Palestine	—	—	8	—	—	—
Peru	—	25	25	—	—	—
Poland	—	365	411	—	460	—
Portugal	—	—	—	—	100	—
Rumania	10	—	36	—	170	—
Russia	—	—	—	—	6,857	5,000
South Africa	—	50	50	—	40	—
Spain	100	240	240	—	1,000	—
Sweden	86	226	293	—	70	—
Switzerland	86	313	152	—	125	—
United States	2,055	—	—	—	5,179	3,700
Yugo-Slavia	16[1]	50	66	—	200	—

[1] Bosnia, Croatia and Serbia.

NOTE.—Some of the above figures should be used with a good deal of caution. They are, however, the best I can get.

VI. *International Trade Federations.*

	Affiliated Membership (in Thousands).		Affiliated British Membership (in Thousands).
	1912.	1922.	1921.
Bookbinders	50	167	24
Building Workers.	419	1,144	—
Carpenters	84	113	—
Clerical, Commercial and Technical Employees.	?	825	100
Clothing Workers.	102	376	128
Diamond Workers	15	18	0·3
General Factory Workers	298	1,787	1,277
Food and Drink Trades.	69	567	—
Furriers	?	24	—
Glass Workers	29	135	23
Hairdressers	5	11	—
Hatters	33	57	8
Hotel, etc., Workers	21	149	27
Land Workers	—	875	210
Leather Workers	106	370	71
Lithographers	36	46	10
Metal Workers	1,106	3,205	513
Miners	?	2,001	900
Musicians	—	53	18
Painters	72	87	—
Postal Workers	?	511	80
Printers	137	181	21
Public Services	72	436	80
Stone Workers	75	147	—
Textile Workers	?	1,726	413
Tobacco Workers.	50	179	5
Transport Workers	882	2,155	650
Woodworkers	393	831	190

VII. National Labour Party.
Membership (in Thousands).

	Trade Unions.		Trades Councils and Local Labour Parties. No.	Socialist Societies.		Total.	General Elections.		
	No.	Membership.		No.	Membership.		Year.	Labour Vote (Thousands).	Members Returned.
1900–1	41	353	7	3	23	376	1900	63	2
1901–2	65	455	21	2	14	469			
1902–3	127	847	49	2	14	861			
1903–4	165	956	76	2	14	970			
1904–5	158	855	73	2	15	900			
1905–6	158	904	73	2	17	921	1906	323	29
1906–7	176	975	83	2	21	998			
1907	181	1,050	92	2	22	1,072			
1908	176	1,127	133	2	27	1,159			
1909	172	1,451	155	2	31	1,486			
1910	151	1,394	148	2	31	1,431	1910 {Jan. Dec.	506 371	40 42
1911	141	1,502	149	2	31	1,539			
1912	130	1,858	146	2	31	1,895			
1913	*	*	158	2	33	*			
1914	101	1,572	179	2	33	1,612			
1915	111	2,054	177	2	33	2,093			
1916	119	2,171	199	3	42	2,220			
1917	123	2,415	239	3	47	2,465			
1918	131	2,960	389	4	53	3,013	1918	2,245	57
1919	126	3,464	418	7	47	3,511			
1920	122	4,318	492	5	42	4,360			
1921	116	3,974	456	5	37	4,010			
1922	108	3,279	547	5	32	3,310	1922	4,237	142
1923	127	3,277	582	5	33	3,310	1923	4,348	191

* Owing to the operation of the Osborne Judgment it was impossible to compile membership statistics for 1913.

VIII. Income, Expenditure, and Funds of 100 Principal Unions.
A.—Pre-War.

Year.	Membership at end of Year.	Income.		Expenditure.		Funds at end of Year.	
	No.	Amount. £	Per Member. s. d.	Amount. £	Per Member. s. d.	Amount. £	Per Member. s. d.
1904	1,207,086	2,129,423	35 3½	2,055,528	34 0¾	4,713,245	78 1
1905	1,226,007	2,235,040	36 5½	2,081,924	33 11½	4,866,361	79 4½
1906	1,313,494	2,371,306	36 1¼	1,987,088	30 1½	5,259,579	80 1
1907	1,478,257	2,528,365	34 2½	2,082,575	28 2	5,705,369	77 2¼
1908	1,448,755	2,777,974	38 1	3,243,675	44 5¾	5,239,668	71 10
1909	1,445,080	2,595,265	35 11	2,716,504	37 7¼	5,118,429	70 10
1910	1,480,993	2,727,880	36 10	2,650,239	35 9½	5,196,070	70 2
1911	1,830,278	2,964,842	32 4¾	2,519,865	27 6½	5,641,047	61 7¾
1912	2,011,017	3,249,048	32 3¾	3,841,694	38 2½	5,048,401	50 2½
1913	2,382,604	3,619,804	30 4½	2,927,095	24 6¾	5,741,110	48 2¼

Income, Expenditure, and Funds of Registered Trade Unions.
B.—Post-War.

Year.	Number of Registered Unions.	Membership at End of Year (Thousands).	Income.		Expenditure.		Funds.	
			Amount (Thousands).	Per Member.	Amount (Thousands).	Per Member.	Amount (Thousands).	Per Member.
			£	s. d.	£	s. d.	£	s. d.
1913	588	3,249	4,554	28 0	2,349	14 5½	6,513	40 1
1919	609	6,693	9,723	29 0½	8,686	25 9	16,045	47 11½
1920	620	7,092	12,963	36 6½	12,883	36 4	15,989	45 1
1921	524	5,454	21,065	77 3	26,004	95 4	10,815	39 7½
1922	514	4,506	15,301	67 11	16,325	72 5½	9,861	39 4

NOTE.—These two tables are not fully comparable, as an examination of the two sets of figures given for 1913 will show. Registered Unions are of all sorts; the 100 principal Unions included a large proportion of societies of skilled workers, with high contributions and rates of benefit.

IX. *Expenditure of 100 Principal Trade Unions Analysed.*
A.—Pre-War.

Year.	Dispute Benefit.		Unemployment Benefit.		Other Benefits and Grants.		Working and Miscellaneous Expenses.	
	Amount.	Percentage of Total Expenditure.	Amount.	Percentage of Total Expenditure.	Amount.	Percentage of Total Expenditure.	Amount.	Percentage of Total Expenditure.
	£		£		£		£	
1904	119,129	5·8	660,273	32·1	849,687	41·3	426,439	20·8
1905	216,480	10·4	528,642	25·4	903,676	43·4	433,126	20·8
1906	157,589	8·0	428,546	21·7	926,222	46·8	465,731	23·5
1907	143,355	6·9	468,922	22·5	981,940	47·2	488,358	23·4
1908	608,192	18·8	1,030,094	31·8	1,068,837	32·9	536,552	16·5
1909	160,659	5·9	952,500	35·1	1,071,385	39·4	531,960	19·6
1910	353,232	13·3	702,973	26·5	1,066,865	40·3	527,169	19·9
1911	318,559	12·7	456,736	18·1	1,161,755	46·1	582,815	23·1
1912	1,379,713	35·9	602,335	15·7	1,151,700	30·0	707,946	18·4
1913	302,985	10·4	493,582	16·9	1,335,309	45·6	795,219	27·1
Average 10 years	375,989	14·4	632,460	24·2	1,051,738	40·3	549,532	21·1

Expenditure of Registered Trade Unions Analysed.[1]
B.—Post-War.

	Dispute Benefit. £000.	Percentage of Total.	Unemployment Benefit. £000.	Percentage of Total.	Other Benefits and Grants. £000.	Percentage of Total.	Working and Miscellaneous Expenses. £000.	Percentage of Total.	Political Fund. £000.	Percentage of Total.
1913	447	12·5	405	11·3	1,376	38·4	1,343	37·5	7	0·2
1919	2,132	24·7	934	10·8	1,650	19·2	3,766	43·7	113	1·3
1920	3,219	25·5	1,406	11·1	1,768	14·0	6,050	47·9	185	1·4
1921	3,427	18·7	7,318	40·0	2,164	11·8	5,225	28·4	160	0·8
1922	1,428	12·9	2,910	26·4	2,045	18·5	4,351	39·5	268	2·4

[1] See note on p. 163.

X. *Pre-War Expenditure of Certain Trade Unions Analysed.*
A.—*Unions of Skilled Workers.*

Name of Union.	Expenditure Total, 1913.	Expenditure on Management, 1913.	Proportion of total spent on Management, 1913.	Expenditure per Head, 1913.			Expenditure on Management per Head, 1913.		
	£	£	Per cent.	£	s.	d.	£	s.	d.
Amalgamated Society of Carpenters and Joiners.	237,950	41,800	17·6	2	14	3	0	9	6½
Friendly Society of Ironfounders.	123,352	12,549	9·8	4	13	10	0	9	4½
London Society of Compositors.	52,567	4,824	9·2	4	10	0	0	8	3½
Amalgamated Society of Engineers.	403,378	66,387	16·5	2	9	2	0	8	2
Steam Engine Makers	30,054	5,587	18·6	1	15	11½	0	7	8½
Amalgamated Association of Operative Cotton Spinners, etc.	90,195	15,881	17·6	3	15	10	0	13	4
Total	937,496	147,028	15·7	—			—		

B.—*Unions consisting largely of Less Skilled Workers.*

Workers' Union	36,467	14,923	40·9	0	8	0	0	3	2½
National Union of General Workers.	48,619	29,845	61·3	0	7	4	0	4	6½
Dock, Wharf, Riverside, and General Workers' Union.	24,543	18,241	74·3	0	10	2½	0	7	7
National Union of Railwaymen.	116,573[1]	72,670[1]	62·4[1]	0	8	8½[1]	0	5	5[1]
Total	226,202	135,679	59·9	—			—		

[1] The year of the amalgamation.

XI. Strikes and Lock-outs, 1909—1923.

(Figures from *Ministry of Labour Gazette*.)

Year.	Number of Disputes beginning in Year.	Number of Workpeople involved in Disputes *beginning* in Year.		Aggregate Duration in Working Days of *all* Disputes *in progress* during Year.	Chief Strikes and Lock-outs of Year.
		Directly.	Indirectly.		
1909	422	168,000	129,000	2,687,000	—
1910	521	384,000	130,000	9,867,000	—
1911	872	824,000	128,000	10,155,000	Seamen, Dockers, Railwaymen, Cotton Operatives.
1912	834	1,232,000	230,000	40,890,000	Miners, Dockers.
1913	1,459	498,000	166,000	9,804,000	Dublin General Strike.
1914	972	326,000	121,000	9,878,000	London Builders, Yorks. Miners.
1915	672	401,000	47,000	2,953,000	—
1916	532	235,000	41,000	2,446,000	South Wales Miners.
1917	730	575,000	297,000	5,647,000	Engineers.
1918	1,165	923,000	193,000	5,875,000	—
1919	1,352	2,400,000	191,000	34,969,000	Railwaymen.
1920	1,607	1,779,000	153,000	26,567,000	Miners.
1921	763	1,770,000	31,000	85,872,000	Miners, Cotton Operatives.
1922	576	512,000	40,000	19,850,000	Engineers, Shipyard Workers.
1923	611	336,000	61,000	10,642,000	Boilermakers.

XII. IMPORTANT TRADE UNION AMALGAMATIONS

(1) Bookbinders, N. U. With (44), formed N. U. of Printing, Bookbinding and Paper Workers.
(2) Bricklayers, Op. S. With (3) and (55), formed Am. U. of Building Trade Workers.
(3) Bricklayers, United Op. (Manchester). With (2) and (55), formed Am. U. of Building Trade Workers.
(4) Builders' Labourers, "Altogether." Formed by (5) and branches of other Socs.
(5) Builders' Labourers, N. Ass. of. Joined in forming (4).
(6) Builders' Labourers' U., United. Now N. Builders' Labourers and Constructional Workers' Soc.
(7) Building and Monumental Workers of Scotland. Formed by (38) and the Scottish Masons and Granite Workers.
(8) Cabinet Makers, Am. U. Joined (9), and now merged in (69).
(9) Carpenters and Joiners, Am. S. Merged in (69).
(10) Carpenters and Joiners, Ass. S. Joined (9), and now merged in (69).
(11) Carpenters and Joiners, Gen. U. Merged in (69).
(12) Civil Service Clerical A. Formed by Clerical Officers' A. and Civil Service U.
(13) Clothiers' Ops., Am. U. Merged in (24) and subsequently in (56).
(14) Co-operative Employees, Am. U. Joined (67) to form (15).
(15) Distributive and Allied Workers, N. U. Formed by (14) and (67)
(16) Dock Labourers, N. U. Merged in (63).
(17) Dock Labourers, Scottish U. Merged in (63).
(18) Dock, Wharf, Riverside and Gen. Workers' U. Merged in (63).
(19) Dyers, N. S. Merged in (60).
(20) Engineering U., Am. Formed by (21), (29), (36), (51), (52), (61) and other Us.
(21) Engineers, Am. S. Merged in (20).
(22) Fawcett A. Merged in (43).
(23) Foundry Workers, N. U. Formed by (33), (34) and Am. S. of Coremakers.
(24) Garment Workers, United. Merged in (56).
(25) Gas, Municipal and Gen. Workers' U. Merged in (27).
(26) Gasworkers and Gen. Labourers' U. Merged in (27).
(27) General and Municipal Workers, N. U. of. Incorporating (25), (26), (35), (39), (68), and other Us.

STATISTICAL APPENDICES 169

(28) Horticultural Workers, N.U. Merged in N.U. of Agricultural Workers.
(29) Instrument Makers, Am. S. Merged in (20).
(30) Iron and Steel Trades A., British. Formed by (31) to take over members of constituent societies.
(31) Iron and Steel Trades A., Confed. Formed by (32), (53), (54), and other Us.
(32) Iron and Steel Workers, Ass. Merged in (31).
(33) Ironfounders, Friendly S. Merged in (23).
(34) Ironmoulders, Ass. of Scotland. Merged in (23).
(35) Labour, N. Am. U. of. Merged in (27).
(36) Machine Workers, United A. Merged in (20).
(37) Marine Workers, Am. U. Formed by (49) and (50).
(38) Masons, Scottish Op. Merged in (7).
(39) Municipal Employees' A. Merged in (27).
(40) Postal and Telegraph Clerks' A. Merged in (43).
(41) Postmen's Fed. Merged in (43).
(42) Post Office Engineering U. Formed by Engineering and Stores A. and engineering members of Am. Telephone Employees.
(43) Post Office Workers, U. of. Formed by (22), (40), and (41).
(44) Printing and Paper Workers, N. U. Formed by Printers' Warehousemen and Cutters, and N. U. Paper Mill Workers, joined with (1) to form N. U. of Printing, Bookbinding and Paper Workers.
(45) Quarrymen, N. Wales U. Merged in (63).
(46) Railwaymen, N. U. Formed by (47), (48), and Signalmen and Pointsmen U.
(47) Railway Servants, Am. S. Merged in (46).
(48) Railway Workers' U., Gen. Merged in (46).
(49) Seafarers' U., Brit. Merged in (37).
(50) Ships' Stewards, Cooks, etc., U. Merged in (37).
(51) Smiths and Strikers, U. K. S. Merged in (20).
(52) Steam Engine Makers' S. Merged in (20).
(53) Steel and Iron Workers, Am. S. Merged in (31).
(54) Steel Smelters, Brit. Merged in (31).
(55) Stonemasons, Op. S. Joined with (2) and (3).
(56) Tailors' and Garment Workers' U. Formed by (24) and (57).
(57) Tailors, Scottish S. Merged in (56).
(58) Textile Workers, Am. S. Formed by several small Unions in Silk Trades.
(59) Textile Workers, Gen. U. Merged in (60).

(60) Textile Workers, N. U.   Formed by (19,) (59), and other Us.
(61) Toolmakers, Am. S.   Merged in (20).
(62) Tramway and Vehicle Workers' Am. A.   Merged in (66) and now in (63).
(63) Transport and Gen. Workers' U.   Formed by (16), (17), (18), (66), and other Us.
(64) Vehicle Workers, London and Prov. U. of Licensed.   Merged in (66) and then in (63).
(65) Vehicle Workers, N. U.   Merged in (63).
(66) Vehicle Workers, United.   Formed by (62) and (64), and now merged in (63).
(67) Warehouse and General Workers' U.   Merged in (15).
(68) Women Workers, N. Fed.   Merged in (27).
(69) Woodworkers, Am. S.   Formed by (9) and (11), incorporating (8) and (10).

XIII. A Summary of Trade Union Organisation arranged in Occupational Groups

(Membership figures are in all cases only approximate)

A.—*Mining*

In all the coalfields, the main body of mine-workers is organised in the district Miners' Association, affiliated to the Miners' Federation of Great Britain (800,000). The M.F.G.B. includes eighteen affiliated district associations in the following areas (approximately in order of size): Yorkshire (140,000), South Wales (130,000), Durham (120,000), Scotland (80,000), Lancashire and Cheshire (65,000), Midland Federation (60,000), Northumberland (40,000), Derbyshire (32,000), Notts. (25,000), North Wales (10,000), Cumberland (9,000), Leicestershire (8,000), South Derbyshire (6,000), Somersetshire (4,000), Cleveland (3,000), Forest of Dean (2,500), Bristol (2,000), Kent (1,600). The M.F.G.B. also includes the National Union of Cokemen and Bye-Product Workers (4,200), and a number of district associations of colliery enginemen (15,000).

Outside the M.F.G.B., a number of district mining crafts have societies of their own in the various coalfields. Thus there are separate societies of colliery enginemen in Scotland (4,000), South Wales, and other districts. The General Federation of Colliery Firemen, Examiners, and Deputies' Associations (12,000), links up associations in nearly all the coalfields. There are also the N. F. of Colliery Mechanics and the N. F. of Colliery Under-Managers.

Other societies connected with mining and quarrying, outside the M.F.G.B., include the following: Cumberland Iron Ore Miners' Ass. (5,000), N. U. of Quarry Workers and Settmakers (8,000), Salt

Workers' Federation (3,000). The general workers' unions have a few members working on the surface of the coal-mines, and many more in tin, lead and other mines and in the quarries. The North Wales Quarrymen's Union (8,000) has recently (1923) amalgamated with the Transport and General Workers' Union. The Am. Engineering Union, the Electrical Trades Union, the N. Am. U. of Enginemen and other craftsmen's societies have also members in the mines.

B.—Railways

By far the largest union is the *National Union of Railwaymen* (350,000), formed in 1913 by the amalgamation of the old Am. S. of Railway Servants with two smaller societies. The N.U.R. aims at organising all grades of railway workers. The locomotive grades (drivers, firemen and cleaners) are divided between the N.U.R. and the *Ass. S. of Locomotive Engineers and Firemen* (60,000), the majority belonging to the latter. The clerical and supervisory grades are mainly organised in the *Railway Clerks' Association* (60,000), though the N.U.R. has a small membership in these grades. The workers in the locomotive and carriage shops are divided fairly equally between the N.U.R. and the various craft unions in the metal and wood working trades (A.E.U., A.S.W., etc.). The general workers' unions have also a small membership in the shops.

C.—Transport

By far the largest society is the *Transport and General Workers' Union* (300,000), formed in 1921 by the amalgamation of most of the unions organising dock and road transport workers. Outside this union there remain only local waterside unions, such as the *Am. Stevedores* (6,000) in London, and the *Coal Trimmers* (2,000) in Cardiff, and three fairly large unions of vehicle workers, the *United Road Transport Workers* (Manchester), the *Liverpool Carters and Motormen*, and the *Scottish Horse and Motormen*, each with about 10,000 members. Some railway carters are in the N.U.R., and some other carters in the Distributive Workers' Union, and in the Unions of General Workers, which have also members at some of the docks.

The seafarers are still organised separately. Their largest society is the *N. Sailors' and Firemen's Union* (60,000), which is in competition with the *Am. Marine Workers' Union* (12,000). Engineers are divided between the *Marine Engineers' Ass.* (?) and the A.E.U. Officers have separate associations of their own.

Shipping and transport clerks are divided between the T. and G.W.U. and the *Shipping Guild* (2,000). Air pilots and mechanics are in the *British Federation of Air Pilots* (?).

The formation of the T. and G.W.U. and the secession of the N.S.F.U. have deprived the *National Transport Workers' Federation* of its former importance. Attempts are now being made to reconstruct it on a broader basis, so as to include railwaymen as well as other transport workers.

D.—*Iron and Steel*

The principal body is the *Iron and Steel Trades Confederation* (103,000), which is virtually a single union (see p. 83). Outside the Confederation is the *N. Union of Blast Furnacemen* (20,000). The mechanics, bricklayers, etc., in iron and steel works are mostly in the unions of their crafts. Enginemen are divided between the Confederation and the N. Am. Union of Enginemen. The general workers' unions have a considerable membership in the industry.

E.—*Engineering and Shipbuilding*

This industry has long been the chosen home of overlapping craft unions and inter-union disputes. The position has been improved by recent amalgamations, such as the formation in 1920, of the *Am. Engineering Union* (256,000), which absorbed the old Am. Soc. of Engineers, the Steam Engine Makers, the Toolmakers, the Machine Workers, the Instrument Makers, the Smiths and Strikers, the Brassfinishers, and some smaller societies. But overlapping the A.E.U. there still remain the *United Patternmakers' Ass.* (12,000), *N. Soc. of Coppersmiths* (3,000), *Associated Blacksmiths' Soc.* (14,000), and a number of others. Three foundry unions (Friendly S. of Ironfounders, Ass. Iron Moulders of Scotland, and Coremakers) joined in forming the *N. Union of Foundry Workers* (40,000); but outside this body remain the *Am. Moulders' Union* (3,000), *Central Ironmoulders' Ass.* (7,000), and the *Stove, Grate and Light Metal Workers* (4,000). Other important societies include the *N. Soc. of Brass and Metal Mechanics* (20,000), *N. Union of Steel Metal Workers* (14,000).

Vehicle builders are divided among three unions, *N. Union of Vehicle Builders* (22,000), *Am. Soc. of Railway Vehicle Builders* (8,000) and the *Wheelwrights, Smiths and Kindred Trades Union* (8,000).

In the electrical trades, the leading union is the *Electrical Trades Union* (25,000). Power station engineers are divided between the E.T.U. and the *Electrical Power Engineers' Ass.* (4,000). The E.T.U. is negotiating for amalgamation with the *N. Am. Union of Enginemen and Electrical Workers* (22,000), which has members in mines, iron and steel works, transport and many other services.

In the shipyards the largest societies are the *United Society of Boilermakers and Iron and Steel Shipbuilders* (90,000), and the *Ship Constructors' and Shipwrights' Association* (39,000). Draughtsmen are in the *Ass. of Engineering and Shipbuilding Draughtsmen* (11,000), and foremen in the *N. Foremen's Ass.* (2,000) and smaller societies.

The less skilled workers in engineering and shipbuilding are largely organised in the general workers' unions. Some of these, and many of the smaller craft unions (but not the A.E.U. or the Boilermakers), belong to the loosely knit and ineffective *Engineering and Shipbuilding Trades Federation*, which also includes other craft unions with members in the industries (*e.g.*, Upholsterers, Furnishing Trades, etc.).

In the minor metal trades, there are very large numbers of small unions, and the general workers' unions have a good many members. The most important society is the *N. Union of Gold, Silver and Kindred Trades* (7,000).

F.—*Building, Contracting, Woodworking and Furnishing*

Most of the leading unions belong to the *National Federation of Building Trades Operatives* (see p. 38), which is the recognised negotiating unit for the industry as a whole, and also conducts organising work, and opens mixed branches of its own in scattered areas. The N.F.B.T.O. is a close federation of craft societies. The two most important are the result of recent amalgamations. Thus, the *Am. Soc. of Woodworkers* (116,000) has absorbed the old Am. Soc. of Carpenters and Joiners, the Gen. Union of Carpenters and Joiners, and the Am. U. of Cabinet Makers. The *Am. U. of Building Trade Workers* (61,000) has similarly absorbed the two unions of bricklayers and the Op. Stonemasons. The *Building and Monumental Workers' Ass. of Scotland* (5,000) has similarly amalgamated two rival Scottish societies. The other important craft unions include the *N. Am. Soc. of Painters and Decorators* (58,000), and the *Scottish Painters* (7,000) ; the *N. Ass. of Op. Plasterers* (13,000) and the *Scottish Plasterers' Fed. U.;* the *N. Am. Op. Plumbers and Domestic Engineers* (24,000), and its rival, which is outside the N.F.B.T.O., the *N. U. of Heating and Domestic Engineers* (4,000) ; the *Am. Slaters and Tilers' Soc.* (2,000), and the *Am. Slaters' Soc. of Scotland* (1,000) ; and the *N. Am. Street Masons and Paviors' Soc.* (3,000).

Builders' labourers are divided between the " *Altogether* " *Builders' Labourers and Constructional Workers' Society* (45,000), the *National Builders' Labourers and Constructional Workers' Soc.* (15,000), and the *Public Works and Constructional Operatives' U.* (2,000). Some are also in the general workers' unions.

In the lesser woodworking trades, the chief societies are the *Am. Soc. of Woodcutting Machinists* (16,000), the *Am. Soc. of Coopers* (4,000), and the *N. U. of Packing-Case Makers* (2,000). In the furnishing trades are the *N. Am. Furnishing Trades Ass.* (22,000), the *Am. U. of Upholsterers* (6,000), and the *United French Polishers' London Soc.* (1,000).

G.—*Printing and Paper*

Practically all the societies belong to the *N. Printing and Kindred Trades Federation* (165,000).

The leading societies are the *Typographical Ass.* (31,000), *London Soc. of Compositors* (15,000), *Scottish Typographical Ass.* (6,000), *Am. Soc. of Lithographic Artists* (4,000), *Am. Soc. of Lithographic Printers* (6,000), *N. Soc. of Electrotypers and Stereotypers* (3,000), *Printing Machine Managers' Trade Soc.* (4,000), *Platen Printing Machine Minders' Soc.* (1,000), *N. Am. Trade Soc. of Op. Printers and Assistants* (17,000), *N. U. of Printing, Bookbinding and Paper*

Workers (70,000), *Am. Soc. of Paper Makers* (2,000), *Ass. of Correctors of the Press* (1,000), *N. U. of Journalists* (4,000).

In the miscellaneous paper trades there are a number of societies, including the *Wallpaper Workers' U.* (2,000).

H.—Cotton

The cotton operatives are grouped in a number of " amalgamations," each uniting the numerous local societies of workers in a particular section of the industry. The chief " amalgamations " are the *Am. Ass. of Card, Blowing and Ring Room Operatives* (76,000), the *Am. Ass. of Op. Cotton Spinners* (51,000), the *Am. Ass. of Weavers, Winders and Warpers* (171,000), the *Am. Ass. of Beamers, Twisters and Drawers* (6,000), the *Gen. U. of Assns. of Power-Loom Overlookers* (9,000), the *Gen. U. of Warp Dressers' Assns.* (3,000), the *Am. Soc. of Textile Warehousemen* (5,000) and the *Bleachers', Dyers', and Finishers' Ass. (Bolton Am.)* (20,000).

Most of the above are grouped for political and general industrial purposes in the *United Textile Factory Workers' Ass.*, which does not, however, usually act as a negotiating body. The weavers, overlookers, beamers, and others on the manufacturing side of the industry are federated for industrial purposes in the *Northern Counties Textile Trades Fed.*, with its local federation in each town.

I.—Wool and Worsted

The leading society is the *N. U. of Textile Workers* (60,000), formed in 1919 by the fusion of the Gen. U. of Textile Workers, the N. Soc. of Dyers, and some smaller unions. The *Am. Soc. of Dyers, Bleachers, and Finishers* (31,000), which remains separate, has members in the cotton and other branches of dyeing besides wool and worsted. The other societies of importance are *N. Soc. of Machine Woolcombers* (8,000), *N. U. of Woolsorters* (1,000), *Managers' and Overlookers' Soc.* (3,000), *Yorkshire Power Loom Overlookers' Ass.* (2,000), *Am. Soc. of Stuff and Woollen Warehousemen* (2,000).

J.—Other Textiles

(1) HOSIERY.—*Leicestershire Hosiery Union* (7,000), *Ilkeston Hosiery U.* (5,000), *Nottingham Hosiery Workers' Soc.* (5,000), *Midland Counties' Hosiery Finishers' U.* (4,000).

(2) JUTE AND FLAX.—*Dundee Jute and Flax Workers' Union* (12,000), and a number of small unions in N. Ireland.

(3) SILK.—*Am. Soc. of Textile Workers* (9,000).

(4) LACE.—*British Lace Operatives Fed.* (5,000).

(5) CARPETS.—*Power Loom Carpet Workers' Ass.* (4,000), *Scottish Power Loom Carpet Trades Ass.* (2,000), *Northern Counties Carpet Trades Ass.* (1,000).

K.—Leather, Indiarubber, and Clothing

(1) LEATHER.—*Am. Soc. of Leather Workers* (4,000), *Saddlers' and Gen. Leather Workers' U.* (1,000).

STATISTICAL APPENDICES

(2) BOOTS AND SHOES.—*N.U. of Boot and Shoe Operatives* (76,000), *Rossendale U. of Boot, Shoe and Slipper Operatives* (5,000).
(3) GLOVES.—*N. U. of Glovers* (1,000).
(4) HATS.—*Am. Soc. of Journeymen Felt Hatters* (4,000), *Am. Ass. of Journeymen Felt Hat Trimmers* (3,000).
(5) INDIARUBBER.—*Am. Soc. of India Rubber Workers* (5,000), *Waterproof Garment Workers' U.* (1,000).
(6) TAILORING.—*Tailors and Garment Workers' Trade U.* (56,000), *Am. Soc. of Tailors and Tailoresses* (14,000), *United Ladies' Tailors' T. U.* (4,000).

L.—Food, Drink, Drugs, and Tobacco

(1) BAKING.—*Am. U. of Op. Bakers and Confectioners* (14,000), *Scottish Bakers' Federal U.* (7,000).
(2) BUTCHERS.—*Journeymen Butchers' Fed.* (6,000).
(3) TOBACCO.—*N. Cigar Makers' and Tobacco Workers' U.* (3,000).
(4) CHEMICALS.—*N. Drug and Chemical U.* (3,000).

M.—Pottery and Glass

(1) POTTERY.—*N. Soc. of Pottery Workers* (21,000).
(2) GLASS.—*N. Glass Workers' Trade Protection Ass.* (4,000).

N.—Distribution

The largest society is the *N. U. of Distributive and Allied Workers* (90,000), formed in 1919 by the amalgamation of the Am. U. of Co-operative Employees and the N. Warehouse and General Workers' U. Next stands the *N. Am. U. of Shop Assistants, Warehousemen, and Clerks* (40,000). Other societies are small. The only body of importance is the *N. U. of Co-operative Officials* (3,000).

O.—Clerks and Commercial Workers

(1) GENERAL CLERKS.—*N. U. of Clerks and Administrative Workers* (8,000), *Ass. of Women Clerks and Secretaries* (3,000).
(2) BANK CLERKS.—*Bank Officers' Guild* (20,000), *Scottish Bankers' Ass.* (3,000).
(3) INSURANCE WORKERS.—*N. Am. U. of Life Assurance Workers* (10,000), *N. Fed. of Insurance Workers* (12,000), *Guild of Insurance Officials* (10,000).

Many of the societies of non-manual workers are federated in the *N. Fed. of Professional, Technical, Administrative and Supervisory Workers*, which includes, as well as some of the above, the Foremen, Draughtsmen, Railway Clerks, Civil Servants, and others.

P.—Post Office

The biggest society is the *Union of Post Office Workers* (80,000), formed in 1920, by the amalgamation of the Postmen's Federation, Postal and Telegraph Clerks' Ass., and Fawcett Ass. The engineering staff is organised separately in the *Post Office Engineering Union*

(15,000). There are a number of associations of the various grades of supervisors, federated in the *Fed. of Post Office Supervisors*. The largest of these is the *Controlling Officers' Ass.* (4,000). Other societies include the *Fed. of Sub-postmasters* (11,000), and the *Fed. of Postal and Telegraph Clerks* (5,000), which is a breakaway from the U.P.W.

Q.—*Civil Service*

The number of distinct societies is very large, each grade having in many cases its own society. The largest and most important body is the *Civil Service Clerical Ass.* (17,000). This, and many other societies, are federated with the Post Office societies in the *Civil Service Confederation*. The *Customs and Excise Fed.* and the *Ass. of Officers of Taxes* (3,000) are among these others. There is also a special *Ass. of Ex-Service Civil Servants* (10,000).

R.—*Local Government*

The largest society is the *N. Ass. of Local Government Officers* a body which is on the border-line between trade unions and professional associations. The *N. Asylum Workers' Union* (10,000), the *Poor Law Officers' Union* (9,000), the *Firemen's Trade Union* (2,000), the *N. U. of Water Works Employees* (2,000), and the *N. U. of Co-operative Workers* (10,000), are all trades unions. Many local Government employees are organised in the transport and general workers' unions. The *Police and Prison Officers' Union* (2,000), has only a nominal membership, as policemen are not permitted to join a trade union, and are organised in the officially controlled *Police Federation*.

S.—*Teaching*

The principal body is the N. U. of Teachers (120,000), which consists mainly of teachers in the elementary schools. Disputes on the question of " equal pay " have led to the formation of two smaller rivals, the *N. U. of Women Teachers* which has stood for strict equality, and the *N. Ass. of Schoolmasters*, standing for sex differentiation. Teachers in secondary schools are organised mainly in the *Assistant Masters' Ass.*, and the *Ass. of Assistant Mistresses*. Uncertificated teachers are mainly in the *N. U. of Class Teachers*, which now forms a distinct section within the N.U.T., and there are numerous specialised associations, such as the *Ass. of University Teachers*.

T.—*Professionals*

It is difficult in some cases to draw the line between trade unions and professional associations. Thus the " Institutes " of Civil and Mechanical Engineers are clearly not trade unions, while the *Soc. of Technical Engineers* (2,000) is. So is the *N. U. of Scientific Workers*, which mainly organises research workers. Trade unionism

STATISTICAL APPENDICES

among professionals is very weak, and the societies are small. Others include the *British Association of Chemists*, the *Architects' and Surveyors' Assistants' Professional Union*, and a number of others. Some of these belong to the *N. Fed. of Professional, Technical, Administrative and Supervisory Workers*.

U.—*Amusement and Sport*

The chief societies in the amusement industry have a joint working arrangement for common action. They are the *Actors' Association* (4,000), *N. Ass. of Theatrical Employees* (7,000), and *Musicians' Union* (20,000). The *Variety Artistes' Fed.* (4,000) is outside this arrangement.

In sport, the only society of any sort is the *Association Football Players' and Trainers' Union* (1,000).

V.—*General Workers*

The two largest societies of general workers are the *N. U. of General and Municipal Workers* (500,000), and the *Workers' Union* (140,000). Two bodies, the *N. Am. Union of Labour* (70,000) and the *Municipal Employees' Union*, have just (June, 1924) completed an amalgamation with the N.U.G.W. The only other British society of any sort is the *United Order of General Labourers* (5,000). The Transport and General Workers' Union has a large general workers' section. The *Irish Transport and General Workers' Union*, by far the largest union in Ireland, is primarily a general workers' society.

Most of the British unions in this group, including the T. and G.W.U., are affiliated to the *N. Fed. of General Workers*, which undertakes negotiating work on their behalf when more than one society is concerned.

W.—*Agriculture.*

The only important Union in Scotland is the *Scottish Farm Servants' U.* (15,000). In England the *N.U. of Agricultural Workers* (30,000) competes for members with the agricultural section of the *Workers U.* Except in Scotland, there has been a heavier slump in Trade Union membership in agriculture than in any other group. There, the N.U.A.W. claimed nearly 150,000 members at the top of the boom in 1920, as against 30,000 in 1923. A revival is now beginning.

XIV. *Trades Union Congress General Council*
Scheme of Representation and Committees

Groups.	Affiliated Membership, 1923 (in Thousands). Men and Women.	Women.	Representatives on General Council.	Sub-Committees of General Council.
Mining	785	—	3	A
Railways	447	6	3	A
Transport	407	—	2	A
Shipbuilding	143	—	1	B
Engineering	449	0·3	3	B
Iron and Steel and Minor Metal Trades	158	1	2	B
Building, Woodworking and Furnishing	382	3	2	B
Cotton	242	120[1]	2	C
Other Textiles	160	62	1	C
Clothing	98	57	1	C
Leather and Boot and Shoe	87	28[1]	1	C
Glass, Pottery, Distribution, etc.	192	43	1	D
Agriculture	30	—	1	D
General Workers	391	45	4	D
Printing	160	46	1	E
Public Employees	170	12	1	E
Non-Manual Workers	68	13	1	E
Women Workers	Included in above		2	F
Total	4,369	437	32	

[1] Estimated.

INDEX

"Abnormal places," 127
Actors' Ass., 100, 177
Agreements, collective, 121
Agricultural workers, 15, 16, 95, 145, 156, 177
Agricultural Workers, N. U. of, 16
"Amalgamated" societies, 5, 6, 8, 77
Amalgamation, 12, 23, 75, 77, 87, 149, 150
Amalgamations, list of, 168
Apportionment lists, 90
Arbitration, 118, 121
  compulsory, 120, 122
Architects' and Surveyors' Assistants' U., 100, 177
Assistant Masters' Ass., 97, 176
Assistant Mistresses' Ass., 97, 176

Bakers, N. Am. U. of, 92, 175
Ballots. See Referendum.
Bamford, S., 2
Bank Officers' Guild, 100, 175
Black Friday, 9, 46
Blacksmiths, Ass. Soc. of, 18, 28, 172
Blastfurnacemen, N. U. of, 19, 22, 86, 172
Boilermakers' Soc., 18, 23, 28, 73, 172
Bonus systems, 131
Boot and shoe operatives, 20, 64, 94
Boot and Shoe Operatives, N. U. of, 23, 92, 96, 175
British Medical Ass., 16, 98
Builders' Guild (1834), 5
Builders' labourers, 19, 28, 32
Builders' Labourers' Soc., "Altogether," 86, 168, 173
Builders' Union (1832), 4, 5, 77
Building Trade Workers, Am. U. of, 23, 86, 114, 168, 173
Building Trades Operatives, N. Fed. of, 19, 36, 38, 92, 93, 157, 173
Building workers, 19, 28, 74, 95, 100, 120, 173

Capitalism, growth of, 10
Cardroom Amalgamation, 21, 23, 27, 41, 174
Carpenters, 29, 86
Casual labour, 92
Chapel, printers', 59
Chartism, 5, 11
Christian Socialism, 147

Civil servants, 17, 20, 69, 70, 86, 99, 175, 176
  women, 97
Civil Service Clerical Ass., 86, 168, 176
Civil Service Confed., 99, 157
Clerks, 16, 29, 101, 156
Clerks, N. U. of, 20, 29, 66, 87, 100, 175
Clothing workers, 94, 156
Clyde Workers' Committee, 61
Coal Commission, 9
Cobbett, W., 2, 4, 11
Cokemen, N. U. of, 17
Collective bargaining, 2, 117, 135
Colliery Under-Managers' Ass., 99
Combination Acts, 3
Commercial Travellers' Ass., 98
Committee on Production, 122
Communism, 62, 150
Compositors, London Soc. of, 19, 50, 173
Conciliation Act (1896), 122
Conciliation Boards, 119, 120
Connolly, James, 34
Conspiracy, law of, 143
Co-operative employees, 111
Co-operative movement, 5, 11, 31, 109, 113
Co-operative Officials, N. U. of, 100, 175
Co-operative Party, 110
Co-operative Wholesale Bank, 110, 111
Corn Production Act, 16, 145
Corresponding societies, 2
Cotton operatives, 20, 21, 27, 86, 93, 148, 156, 158, 174
Council of Action, 42, 126
Craft representation, 56
Craft unionism, 24, 26, 27, 28, 62, 70, 73, 80

Daily Herald, 41, 43
Demarcation, 87
Dilution of labour, 9, 90
Direct action, 9, 126
Discipline, 137
Dispute pay, 118
Distributive workers, 15, 156
Distributive Workers, N. U. of, 20, 23, 33, 85, 86, 92, 96, 100, 114, 168, 171, 175
District committees, 22, 51, 65

INDEX

District councils, 55, 66
Dock strike (1889), 7, 39, 148
Dockers, 7, 91
Dockers' Union, 8, 166, 168
Doctors, 16, 98
" Document," 4
Dorchester labourers, 4
Draughtsmen's Ass., 16, 99, 118, 172, 175
Dyers, 20, 174

Education, working-class, 48, 112
Electrical Power Engineers' Ass., 100, 118, 172
Electrical Trades U., 17, 18, 171, 172
Electricians, Ass. of Supervising, 100
Employment Exchanges, 146
" Employment " unionism, 31
Enclosures, 11
Engineering and Shipbuilding Trades Fed., 36, 85, 89, 157, 172
Engineering workers, 18, 20, 26, 28, 82, 95, 128
Engineering Union, Amalg., 17, 18, 23, 28, 35, 51, 67, 70, 80, 85, 126, 168, 171, 172
Engineers, Amalg. Soc. of, 5, 8, 9, 63, 69, 85, 166, 168
Enginemen, N. U. of, 17, 29, 172.
Entry to a trade, 92

Fabianism, 148
Factory Acts, 144
Federation, of Trade Unions, 2, 22, 35, 77, 84, 105, 157
Foremen, engineering, 99, 103
Foremen's Ass., N., 99, 103, 172
Foremen's Mutual Benefit Ass., 103
Foundry Workers, N. U. of, 18, 86, 168, 172
French Revolution, 2
Funeral benefit, 72

Gasworkers' Union. See *General Workers, N. U. of.*
General workers, 7, 9, 19, 20, 21, 24, 25, 27, 32, 69, 70, 78, 82, 92, 156, 158, 172, 177
General Workers, N. Fed. of, 36, 157, 177
General Workers, N. U. of, 7, 8, 23, 33, 85, 86, 97, 166, 168, 177
Grand National Consolidated Trades Union (1834), 4, 5, 11, 77
Guild Socialism, 62, 148, 149

Hardy, T., 2
Harrison, Frederic, 147
Hours of employment, 133
Hughes, Thomas, 147
Hume, Joseph, 3

Imperialism, economic, 12
Independent Labour Party, 8, 12, 108, 148, 150
Industrial Conference, N. (1919), 134
Industrial Courts Act, 122
Industrial legislation, 136, 144
Industrial revolution, 2, 10
Industrial truce, 9
Industrial unionism, 25, 27, 30, 62, 80, 81, 82, 138, 148, 150
Industrial Workers of the World, 33, 63, 149
Insurance Acts, 16, 98, 146
Insurance Officials, Guild of, 100, 175
International Labour Office, 48, 134
International of Labour Unions, Red, 48
International Trade Unionism, 46, 158, 159
International Working Men's Ass., 47
Ireland, Trade Unionism in, 34, 66, 155
Irish Trade Union Congress, 35, 43
Irish Transport and General Workers' U., 34, 177
Iron and Steel Trades Confed., 19, 22, 23, 83, 86, 113, 157, 169, 172
Iron and steel workers, 19, 127

Joint Board, 44
Joint Committee of Trade Unionists and Co-operators, 110
Joint Council, N., 44, 111
Joint Labour and Co-operative Assns., 110
Journalists, N. U. of, 16, 174
Junta, the, 6
Jute and Flax Workers' U., 96

Labour College, 114
Labour Colleges, N. Council of, 114, 115
Labour Government (1924), 109
Labour parties, local, 15, 38, 107, 110, 113, 161
Labour Party, 8, 10, 12, 39, 43, 47, 97, 107, 112, 143, 161
women in, 97
Labour Research Department, 45
Larkin, James, 34
Law Clerks' Fed., 100
Local Government Officers, N. Ass. of, 98, 176
Lock-outs, 123
Locomotive Engineers, Ass. Soc. of, 18, 23, 26, 81, 86, 91, 171
Luddites, 11

Macdonald, Alex., 148
" Machine question," 91, 137
Maintenance, industrial, 93
Management expenses, 72
Management, interference in, 137

INDEX

Marine Workers' U., Am., 87, 169, 171
Mann, Tom, 148
Marxism, 7, 12, 114, 148
Metal Amalgamation Committee, 81
Metal workers, 9, 19, 95, 156, 172
Miners, 2, 6, 9, 25, 74, 128, 133, 148, 156, 170
  craft unions of, 17, 25, 170
Miners' Fed. of G. B., 17, 21, 23, 36, 37, 45, 57, 69, 92, 107, 151, 157, 170
Miners' Fed., International, 47
Miners' Fed., S. Wales, 114, 170
Mines Acts, 145
Mines for the Nation Campaign, 44
Minimum wage, 144, 145
Mining deputies, 17, 25, 102
Munitions Acts, 60, 122
Musicians' U., 86, 100, 177

New Unionism (1889), 7
Night shift, 134
Non-manual workers, 16, 22, 23, 41, 94, 97, 175, 176

" One Big Union," 148
" Open shop," 118
Osborne Judgment, 108, 140, 142
Overlapping, 36, 37, 40, 86
Overlookers, Ass. of Loom, 28, 174
Overtime, 134
Owen, Robert, 3, 5, 11
Owenism, 3, 4, 5

Painters, N. Soc. of, 23
Paper Makers, Am. Soc. of, 51, 174
Parliamentary Reform Movement, 2, 4, 11
Patternmakers' Ass., 28, 81, 172
Payment by results, 126, 129
Picketing, 6
Piece-work, 127, 129
  collective, 131
Place, Francis, 2, 3
Plasterers' Ass., 28, 173
Plebs League, 114
Plumbers' Ass., 28, 88, 173
" Poaching," 91
Political action, 6, 7, 10, 106, 142
Political Fund, 108
Positivists, 147
Postal workers, 16, 20, 69, 70, 83, 99, 102, 150
Post Office Workers, U. of, 23, 70, 96, 98, 103, 113, 118, 169, 175
Potters' Union (1832), 4
Premium bonus system, 131, 132
Price-cutting, 132
Price lists, 2, 130
Printers and Assistants, N. Soc. of, 19, 173

Printing, Bookbinding and Paper Workers, N. U. of, 19, 23, 33, 86, 169, 173
Printing Trades Fed., 16, 19, 36, 92, 157, 173
Producers' societies, 5
Professional associations, 98, 100, 176
Professional Workers' Fed., 17, 101, 157, 175, 177
Public employees, 31, 73, 94, 99, 156, 158

Railway Clerks' Ass., 18, 23, 26, 82, 100, 102, 113, 171, 175
Railway shopmen, 18, 26, 66, 92
Railway strike (1919), 9
Railway Women's Guild, 97
Railwaymen, 7, 17, 25, 121, 150, 156
Railwaymen, N. U. of, 8, 17, 18, 23, 26, 45, 54, 67, 69, 78, 79, 81, 83, 86, 91, 95, 100, 114, 121, 166, 169, 171
" Rank and file " movements, 77, 105
Recognition, 2
Referendum, 54, 68, 104
Reform Act (1832), 4
Ricardo, D., 4
Ruskin College, 112, 113, 115
Russian Revolution, 150

Sailors and Firemen, N. U. of, 23, 87, 171
Schoolmasters, N. Ass. of, 97, 176
Scientific management, 131
Scientific Workers, N. U. of, 100, 176
Scottish Farm Servants' Union, 16
Scottish Trades Union Congress, 34, 43
Scottish Typographical Ass., 19, 173
Scotland, Trade Unionism in, 34, 66
Seamen, 7
Sheet Metal Workers, N. U. of, 22, 86
Shipping Guild, 100, 171
Shipwrights' Ass., 18, 172
Shipyard workers, 18, 88, 127
Shop Assistants' Union, 20, 33, 86, 96, 100, 175
Shop stewards, 49, 60, 61, 62, 63, 150
Sick benefit, 71
Skilled and unskilled, relations of, 5, 24, 82, 90
Social Democratic Federation, 8
Socialism, rise of, 7, 8, 148
Socialist Bureau, International, 47
Spinners' Amalgamation, 21, 23, 27, 73, 166, 174
Spinners' Union (1829), 4
Standard rates of wages, 126
State, theory of, 149
Stationmasters, 18, 102
Steel Smelters' U., 70, 169
Stevedores, Am. Soc. of, 91

INDEX

Strike policy, 118, 121, 123
  right to, 6, 119, 125
  statistics, 167
Sunday labour, 134
Superannuation, 71, 72
Supervisors, 18, 97, 101, 117
Sympathetic strikes, 126
Syndicalism, 148

Taff Vale case, 140, 143
Tailors' and Garment Workers' U., 23, 86, 92, 96, 169
Teachers, 16, 94, 156, 158, 176
Teachers, N. U. of, 23, 97, 98, 99, 118, 176
Teachers, N. U. of Women, 97, 176
Textile Factory Workers' Ass., United, 157, 174
Textile trades federations, local, 37
Textile Trades Fed., N. Counties, 36, 174
Textile Trades, N. Ass. of Unions in, 157
Textile workers, 2, 6, 127, 156, 158, 174
Textile Workers, N. U. of, 23, 85, 96, 170, 174
Thomas, J. H., 57
Torts, law of, 143
Trade Boards Acts, 144, 145
Trade clubs in eighteenth century, 2, 10
Trade Disputes Act, 140, 143
Trade Union
  Acts, 74, 78, 107, 108, 140
  benefits and contributions, 69
  branches, 64
  expenditure, 73, 74, 75
  finance, 68, 162–166
  officials, 66, 75, 80, 104
  reserve funds, 71, 74, 75, 162, 163
  rules and regulations, 123, 135
Trade Unionism,
  classification of, 28
  geographical distribution, 15
  Government of, Part III.,
  History of, Part I., 24
  industrial distribution, 15, 156
  numerical growth, 7, 9, 14, 154, 155, 156
  units of organisation, 21
Trade Unions
  as benefit societies, 5, 7, 25, 68, 79, 118
  legal position of, 140
  local, 49
  national, 51
  registration of, 144
  sectional International federations, 46, 48, 160
Trade Unions, Gen. Fed. of, 44, 46, 71

Trade Unions, International Fed. of, 44, 46, 158, 159
Trades Councils, 6, 12, 15, 38, 41, 43, 106, 107, 113, 115, 154, 155
  federations of, 39
Trades Councils, N. Fed. of, 39
Trades Union Congress, 6, 8, 12, 16, 17, 24, 39, 41, 42, 46, 47, 91, 92, 97, 101, 106, 107, 112, 154, 155
  General Council, 12, 39, 41, 80, 97, 106, 114, 178
Transport and General Workers' U., 20, 23, 37, 84, 85, 91, 93, 100, 170, 171, 177
Transport workers, 9, 20, 73, 78, 92, 156
Transport Workers' Fed., 20, 37, 45, 78, 84, 93, 128, 157, 171
  International, 47
Triple Alliance, 9, 45
Tutorial classes, 113, 115
Typographical Ass., 19, 173

Unemployed, the, 40
Unemployed Workers' Committee, N., 40
Unemployment, 87
  post-war, 9
  benefit, 70, 71, 72
  Insurance Acts, 71, 146

Vigilance committees, 55

Wages, incremental scales of, 127
  rates of, 126, 134
Wales, Trade Unionism in, 35
War, effect of, 9, 12, 19, 84, 90, 93, 128
Washington Hours Convention, 134
Weavers, handloom, 2, 11
Weavers' Amalgamation, 21, 23, 27, 28, 33, 36, 73, 96, 174
Week-end schools, 113
Whitley Councils, 84, 99, 120
Women Clerks' and Secretaries' Ass., 97
Women's Co-operative Guild, 97
Women in Trade Unions, 14, 15, 93, 158
Women's Industrial Organisations, Standing Joint Committee of, 97
Women's Trade Union League, 97
Women's unions, 32
Women's wages, 95
Women Workers, N. Fed. of, 33, 97, 170
Woodworkers, Am. Soc. of, 19, 23, 29, 35, 66, 86, 170, 173
Wool operatives, 20, 85
Workers' control, 135, 149
Workers' Educational Ass., 112
Workers' Educational Trade Union Committee, 113, 114
Workers' Union, 23, 86, 92, 166, 177
Workmen's Compensation, 146
Workshop organisation, 59, 65

For Product Safety Concerns and Information please contact our EU representative GPSR@taylorandfrancis.com
Taylor & Francis Verlag GmbH, Kaufingerstraße 24, 80331 München, Germany

www.ingramcontent.com/pod-product-compliance
Lightning Source LLC
Chambersburg PA
CBHW052031300426
44116CB00024B/1730